Fake Gods and False History

Fake Gods and False History

Being Indian in a contested Mumbai neighbourhood

Jonathan Galton

UCLPRESS

First published in 2023 by
UCL Press
University College London
Gower Street
London WC1E 6BT

Available to download free: www.uclpress.co.uk

Text © Author, 2023
Images © Author, 2023

The author has asserted his rights under the Copyright, Designs and Patents Act 1988 to be identified as the author of this work.

A CIP catalogue record for this book is available from The British Library.

Any third-party material in this book is not covered by the book's Creative Commons licence. Details of the copyright ownership and permitted use of third-party material is given in the image (or extract) credit lines. If you would like to reuse any third-party material not covered by the book's Creative Commons licence, you will need to obtain permission directly from the copyright owner.

This book is published under a Creative Commons Attribution-Non-Commercial 4.0 International licence (CC BY-NC 4.0), https://creativecommons.org/licenses/by-nc/4.0/. This licence allows you to share and adapt the work for non-commercial use providing attribution is made to the author and publisher (but not in any way that suggests that they endorse you or your use of the work) and any changes are indicated. Attribution should include the following information:

Galton, J. 2023. *Fake Gods and False History: Being Indian in a contested Mumbai neighbourhood*. London: UCL Press. https://doi.org/10.14324/111.9781800085787

Further details about Creative Commons licences are available at https://creativecommons.org/ licenses/

ISBN: 978-1-80008-580-0 (Hbk.)
ISBN: 978-1-80008-579-4 (Pbk.)
ISBN: 978-1-80008-578-7 (PDF)
ISBN: 978-1-80008-581-7 (epub)
DOI: https:// doi.org/10.14324/111.9781800085787

For my parents, Carol and Antony Galton:
thank you for everything

Contents

List of figures ix
List of abbreviations xi
Acknowledgements xiii

Introduction: a neighbourhood on the edge of history 1

1 'Chawlness': a folk history of (un)locked doors 29

2 'Ganesh is a fake god': the ambiguous humanity of Dr Babasaheb Ambedkar 51

3 Adrift in history? Living between village and city 76

4 'We are Indians, firstly and lastly': Buddhist nationalism and the true history of India 100

5 Village histories, urban futures 130

6 Shivaji contested: on being Maharashtrian 149

7 'Smiles or fraud?': when chawlness falls apart 176

Epilogue: a neighbourhood at the end of history? 189

Bibliography 202
Index 214

List of figures

0.1	View of the BDD Chawls from the central crossroads.	3
0.2	One of the BDD Chawls buildings at Delisle Road (N. M. Joshi Marg).	6
1.1	Map of the BDD Chawls neighbourhood.	30
1.2	(a) One end of the 'gallery' of Chawl F, afternoon (b) The same gallery during a wedding party.	37
2.1	The Jay Bhim Katta.	55
3.1	Katkarwadi Gramastha Mandal room, BDD Chawl K, Delisle Road.	77
3.2	Bandya Maruti Seva Mandal's Dahi Handi pyramid, BDD Chawls, Delisle Road.	91
4.1	Back of a custom-made t-shirt produced by the BDD Chawls RPI(A) Ambedkar Jayanti committee for Ambedkar Jayanti 2015 celebrations.	102
4.2	Renovated facade of the BDD Chawls Buddha Vihar.	122
6.1	Dalit Buddhist bikers from the BDD Chawls en route to celebrate the Battle of Koregaon, 31 December 2017.	153

List of abbreviations

BDD   Bombay Development Department
BJP   Bharatiya Janata Party
BMC   Brihanmumbai Municipal Corporation
MHADA   Maharashtra Housing and Area Development Authority
MLA   Member of the Legislative Assembly
MNS   Maharashtra Navnirman Sena
OBC   Other Backward Class
RPI(A) Republican Party of India (Athawale)
RSS   Rashtriya Swayamsevak Sangh
SC   Scheduled Caste

Acknowledgements

In writing this book I have stood on many shoulders for which I can only begin to express my gratitude. Firstly, funding the PhD research that forms the basis of the book, I benefitted from an Economic and Social Research Council (ESRC) studentship and a SOAS fieldwork grant. Additional thanks go to the ESRC for providing generous funding towards Marathi lessons and several conferences. An even bigger thank you goes to my PhD supervisor Edward Simpson. Thank you, Ed, for your insight and generosity, for usually turning out to be right, and for including me in such an amiable community of scholars.

There are many others I need to thank at SOAS. Julia Sallabank and Shabnum Tejani for secondary supervision. Mina Sol for early ethnographic inspiration. Kevin Latham, Richard Fardon and Naomi Leite for all the research seminars before and after fieldwork. Caroline Osella and David Mosse for your invaluable feedback on what have become Chapters 3, 4 and 5. And of course to my fellow students in anthropology and other disciplines, including but by no means limited to Imran Jamal, Mustafa Ahmed Khan, Liana Chase, Francesca Vaghi, Elisa Tamburo, Marcello Francioni, Lyman Gamberton, Maria Nolan, Alina Apostu, Zoe Goodman, Keval Shah and Zaen Alkazi. Particular thanks to Himalay Gohel for your feedback on Chapter 2 and, more importantly, your friendship.

Elsewhere in the academic world I have a particular debt of gratitude for feedback, in all shapes and sizes, from Ashraf Hoque, Victoria Redclift, Sondra Hausner, Joël Cabalion, Delphine Thivet, Sagnik Dutta, Ritanjan Das, Thomas Blom Hansen, Alison Lamont and an assortment of anonymous reviewers at various journals. Warm wishes and thanks also to my language teachers – Varsha Joshi-Ganu (Marathi) and the late Rakesh Nautiyal (Hindi). To my PhD examination committee, Atreyee Sen and Prashant Kidambi, a heartfelt thank you for your engagement, feedback and generosity of spirit.

To my publishers at UCL Press, and Chris Penfold in particular, I can only say an enormous thank you for taking me on. I am especially grateful to my anonymous reviewers for all of your suggestions that have made this a better book.

Meanwhile there are many to whom I am indebted in Mumbai and elsewhere in India. Some are cited in the body of the thesis, but thank you again here to Neera Adarkar, Rahul Srivastava, Matias Echanove, Mridula Chari, Sumeet Mhaskar, Babasaheb Kambale, Vanessa Caru, Prasad Shetty, Chhaya Goswami and all at CAMP for your collective insight. Likewise, thank you to everybody at the Tata Institute of Social Sciences (TISS), to which I was affiliated for a year.

Particular thanks also go to Abbas Ali Hitawala for first telling me about the BDD Chawls, Shoaib Daniyal for fanning the flames of my initial linguistic interests, Kaushik Lele for your tireless commitment to teaching and demystifying Marathi and Naresh Fernandes for allowing me (twice) to sully the pages of *Scroll* with my musings. And to all those other friends who kept me sane throughout 2017 and beyond with conversation, beer, insight and occasionally music – Simin Patel, Gauri Patil, Ram Kamath, Sucharita Kanjilal, Sameer Gardner, Prasad Dandekar, Shripad Ranade, Frazan Kotwal, Nidhi Shah, Lakshya and Sreya Tak, Monish Barua, Siddharth Sanapathi, Nitesh Tigga – thank you for making the fieldwork year infinitely richer and more exciting!

Back home, there are still others who deserve much gratitude from me: Constance Smith, who inspired me to become an anthropologist, Ida Roland Birkvad for making the journey so much more fun and Kaunteya Shah for keeping the Mumbai enthusiasm alive (and reviewing a highly complex draft of Chapter 6). A significant thank you to my parents, Carol and Antony Galton, for more than you can possibly imagine, but above all for your love, support and feedback. Big thanks also to Simon, Clare and Rosemary Galton and Matthew Thomas for your Mumbai visits. And as for Tom Littler, Ursula Sagar, Costas Mistrellides and Meng Wang – words are not enough. Thank you for being there when I needed you.

Finally, to the group of people without whom this project would quite literally not have been possible. Yes, convention dictates that I change your names and refer to you as 'interlocutors' throughout the thesis, sometimes doubting or respectfully disagreeing with the information and opinions you so generously provided me with, but please know that first and foremost you are my friends. This book is for all of you:

Akshay Dongre, Akshay Soutar, Albert Lobo, Alpita Manwadkar, Amar Katkar, Amar Shingte, Ananda Katkar, Aniket Chavan, Aniket Manwadkar, Anil Atyalkar, Anil Kamble, Anil Patil, Atish Kadam, Atul Katkar, Avinash Patil, Darshan Pawar, Irfan Bilakhiya, Komal Mane, Mahesh Jadhav, Makarand Tasgaonkar, Mangesh Pawar, Maruti Chavan,

Mayur Desai, Nitin Kamble, Nivrutti Desai, Omkar Hodage, Popat Nangare, Pramod Jadhav, Pravin Done, Priyanka Jadhav, Rahul Katkar, Raj Kupekar, Rakesh Gamre, Ramesh Redekar, Ratnadeep Jadhav, Rohini Mane, Sandeep Gurav, Sandeep Patil, Sanjay Pawar, Satish Injal, Sharad Patil, Shashikant Done, Shrikant Chavan, Siddhesh Kadam, Sudhir Waigankar, Suhas Sawant, Sujata Jadhav, Sunil Shetye, Suresh Chavan, Tejas Katkar, Tejaswini Manwadkar, Vaibhav Katkar, Vijay Kumbhar, Vijay Manwadkar, Vikas Patil, Vinayak More, Vishal Killedar.

Introduction: a neighbourhood on the edge of history

One evening in August 2017 I went to a book launch. I was not so much interested in the book – a dense-sounding economic history of modern India – as I was in the chance to visit the ballroom of Mumbai's Taj Mahal Palace hotel where the launch was being held. I found a seat in the packed hall, shivering due to the cranked-up air conditioning, and made small talk with the man sitting next to me. He worked for an international bank and spoke with the unassailable confidence of a senior financial executive. This event was clearly more his milieu than mine and he seemed surprised that I knew so little about the author whose work had ostensibly drawn me there. Gradually I let on that I was conducting fieldwork for a PhD in anthropology, and he asked the question that I had come to dread:

'What are you working on?'

'Well, I guess you could say it's a study of social interaction and identity in a neighbourhood in Mumbai,' I told him, sounding less convincing than I had intended.

'Which neighbourhood?' he asked, not unreasonably.

'The BDD Chawls in Delisle Road?' I ventured, unsure whether he would be familiar with a location so removed from the deluxe split-level apartment I pictured him living in. He flashed me a sceptical half smile.

'But how could you possibly know that place even exists? What are you trying to find there, anyway?'

Again, these were reasonable questions, but not ones for which I had ready responses. Before I could even try, some grandee of the Mumbai commerce scene started booming words of welcome into a microphone, and I sat back, relieved. Three-quarters of an hour in, bored and uncomfortably cold, I crept out into the warmth of the night. Remembering the man's questions, I started thinking about how I might have best replied. Here, six years on and with all the benefits that hindsight brings, is my attempt at an answer.

First encounters

Every anthropologist has an arrival story. Ever since Malinowski was 'suddenly set down' with his 'gear, alone on a tropical beach' (1922, p. 4), both imitators and detractors have sought to capture the process by which they, too, got swept up from the sidelines into the magic of ethnographic fieldwork. Clifford and Hildred Geertz found their feet running from a police raid in the wake of a Balinese cockfight (Geertz, 2000), while Atreyee Sen was tailed by a detective before being allowed to conduct fieldwork in a Mumbai slum (2007, p. 188). My story is markedly less dramatic than Sen's or the Geertzes', and my arrival less abrupt than Malinowski's. There were multiple starting points, in fact, each complementing the other before I realised quite certainly that the central Mumbai neighbourhood known as the Delisle Road (or N. M. Joshi Marg) BDD Chawls had *already become* my fieldsite.

I first encountered this neighbourhood on a humid afternoon in early June 2016. The monsoon was a week or more away, and I drew a self-punishing sort of pleasure from the stickiness of the air, my trousers uncomfortably clenching my legs, my sweat-stained facecloth in regular but futile contact with my face. I was on a short pre-research jaunt, searching central Mumbai for a neighbourhood suited to what at that point was my proposed research project: an exploration of everyday language use in a small neighbourhood that would help answer broader questions about language attitudes and social identity.[1]

I had built up a mental image of a suitable neighbourhood: a small, peaceful knot of streets with easily accessible entry points such as tea stalls or public benches. Above all, I sought evidence of community diversity – perhaps a mosque near a Hindu temple, or signs in different languages in close proximity. My explorations had taken me to a road, known officially as N. M. Joshi Marg and unofficially as Delisle Road (its former name), running past Lower Parel station. This is in the heart of what is sometimes called Girangaon, or 'Village of Mills', sandwiched between the grand colonial downtown of 'South Bombay'[2] and the suburbs that stretch for more than 20 miles to the north. Walking down the noisy road past little snack bars and hole-in-the-wall shops I caught glimpses of a blue-glass tower beyond, with a Starbucks on the ground floor. I filed it away in my mind as evidence of gentrification in this part of the city where defunct textile mills were being replaced with malls and office blocks, and carried on until I came to a turn-off into a promising criss-cross of streets I had spotted on Google Maps.

I immediately started ticking boxes in my head. There was a mosque on the corner, mostly obscured by shops, opposite a small Hindu shrine. There was a group of men sitting and drinking tea on the steps outside a snack bar. There were motorbikes and a few cars by the side of the road and plenty of people, but compared to Delisle Road itself it was quiet, and further down the road were trees on either side (Figure 0.1). I took a walk around the perimeter of the neighbourhood, noting the uniformity of the buildings – four-storey concrete cuboids, some grey, some painted a dull yellow or salmon colour, with large rectangular openings at the bottom and barred windows along each storey. In the centre was a crossroads, not far from which was an outdoor seating area, seven benches under a slanting corrugated roof supported by poles, next to a dusty park. I sat for a while considering my next move.

Figure 0.1 View of the BDD Chawls from the central crossroads. © Author.

A NEIGHBOURHOOD ON THE EDGE OF HISTORY

There was a young man sitting near me and I racked my rains for a pretext to talk to him, so I could come away from the area with at least one encounter under my belt. After 10 minutes of self-conscious silence I got up to move away and made some banal remark about the weather in Marathi, the regional language of Maharashtra State in which Mumbai is situated. It was enough. He asked me who I was, where I was from, and how come I could speak Marathi, and gradually a group gathered around us. I explained that I had learned Hindi on previous visits to India and had spent the previous two years trying to learn Marathi. His name was Bharat,[3] and his friends told me he played *kabaddi*, a popular Indian contact sport. His friends Vinod and Anish were a Marathi-language journalist and real-estate broker respectively, and all three lived in the buildings directly across the road.

Unexpectedly, since I had imagined they were probably Hindu, they told me they were Buddhists. They belonged to the traditionally 'untouchable' Mahar caste that had taken part in a mass conversion movement led by the Mahar-born social reformer Dr Bhimrao 'Babasaheb' Ambedkar in 1956 in an attempt to escape the stranglehold of the Hindu caste system. In a Marathi conversation that constantly slipped back into my comfort zone of Hindi, they told me that they preferred to refer to themselves as Dalit. This is a generic term for untouchable castes popularised in the twentieth century by Ambedkar and others (Teltumbde, 2017, p. 2). They stressed that as Buddhists they don't believe in god(s), but rather believe in self-determination, and they made a number of resentful comments about Hinduism and the caste system. Having hitherto envisaged Mumbai's social dynamics largely in Hindu–Muslim terms, I was unprepared for this Hindu–Buddhist dimension, and earmarked it to follow up in future.

Aside from this, they mostly talked to me about Ambedkar and the social upliftment work he had done for their community during the first half of the twentieth century. So much do Dalits – Mahars in particular – respect him, in fact, that Ambedkar's birthday is celebrated every year on 14 April, a national holiday called Ambedkar Jayanti. My new friends showed me pictures of the most recent celebrations, which took place on the street just in front of where we were sitting, behind which a huge banner with Ambedkar's image hung from the building directly opposite. After a round of group photos, I rose to leave a second time, pausing as I said goodbye to ask the name of the neighbourhood. 'The BDD Chawls', said Anish.

The BDD Chawls

Coincidentally, I had heard the name 'BDD Chawls' a few days earlier, when an architect friend told me that if I really wanted to understand the changing nature of Mumbai I should visit this locality, which had been locked for over a decade in a cycle of redevelopment proposals that emerged and subsequently foundered owing to political wrangling. Chawls are an indispensable part of Mumbai mythology. A tenement-like housing archetype, the chawl is 'ubiquitous' across the city, 'defining the roads, enhancing the street junctions, encircling the maidans [public squares] and forming clusters around the courtyards' (Adarkar, 2011, p. xi). Chawls are characterised by long external or internal corridors lined with small residential units, often comprising a single room that can house a large family or group of individuals. There are usually shared toilets at one end of the corridor. Several hundred residents may live in one relatively compact chawl building. This close-knit mode of living is etched into the city's psyche in chawl-based novels such as P. L. Deshpande's (Marathi) *Batatyachi Chal* and Kiran Nagarkar's (English) *Ravan and Eddie*, and chawls form the backdrop to countless Hindi- and Marathi-language films.

Many chawls were constructed in the late nineteenth or early twentieth century in an attempt to meet the housing demands arising from an influx of migrant labour (Caru, 2011, p. 26). Much of this migration was from the districts immediately surrounding Mumbai,[4] linked to the textile mills that dominated the city's economy until the late twentieth century. Indeed, some chawls were directly owned by the mills themselves, while many more were privately owned and others were constructed by public bodies linked to the colonial administration. The Bombay Development Department, or Directorate (BDD) was one such body, initially proposed by Sir George Lloyd, Governor of Bombay, in an attempt to reassert British colonial control over issues of housing and sanitation in the face of an increasingly devolved municipality dominated by Indian landowners (Prakash, 2011, p. 82).[5] The BDD was tasked *inter alia* with the construction of 50,000 dwellings (Caru, 2019, p. 228), a project that was never fully realised. Nevertheless, four clusters of BDD Chawls were built in the early 1920s across Girangaon in Worli, Delisle Road, Naigaon and Sewri, and are famed for the strength of their reinforced concrete walls (Srivastava and Echanove, 2014). The Worli site is by far the largest, with 121 individual chawl buildings, while in the Delisle Road BDD Chawls, where Bharat and his friends live, there are only 32 buildings, each comprising four storeys (Figure 0.2) on which ten 180 sq. ft. dwellings are lined up either side of a wide central corridor.

Fieldwork begins – an invitation

I came back to Mumbai for a full year of fieldwork in January 2017 and, although I had several candidate fieldsites in mind, it was not long before I returned to the BDD Chawls. On my first return visit, nobody was sitting at the 'Buddhist seating area' (as I thought of it) and I had limited success in interacting with anybody elsewhere in the neighbourhood. People were staring at me and I left, feeling awkward and disheartened until I hit on the idea of next time getting a haircut at one of the poky little open-fronted barber's shops I had noticed.

This turned out to be a good decision. The barber I selected, a man called Maruti, was talkative and seemed to have a large number of friends in the area who would drop by for a chat. Just as I was paying, a man I recognised walked up. After a few seconds I placed him as Vinod, the Buddhist journalist, and hastily scrolled through my phone gallery to find the picture I had taken the previous June. He laughed and found the

Figure 0.2 One of the BDD Chawls buildings at Delisle Road (N. M.Joshi Marg). © Author.

equivalent photo on his phone, urging me come with him to the seating area which he referred to as the 'Jay Bhim Katta'.

Here I was invited to sit down, and reintroduced to Anish, who I remembered as the most vocal of the group, and newly introduced to his quieter friend Manish. Both were unmarried and in their early thirties and described themselves as social workers, although I later remembered that Anish also worked in real estate and learned that Manish had a clerical job. We were joined by a slightly older man, with a fierce face and assertive posture who apparently commanded the respect of the others. I explained my proposed research as inoffensively as my command of Marathi allowed, and the man, called Mahendra, asked me if I had heard of an academic called 'James Klein'. I had not, and his response sounded like a friendly warning about the trouble I could get into for not conducting rigorous research, although I struggled to follow his rapid Marathi. Long afterwards, I realised he had been referring to James Laine whose 2003 book *Shivaji: Hindu King in Islamic India* had been banned in India after it caused an outcry among certain grassroots organisations. Even at the time, however, the fact that here, deep in what I regarded as the 'field', academic writers and their shortcomings were an apparently familiar topic of discussion sent a wave of anxiety through me.

Mahendra continued to hold court and told me that to understand the true history of India I must read Nehru's *The Discovery of India*, and a text by Ambedkar called *Manav Vansh Shastra*. He then gestured around him and explained that most of the people sitting at the Jay Bhim Katta were Dalit Buddhists, like him, although in the surrounding neighbourhood Hindus were in the majority. In any case, he argued in a convoluted fashion that I found difficult to understand, all religions are the same and nationalism is more important, a claim that surprised me in a country where social life is so woven through with religiosity. For that reason, he added, I must come back in two days' time (26 January) to join the community in their Republic Day programme, celebrating the date on which the Constitution of India came into force in 1950.

Fieldwork begins? Another invitation

Alongside these research trips, I was easing myself into Mumbai life in other ways, from visits to my favourite city haunts to finding a flat (adjacent to the BDD Chawls in Worli, as it happened) and picking up threads with old friends. One of these was Vikas, a Maharashtrian Hindu in his early twenties, who I had met through an online language exchange platform.

He told me he lived in Lower Parel in a room with other 'bachelors', a term used in India to describe men who live together, regardless of their actual marital status. It was only when he invited me to the room that I discovered, to my astonishment, it was in the BDD Chawls.

It was with Vikas that I first saw the inside of a chawl. He took me on an unfamiliar route past a chai stand into a roughly paved space from which we took a side entrance into his building. We went straight up the wide stairway, passing a long, wide corridor on the first floor up to a similar corridor on the second. It seemed a gloomy space, the only light coming in from the barred windows at either end but, adjusting to the light, I noticed the rough paving stones and the way the wall was painted in different colours outside each room – beige, blue, yellow and green. In front of each door was a cluster of shoes and a small plastic bucket; in some cases clothes were hanging above these. Vikas' room was near the end of the corridor and as we came to the door he pointed out the six common toilets beyond it that were shared by all the residents of that floor. The purpose of the plastic buckets became clear.

The room itself was shockingly small and bare, given the 15 or so people that lived in it, with no furniture beyond a single plastic chair. Clothes were hanging on a row of pegs that ran three sides around the room, and at the far end, underneath a wooden platform full of trunks and suitcases, was a partially enclosed area where somebody was washing stainless steel pots. I assumed – correctly as it later turned out – that this was also the place where room residents washed their bodies and their clothes. There were several men inside, sitting on bedsheets, and Vikas introduced me to them. One of them told me he had been living in the room for 10 years and worked as a cashier in a south Mumbai mall, while his wife and son lived in a village called Amrutwadi,[6] in Kolhapur District which is a few hundred miles southeast of Mumbai. Vikas explained that everybody in the room came from the same village, and I brushed this off as a delightful curiosity, having no notion that this particular mode of living would form a major component of my research.

In the weeks that followed I also became a regular visitor in many of the Dalit Buddhist families' homes. Although the dimensions of these 180 sq. ft. rooms were the same as those of Vikas' room, as spaces they felt very different. Aside from symbolic differences, like the pictures of Ambedkar and the Buddha, there were striking material differences. Notable among these was the presence of bulky furniture in the family rooms, such as single beds or banquettes, cabinets full of photographs and memorabilia, metal chests and cupboards. Where Vikas' room had felt like a single space, the washing area (or *mori*) separated only by a waist-high wall, the family rooms were generally subdivided into a few discrete enclosures. In place of the open-fronted mezzanine storage space there was usually a fully enclosed attic on top of an enclosed *mori*, with a tiny kitchen beyond.

In short, I was not 'suddenly set down' on a Malinowskian beach but rather was drawn gently into the life of the BDD Chawls until I reached a point where I could not imagine another fieldsite. Although my intention had been to conduct an ethnographic study of linguistic identity, it became increasingly clear to me that my Marathi skills were far from sufficient for this, and correspondingly *unclear* where I should be focusing my attention instead.

A rooftop interlude: three tales of the city

But this is Mumbai! Where is the Gateway of India? Where is Bollywood? Where, above all, is the super dense crush load of the local trains wheezing southwards from the outermost suburbs? 'Everyone has a Bombay story,' write two of its best loved citizen-chroniclers, Jerry Pinto and Naresh Fernandes, 'and everyone's Bombay is not the Bombay we thought we knew' (Pinto and Fernandes, 2003). Bollywood features little in my story, and the Gateway of India not at all, although the famously crowded local trains can sometimes be heard faintly offstage as they suck in and later disgorge my research participants at Lower Parel station.

I first visited Mumbai in 2003, having spent the preceding months teaching English in the southern state of Tamil Nadu. I found the city both exhilarating and intimidating. The immediate warmth and open curiosity of small-town south India had lulled me into a comfortable sense of being in a world away from home. Mumbai shocked me out of this orientalist cocoon, its luxury hotels and fancy coffee shops and aloof worldliness all disconcertingly familiar and strange at the same time. Nevertheless, the city drew me in, and I returned many times in the ensuing years. At first, I found it glamorous and sexy, an impression magnified by texts such as Suketu Mehta's *Maximum City* and the novels of Rohinton Mistry that I devoured between trips. It was only when I turned seriously to Mumbai as a subject of academic study that I began to appreciate the city's proud working-class history and the stories it told of itself.

'No city can be fully known,' Hansen and Verkaaik (2009, p. 8) warn us, a warning that rang ever louder in my ears as the fieldwork year went on. Mumbai, in particular, is 'too multi-layered and overflowing in history and meanings to be fully captured by a single narrative or name' (Hansen and Verkaaik, 2009, p. 8). Groping around for a coherent narrative of my own, I often climbed to the rooftop terrace of one of the chawls for some headspace. From this vantage point, let us peel back a few layers to tell three of the city's most famous stories that nestle in this book's shadows. First, the shift from Bombay to Mumbai as a result of a consolidated Maharashtrian claim on the city. Second, the decline of the textile mill industry and the urban redevelopment that has ensued. Third, the religious riots of 1992–3 and the ethnic segregation that these riots are generally held to have set in motion.

When Bombay became Mumbai: Marathas and the Shiv Sena

From one rooftop it is possible to see the roofs of many of the other 31 BDD Chawls. Of these, around 13 have a sizeable Dalit community[7] which includes both Anish's community, the Dalit Buddhist Mahars, but also a Dalit Hindu community referred to as Chambhar, or Chamar. Some of the other buildings are almost exclusively occupied by another Hindu community, known as the Maratha, to which Vikas and his roommates belong. All three groups speak Marathi as a first language and mostly trace their roots either to the Konkan region due south of Mumbai, or to Kolhapur, a wealthy inland district known for its sugarcane industry and part of the wider Ghats (mountain passes) region.[8] Some of the Maratha-dominated chawls mostly house Kolhapuri families while some others have a strong Konkani demographic but, overall, the Delisle Road area is known as a 'mini-Kolhapur'.

The Maratha community is sometimes referred to as a 'caste cluster' and comprises a group of Hindu clans widely regarded as the dominant peasant-cultivators of rural Maharashtra. While most of the Marathas I met told me their community belonged to the Kshatriya *varna*, a broad caste classification associated with rulers and warriors, many of my Dalit Buddhist friends dismissed this as a bogus claim, and insisted that Marathas were actually Shudras, or labourers.[9] This is an old debate that I shall return to in Chapter 6, but throughout this book I shall avoid using the conventional term 'upper caste' in connection with Marathas. Instead, I follow historian Babasaheb Kambale and use the term 'dominant caste' as an umbrella category, roughly comprising those communities not deemed sufficiently disadvantaged to be eligible for government affirmative action schemes such as reservations (quotas) in employment and education at the national level.

Even this usage is contentious. Eligibility for reservations was originally granted in the 1950 Constitution of India to Dalits (officially referred to as Scheduled Castes) and *adivasi*, or tribal, communities (Scheduled Tribes). Since 1992, reservations have been extended to an additional group referred to as Other Backward Classes (OBC) which includes certain communities sometimes considered part of the Maratha cluster, such as the Kunbi. More recently, larger sections of the Maratha community have campaigned to be designated as OBC to take advantage of reservations in employment and education, a claim to backwardness that has been disputed on empirical grounds (Deshpande and Ramachandran, 2017, p. 81; Kumar, 2009, p. 12). In response, a bill was introduced in November 2018 by Maharashtra's Chief Minister Devendra Fadnavis, which reserved 16 per cent of public sector positions and educational places for the Maratha community, newly designated as a Socially and Educationally Backward Class (SEBC) (Bare Acts Live, 2018; Srivastava, 2019).[10]

The Marathas are at the centre of many narratives of Maharashtra, historical and contemporary (Hansen, 2001, pp. 20–36). One Maratha looms particularly large: Shivaji Bhonsle, the subject of James Laine's biography that so exercised Mahendra. Known as Chhatrapati Shivaji Maharaj, in the mid-seventeenth century he established a Maratha Empire, which went on to control much of western and central India at its height in the eighteenth century. His image, that of a handsome, bearded figure in a *pagdi* (turban) and often on horseback, is found all over Maharashtra. I encountered Shivaji thus in private homes and public spaces across the BDD Chawls.

Shivaji is also the namesake of the most powerful regional political party, the Shiv Sena or 'Army of Shiva[ji]'. To appreciate the niche that the Shiv Sena has been able to carve for itself, it is necessary to understand that Mumbai, or Bombay as it was before 1995, has never been a genuinely Maharashtrian city. From Bombay's earliest days as a sizeable urban centre under East India Company control in the seventeenth century, merchants from Gujarat and elsewhere were 'assiduously induced' to settle in the city (Kosambi, 1995, p. 7). By the mid-nineteenth century, commerce in Bombay was 'notable for its ethnic diversity', dominated by Gujarati communities including Parsis, Bohra Muslims and (Hindu and Jain) Banias (Kidambi, 2007, p. 25), meaning that it was always regarded as an 'alien substance in the land' by the Marathi-speaking intelligentsia, and a 'bridgehead of imperial culture' (Hansen, 2001, p. 37).

When, after Independence, the city was incorporated into the newly formed and territorially extensive Bombay State, its fate became bound up in competing claims. There was the mostly left-leaning Samyukta Maharashtra movement, which lobbied in the 1950s for a separate Marathi-speaking state called Maharashtra with Bombay at its heart.

A parallel movement campaigned for a Gujarati-speaking state to the north of Maharashtra and made its own claim to Bombay, arguing that despite the city's location within the proposed borders of Maharashtra, nearly 150 km to the south of their envisioned Gujarat, it was a 'leading centre in the formation of modern Gujarati culture' (Hansen, 2001, p. 38). Maharashtrians, they argued, 'had no claim whatsoever to the city' (Adarkar and Menon, 2004, p. 222).

The Samyukta Maharashtra claim prevailed and Bombay became the capital of the newly-formed Maharashtra state in 1960. However, the expectation that Maharashtrian 'job prospects in the city would substantially improve' was not met (Lele, 1995, p. 189). In 1966, therefore, political cartoonist Bal Thackeray established the Shiv Sena as a social welfare organisation promoting the interests of Maharashtrian (but not specifically Maratha) 'sons of the soil' in an employment market crowded with 'outsiders', notably migrants from South India (Chandavarkar, 2004, pp. 51–4). In the decades that followed, the organisation grew into a fully-fledged right-wing political party with strong Hindu nationalist leanings, and it is now a dominant force in municipal and regional politics. It has a strong voter base among the Marathas and Chambhars of the BDD Chawls, although the appeal does not extend in any significant way to the Dalit Buddhist community.

In 1995 the party came to power in the Maharashtra Legislative Assembly in alliance with the Hindu-nationalist BJP (the Bharatiya Janata Party, currently incumbent at a national level under Prime Minister Narendra Modi). Once in power, the Shiv Sena swiftly engineered the renaming of the city from Bombay to Mumbai with a view to emphasising the Marathi origins of the city's name from the local goddess Mumbadevi (Hansen, 2001, p. 1). For many this dealt a symbolic blow to the cosmopolitan, progressive 'Bombay' in favour of a Marathi-speaking Hindu monoculture (Kamdar, 1997, p. 76). In such circles, often liberal and Anglophone, this move is regarded as an ahistorical 'aberration' (Gavaskar, 2010) rather than a way to remove the stain of colonialism. In this book, however, I use the official name Mumbai, unless specifically referring to the pre-1995 city of Bombay,[11] and I will return to this phase of the city's history in Chapter 6.

Village of mills to city of malls

I found the view from the roof particularly magical in the early evening light, but I knew that I ought to find it terrifying. The gleam of the towering office blocks and luxury residential high-rises tell what for many commenters is the defining story of contemporary Mumbai: the 'murder of the mills' (Krishnan, 2000). The blue-glass Marathon Futurex complex, for example, home of Zee TV and L'Oréal as well as the Starbucks I saw on my first visit, occupies the site of what used to be Mafatlal Mills. In the other direction, a disused chimney is dwarfed by the Lodha Excelus residential tower that stands where Apollo Mills once stood.

Bombay's relationship with cotton began to flourish in the mid-nineteenth century, and by the 1860s the city had become one of the world's major cotton exporters. In a symbiotic development, a textile manufacturing industry emerged in Bombay, a largely Indian-run enterprise as exemplified by the Parsi entrepreneur, Cowasji Davar, who opened the first cotton mill in 1854 (Kidambi, 2007, p. 19). Although the growth of this industry was far from smooth, within a few decades it had become the dominant industry in Bombay, attracting migrant workers from across western India.

By the 1930s, three-quarters of the city's population worked in the mills (D'Monte, 2002, p. 14), ninety per cent of whom lived 'within a fifteen-minute walk of their factories' (Fernandes, 2013, p. 55), many in the chawls that were being constructed to house them. The biggest concentration of textile mills was in the neighbourhoods directly to the north of the colonial commercial centre, such as Parel, Lalbaug and Dadar. This was Girangaon (literally 'village of mills'), a district with a distinctive working-class culture which had strong roots in the Konkan and Ghats (Adarkar and Menon, 2004, p. 110).

Filthy, overcrowded living conditions made the neighbourhood a fertile incubator of disease, and at many points tensions due to differences in caste, religion and language wore down the bonds of working-class solidarity (Adarkar and Menon, 2004; Chandavarkar, 1994, pp. 112–13; Shaikh, 2005, p. 1899). Nevertheless, Girangaon was also a place in which civil society and artistic endeavour flourished, producing 'many singers, actors, writers, poets [and] artistes' (Adarkar and Menon, 2004, p. 114). Above all, there was an active and diverse trade-union movement, including the city's first worker-tenants union established in the BDD Chawls in 1935 (Caru, 2019, p. 233), and, more generally, striking became 'an integral part of the social experience of Girangaon' (Chandavarkar, 2004, p. 34).

Indeed, there were numerous textile workers' strikes over the lifetime of the industry, but it is the general strike of 1982–3 that Mumbai remembers as definitive. By the 1970s, the textile mills were facing difficulties on multiple fronts: job losses due to a growing powerloom sector (D'Monte, 2002, pp. 96–7), job insecurity linked to an increase in surplus workers (Shaikh, 2005, p. 1899) and indiscriminate diversion of funds by mill-owners into 'more profitable industries' (Adarkar and Menon, 2004,

p. 320). After a great deal of persuasion, renowned trade unionist Datta Samant agreed to lead a strike in 1982, calling for better wages and the scrapping of legislation that restricted unionisation. The strike lasted for over a year, affected a quarter of a million workers and was never officially called off (Adarkar and Menon, 2004, p. 337).

Many striking millworkers actually joined the powerloom industry to make ends meet, which not only sustained the strike but also meant that it had 'no appreciable decline in the availability of or output of cloth' (Chandavarkar, 2004, p. 70). Following an unofficial declaration by government-affiliated unions and mill-owners that the strike was over in 1983, many mills reopened, but 'never recovered their former vitality' and over a hundred thousand workers were not rehired (Prakash, 2011, p. 294). Many returned to their villages, while others found work as security guards, drivers, waiters and similar roles in a job market that was becoming increasingly casualised and precarious (cf. Krishnan, 2000, p. 20; Mhaskar, 2013, pp. 152–3).

In the climate of economic liberalisation of the early 1990s, mill-owners turned their attention to their most valuable remaining asset, what Appadurai has evocatively called a 'feast of hidden real estate just beyond the famine of the streets' (2000, p. 641). Development Control Regulations were initially formulated with the public good in mind by requiring one-third of any vacant mill land to be handed over to the Maharashtra Housing and Area Development Authority (MHADA) and another to the municipal corporation (BMC) but this requirement was watered down significantly in 2001. The result of these policy changes is the efflorescence of concrete and steel and glass: offices, luxury apartments, malls and entertainment complexes. Some of these, like Kamala Mills, have retained their old names to add a sophisticated hint of urban grit to the dim-sum restaurants and craft-beer bars inside.

The chimney of Phoenix Mills, just visible from the BDD Chawl roofs, bears witness to one of the most famous examples of corporate greed chronicled meticulously in Shekhar Krishnan's 2000 report, *The Murder of the Mills: A case study of Phoenix Mills*. In early 1998, the mill management began to lay off staff in certain departments and phased out the second and third work shifts (Krishnan, 2000, p. 7). At the same time, supposedly in response to millworkers' demands for recreational facilities, a bowling alley and disco were constructed on mill premises. These became a 'favourite site for photo-ops of famous film stars and celebrities' and a 'hang-out for upper-class youth … Hardly a place for mill-workers to unwind after a long day at work', as Krishnan caustically observes, not least considering the prohibitive admission charges (2000, p. 5).

Today, rebranded as High Street Phoenix, the site is 'India's first premium luxury retail and entertainment' complex set in 'an atmosphere of sophistication and refinement under one elegant roof' (Phoenix Palladium, n.d.). The chimney remains, now painted a cool white and branded with the mall logo; at its base is a McDonald's. The 'mill to mall' narrative so poignantly illustrated by this chimney will be revisited, and in places challenged, in Chapters 1, 3 and 5.

Cosmopolis lost? Religious riots and segregated neighbourhoods

Standing on the roof at dusk, a nearby muezzin calls to mind another painful episode in Mumbai's recent history. The source of the *azan* is the Bawla Masjid which sits at the Delisle Road turnoff into the BDD Chawls, the pale green minarets visible in front of the Marathon Futurex building. It is the second biggest mosque in Mumbai, although very few in the city are aware of its existence. Moreover, its size is no longer matched by that of the area's Muslim population which haemorrhaged following religious riots that engulfed Mumbai in the early 1990s.

In December 1992, after a protracted political campaign, fundamentalist Hindus in the North Indian town of Ayodhya destroyed the Babri Masjid, a mosque they believed to have been built on the birthplace of Lord Ram, *avatar* (incarnation) of the god Vishnu. Hindu–Muslim riots broke out across the country, and Mumbai in particular 'witnessed large-scale death, destruction and unfettered violence' (Sen, 2007, pp. 5–6). Darryl D'Monte draws a direct link between the sense of hopelessness that followed the mill closures and the violent energy unleashed in the religious riots a decade later (2002, p. 17). Few would dispute that the Shiv Sena was complicit in this violence, and the party came to be seen by the city's middle-class Hindus as their 'ultimate defender[s]' – 'bastards', admittedly, but 'our bastards' (Hansen, 2001, p. 125) – partly explaining its electoral success in 1995.

It is frequently argued that the riots mark a turning point in Mumbai's trajectory from a city of 'ethnically mixed neighbourhoods' to one where religious communities, Muslims above all, have been driven to self-segregate in 'spatially concentrated' areas (Hansen, 2001, p. 160; see also Phadke et al., 2011, p. 12; Sen, 2007, p. 13; Shaban, 2010). It is worth noting, however, that to an extent the city's neighbourhoods have always been differentiated along linguistic and religious lines (Kosambi, 1995, p. 8; Masselos, 2019, p. 311; Wacha, 1920, pp. 425–8) and, as pioneering urban biographer Govind Narayan recorded in 1863, 'though most of the settlements in Mumbai are fairly mixed, most people prefer to stay close to members of their own caste' (Ranganathan, 2008, p. 130).

This appears to be true of the BDD Chawls, where – as already indicated – a loose spatial segregation between communities is evident and, by all accounts, it long predates the 1992–3 riots. The impact of the riots can most clearly be observed in Chawl E,[12] which once hosted a large Muslim community that has now dwindled to a few families. Mahadev, a Hindu resident of the building, told me that most of his Muslim neighbours have moved to the suburb of Mumbra, where he occasionally visits them. Only a handful of Muslim-owned shops remain on Delisle Road. We will briefly encounter Ayodhya again in Chapter 4, and questions of spatial segregation dominate Chapter 5, but for the most part it is Hindu–Buddhist relations rather than Hindu–Muslim relations that form the basis of my study.

About this book: fake gods, false histories and ambiguous futures

Anthropologists sometimes quip that entire careers are built around unpacking the first hours of fieldwork in ever more theoretical ways. For my part, I found myself returning again and again to the first conversation I had with Mahendra when he talked about 'true history', the writing of Ambedkar, the relationship between religion and nationalism, and the problems faced by researcher James Laine. Likewise, my first visit to Vikas' room exposed me, quite casually, to the phenomenon of the Gramastha Mandal, a dormitory room established to house migrants from a specific village, which became a recurrent motif during my research. Finally, the prospect of redevelopment – first mentioned to me in passing by a friend – hung over the fieldwork like a cloud that never quite burst.

This book has ultimately emerged as a study of how people talk about history and how this shapes their everyday lives, their politics and their cultural identities. History has always been a battleground, but with the massive expansion of the public sphere into the worlds of social media and 24-hour news cycles, the scale and intensity of such battling is arguably greater today than ever before. In the UK, where I live, academics, politicians, artists and activists debate the legacy of British imperialism and reexamine the heroic status once accorded to figures such as Horatio Nelson, Cecil Rhodes and Winston Churchill. In North America and parts of Oceania such debates are complicated further by indigenous claims to the land that frame the very presence of white majorities as settler colonialism and contest the meaning of celebrations like Thanksgiving and Australia Day. A particularly raw and recent example, at the time of writing, is the way in which differing narratives of history have been weaponised to bolster competing claims to the territory of Ukraine in the current Russia–Ukraine war (Kasianov, 2022).

Such discursive wars are also being waged across India with very real consequences for its future. Do inclusive traditions of Indian nationhood that make room for Muslims, Christians, Dalits, socialists and others stand a chance when pitted against the strident majoritarian Hindu nationalism of the present moment? Have all vestiges of the social democracy that characterised independent India's first decades been swept away in a tide of neoliberal hypercapitalism? In November 2022, Minister for Home Affairs Amit Shah took to Twitter, to:

> urge our historians and students of history to identify 30 great empires in Indian history and 300 warriors who showed exemplary valour to protect the motherland and write extensively about them. This will bring out the truth and the lies will vanish on their own.
> (Shah, 2022)

The wider context was a speech Shah gave in Assam, northeast India, celebrating the 400th birth anniversary of Lachit Barphukan, an Assamese general who had defeated the Mughal army in the Battle of Saraighat, thereby saving (according to Shah) 'entire Southeast Asia from religiously fanatic invader Aurangzeb' (PTI, 2022). He went on to place Barphukan in a long tradition of Indian heroes, including Shivaji, who had fended off Islamic invaders. But many Assamese historians reject this characterisation, pointing out that Barphukan followed the Tai religion and led an army that comprised Muslims as well as Hindus, against Aurangzeb's troops that actually included many Hindus and were even led by a Hindu Rajput general (Zaman, 2022). Any implied cosmological struggle between the forces of Hinduism and the forces of Islam is simplistic propaganda, they argue.

Disputes like these often play out publicly in political speeches – think of Vladimir Putin's angry jeremiads on Russian history and British politicians' varied pronouncements about empire – or debates on television, news outlets and social media. They frequently feature prominent opinion formers, often with glaring disparities of power, with some arguing from a privileged majoritarian perspective and others from a more marginalised position. No matter how complex and nuanced the individual contributions, the collective debate typically clusters into ever-more polarised camps over a single issue – 'Was the British Empire a force for good or evil?' or 'Was Winston Churchill a war hero or a racist?' While attempts to 'see both sides' to many questions of this kind are often banal at best and invidiously reproduce existing power structures at worst, the opposite tendency to seek purity in binaries can result in stalemates that hamper coalition-building and foreclose the possibility of progress.

Is there a role for anthropology in unpicking these debates? Anthropologists Stephan Palmié and Charles Stewart threw down a gauntlet in 2016, when they proposed that a 'concerted anthropology of history', that 'turn[s] history itself, as a form of knowledge and social praxis, into an object of anthropological inquiry' is yet to emerge (Palmié and Stewart, 2016, p. 207).[13] My own anthropological study responds to this challenge by exploring the ramifications of such debates at the more mundane level of a neighbourhood away from the public glare and examining how its residents live with a multiplicity of historical narratives that cut across different geographies and timescales and, in doing so, how they invoke the legacies of certain godlike figures. 'Fake gods' and 'false history' were expressions used by my Dalit Buddhist interlocutors in reference to the Hindu beliefs and practices of their Maratha neighbours. In contrast, the true, or alternative history of India – so eagerly impressed on me by Mahendra – cuts to the heart of their understanding of what it means to be Indian, and to be Maharashtrian, Dalit and Buddhist. As we shall learn, they consider themselves the heirs to an ancient Buddhist utopia of rational egalitarianism that was invaded thousands of years ago by 'Aryans' who subjugated the indigenous population by imposing Hinduism with its caste hierarchies, invented deities and false narratives of history.

A marginalised minority declaring their allegiance to the nation in spite of the majoritarian state, this is quite distinct from the Hindu nationalism of Amit Shah and his fellow ideologues and does not comfortably fit the familiar moulds of nationalism proposed by foundational scholars such as Ernest Gellner and Benedict Anderson. The Dalit Buddhists argue that it was through the intervention of Ambedkar that this alternative history was uncovered, allowing them today to apply a rational lens to neighbourhood issues, unlike their superstitious, easily-duped Hindu neighbours. But Ambedkar's own history is contested too: to my Dalit Buddhist friends he appears to be something more than human, whereas one former BJP politician has described him as a 'false god' (Shourie, 1997) and, more generally, the Hindu nationalist movement makes frequent attempts to appropriate his legacy.

Tensions between shared and divergent histories are also found among the migrant residents of Gramastha Mandals, the village-linked dormitory rooms like the one Vikas took me to. Many of these migrants do not feel at home in Mumbai at all and occupy a liminal space between village and city. Their ties to the village are bolstered by a strong sense of shared history, but this history encodes deeply-rooted divisions between communities (notably Hindu and Buddhist) which are reproduced and reconfigured in the built structures of the BDD Chawls.

Meanwhile, at the neighbourhood scale, history can bind communities together, and there is a strong sense of a common chawl history shared by both Dalits and Marathas. However, this togetherness is fragile and constantly at risk of fraying in the face of disputes over the state-led neighbourhood redevelopment plans and contestations over the use of local space. Indeed, an important secondary aim of the present study is to capture, ethnographically, the last years of the BDD Chawls' life. There is a rich existing literature on Mumbai chawls – of particular note is Neera Adarkar's edited volume, *The Chawls of Mumbai: Galleries of Life* – but few anthropological studies that focus on a single chawl neighbourhood, especially in the closing moments of its existence.

It is through this lens that I shift the focus away from the depressingly familiar anti-Muslim manifestations of contemporary Hindu nationalism and put the 'tales of the city' outlined earlier partially to the side, to tell a more ambiguous story of neighbourhood and nation. This fine-grained, zoomed-in perspective matters precisely because the highly public discourse of politicians and thought leaders is so pervasive and influential that it is tempting to read it as a scaled-up reflection of the localised, everyday conversations that unfold away from the spotlight. While the popular dictum that 'Twitter is not real life' erases the many and varied ways in which Twitter (or social media and the internet *tout court*) both represents and shapes offline social reality, it nevertheless reminds us of the innumerable stories and conversations that never gain global online prominence and yet have much to tell us about why people live, and think, and act, and vote in the ways that they do – often in ways that outsiders might not expect them to. It is in this hinterland that my ethnography is situated.

The material is tightly linked to the BDD Chawls and embedded in an emphatically Indian context, but since – as already discussed – history-telling is an essential weapon in political and cultural armouries worldwide, readers from outside India are encouraged to draw connections with their own experiences of the way history impinges on their lives. The contested legacies of godlike humans such as Ambedkar and Shivaji, discussed in Chapters 2 and 6 respectively, might prompt readers to consider comparable debates over the legacies of towering historical figures closer to home. Meanwhile, the complex account in Chapter 4 of how history-making entwines with nationalism and imperialism will likely resonate far beyond India's borders, as will the reflections in Chapters 3 and 5 on what happens when village identities are transposed to the city.

Outline of chapters

Chapter 1 introduces the BDD Chawls as a site living on borrowed time and shows how the prospect of redevelopment and rehousing has intensified a nostalgic interest in the neighbourhood's history on the part of its residents. There is a strong idea, common to Dalits and Marathas, of what it means to be a chawl resident which I label 'chawlness'. Chawlness is predicated on a narrative that the chawls were originally built as prisons, and also on a rather generic sense of a close-knit community that keeps its doors open and maintains social ties strong enough to subsume minor temporary disputes within a longer-term peace. Although this open-door culture is sometimes framed in opposition to the closed-door culture of middle-class flats, there is nevertheless a perception among many BDD Chawls residents that they themselves now belong to the middle class. At the end of the chapter I explore why chawlness might in fact be rather weak in the face of the manifold social differences that mark the neighbourhood, themes that will be returned to throughout the rest of the book.

Chapter 2 opens with Ganesh Chaturthi, a popular festival celebrating the Hindu deity Ganesh, who my Dalit Buddhist interlocutors regard as a 'fake' god, a superstition that distracts India from the real work of nation-building. For them, the only 'god' worth following is Ambedkar and this chapter explores Ambedkar's ambiguous position in their lives, constantly slipping between human and superhuman, and the way his ideas underpin their social structures. I also consider the tension between the narratives, both commonly voiced, of Dalit emancipation following the social-upliftment work of Ambedkar, and of continuing caste-based atrocities across India. Ultimately, I conclude that this comfortable coexistence of contradictory ideas, a marked contrast to the polarisation that characterises much public wrangling over history, yields valuable insight into the position occupied by Dalit Buddhists in contemporary Mumbai.

In Chapter 3, the scene shifts to the Gramastha Mandals, the dormitory-style rooms owned by village-linked associations that are only open to migrant bachelors from that village. These young men retain strong links to their natal villages, reinforced by living with fellow villagers in Mumbai, and only participate in an extremely limited way with the wider social life of the BDD Chawls. In stark contrast to the more familiar worldwide story of ethnic, religious and other differences between migrants and host communities, the migrants typically belong to the same communities (mostly Maratha Hindu) as the families living around them. After several generations in Mumbai, however, the families have developed their own networks of urban belonging, notably in the form of social clubs called Mitra Mandals, many of which were in fact established by the ancestors of today's Gramastha Mandal migrants. While Mitra Mandal members celebrate their clubs' histories of sporting achievements and social service, the Gramastha Mandal members tell histories of exclusion and fights between migrants and families. Trapped in often tedious jobs, repetitive social lives and nostalgia for their village childhoods, while being excluded from the organisations their ancestors helped to create, the Gramastha Mandal migrants appear to be adrift in history, although I complicate this picture in the final section of the chapter.

Chapter 4 opens with a dispute over space outside the local Buddhist temple and cuts to the heart of my Dalit interlocutors' claim that while Hindus are primarily loyal to their community (caste and religion), Buddhists consider themselves Indians 'firstly and lastly'. I endeavour to understand this claim and the work it does by picking apart the reasons it initially disconcerted me, showing in the process how closely this version of nationalism is bound up with Ambedkar's legacy. Above all, it is entwined with a conception of the 'true history' of India, a narrative that places Dalits as the autochthons of an ancient Buddhist India governed by principles of rational egalitarianism. This utopia was shattered by the arrival of 'Aryans' from outside who were the ancestors of today's Brahmans (traditionally the uppermost Hindu caste)[14] and who introduced the caste system as a tool of oppression and practised thought-control with invented gods and 'false history'. This discussion is embedded into a broader debate about nationalism that places contemporary Hinduism within the global context of rising majoritarian populism.

In Chapter 5, we return to Gramastha Mandals and ask whether a shared village history brings disparate communities from the same village closer together once in Mumbai, a commonly-found trope in studies of village-to-city migration in India. Membership of most of the Gramastha Mandals is actually allocated on the basis of community, with Hindu-only or even Maratha-only Gramastha Mandal rooms, as well as a few (Dalit) Buddhist-only rooms in different buildings. Moreover, Dalits and Marathas will have experienced their villages differently, living in different locations with different social networks and religious functions, a difference that has been imported and reconfigured in the built layout of the chawls. Spending time in both Hindu and Buddhist Gramastha Mandal rooms, this chapter demonstrates that the spatial configuration of migrants' BDD Chawls lives makes interaction with one's own community a daily reality in contrast to the time and effort needed to mix with the other community. There are signs of slow change here, however, and many migrants are beginning to construct (sub-)urban futures for themselves far from the neighbourhood.

Chapter 6 opens with an account of Dalit commemorations of the 1818 Battle of Koregaon in which a Mahar battalion, fighting on behalf of the British, defeated the forces of the local Brahman rulers. The celebrations ended in violent attacks from dominant-caste Hindus who regarded it as antinational. The spotlight turns to Chhatrapati Shivaji, icon of the Shiv Sena and the Marathas, who is perhaps surprisingly an object of reverence for the Dalit Buddhists too. In contrast to the 'for' or 'against' positions that contestations over revered historical figures often assume, there is a degree of overlap in the narratives that circulate in these communities, likely a product of shared school textbooks, linked to Shivaji's religious tolerance and egalitarian rule. However, among the Dalit Buddhists, who are proud Maharashtrians as well as proud Indians, he is typically claimed as a low-caste peasant ruler whose core ideological mission was to oppose Brahmanic hierarchy. For the Marathas, it is Shivaji's identity as a high-caste Maratha Hindu that is highlighted, his tolerance explicitly framed in contrast to the perceived fanaticism of earlier Islamic rule. This proprietorial view of Shivaji is deeply entangled in the Marathas' own status anxieties as Indians and as citizens of Mumbai, and linked to their support for the Shiv Sena. Regional history is as fiercely contested as national and local history and does not provide enough common ground to bring disparate communities together.

Chapter 7 revisits the chawlness introduced in Chapter 1, to show how the neighbourhood redevelopment proposals highlighted that a deeply-felt shared sense of belonging is insufficient to transcend the ideological divisions between the Dalit Buddhist and Maratha communities. Ideas of falseness and fakery abound here too. A protest movement against the redevelopment proposals arose that was significantly, but not exclusively, spearheaded by members of the Dalit Buddhist community. They were sceptical of the government's promises to rehouse existing residents and frustrated by the lack of clarity on these and other issues, while the Maratha community largely dismissed these concerns. The title of a well-known Marathi play (*Hasva Fasvi,* or 'smiling deceit*)* was adapted by the Dalit protestors in one of their banners to *Hasvi ki Fasvi?* (smiles or fraud?) which asked whether the state government's promises could be trusted.

There are no neat endings here and the Epilogue reflects this. I provide an update to the major strands of the ethnography following my departure from the fieldsite, showing how the site redevelopment plans remained mired in inertia until very recently, while the village-wards orientation of the Gramastha Mandal migrants was further underlined by their exodus from Mumbai during the covid lockdowns of 2020–1. Just as debates over the history and future of the BDD Chawls continue, the Bhima Koregaon celebrations and their aftermath are now hot topics in South Asian studies as a symptom of how profoundly contested India's history and future have become. I also reflect again on my own role in producing the knowledge that underpins the book's argument, and the anxieties that have accompanied this. Finally, I ask why history matters to my interlocutors and why I found this so alien. Concluding that this is in part a reflection of my own background and the lens through which I view the BDD Chawls, and in part the result of centuries of instrumentalising and contesting history in India, I draw on parallels from other parts of the world (including my own) to make sense of it.

The 'why' and the 'how': on ethics and methods

In the unlikely event that he was still listening, my book-launch neighbour might reasonably be expected to ask a further question: *why* are you doing this? The best answer I can give begins with language, which has been an obsession of mine for much longer even than India has. On that first visit to Mumbai in 2003, knowing little of the city's history, I was puzzled that, despite being in Maharashtra, I seemed to encounter Gujarati at every turn. Later, I was intrigued to read Suketu Mehta's description of a Bombay-specific Hindi which he used even when talking to fellow Gujarati speakers (Mehta, 2004, p. 9). Still later, I was fascinated by a comment I overheard (paraphrased here) from a wealthy non-Maharashtrian: 'Of course the city really belongs to the Maharashtrians, doesn't it? They're friendly, but you can never properly *know* them, can you?'

All these threads fed into my preoccupation with the city's linguistic life that bloomed into the research proposal I took to Mumbai before ultimately discarding. Still, if somebody had asked me *why* I was undertaking this research, I would have been at a loss. 'I find it interesting' would have been the truest answer I could have given, although I would have probably couched this in terms of the potential benefits it might bring to policymakers or social workers. If they had asked why *I* was undertaking the research, I would have been even harder pressed for an answer. 'I'm sceptical about white men going off to research in Papua New Guinea, or wherever,' a sociolinguist once told me, 'You just don't blend in.' I was taken aback: it had not occurred to me that 'blending in' was a necessary or even desirable part of the research I wanted to conduct. Surely, I answered her eloquently in my head several days later, the academic world depends on the richness of multiple perspectives – insiders, outsiders and everything in between.

Although I stand by this answer in theory, I acknowledge that due to my many identity-based privileges – of race, class, mother tongue and gender among others – the odds are disproportionately stacked in my favour when it comes to making my voice heard. Moreover, and with the safety of hindsight, I admit that I am now less, rather than more, convinced that I had any 'right' to choose the BDD Chawls as a fieldsite in the first place. There is something especially uncomfortable about a British anthropologist conducting research in a former British colony and yet, as we shall see in Chapter 6, my interlocutors' own relationship to the idea of British rule was far from simple, and I frequently found myself in the position of arguing against colonialism with Dalit Buddhist friends who regarded the British as benevolent liberators.

I have no convincing response to offer to any of this, other than noting that in analysing my fieldnotes and converting them into prose I have deliberately drawn heavily on the work of Indian academics, especially female and Dalit scholars. This is in any case no more than a bare minimum and, had I been familiar with Linda Tuhiwai Smith's *Decolonizing Methodologies* when developing my research proposal, I might have approached critical questions such as 'Whose research is it?', 'Who owns it?', 'Who will benefit from it?' and 'How will its results be disseminated?' more mindfully, rather than in the spirit of box-ticking (Smith, 2021, p. 10). Tuhiwai Smith's recommendations on sharing knowledge and reporting back will be returned to in 'An anthropologist's anxieties' in the Epilogue.

There is no question that I was viewed as an outsider in the BDD Chawls. Of course this comes with disadvantages. Despite my familiarity with India, including Mumbai, prior to beginning my research, I could never have hoped to have acquired anything close to the depth of embodied understanding of a researcher brought up in Mumbai or even elsewhere in India.

Meanwhile, conceding that my spoken Marathi was not sufficient to conduct the research as proposed was not merely humiliating but threw up a host of practical problems. Much of the ambient conversation around me in the BDD Chawls simply went over my head, as did the substance of many of the speeches I listened to at events. The bulk of my conversations took place in Hindi, and in some cases English, meaning that an epistemological distance was hardwired into these interactions. These are serious shortcomings and as such the entire study comes with a heavy caveat.

Nevertheless, there are also benefits to being an outsider, and I sometimes took advantage of this status in order to ask questions that were, in retrospect, rather impudent. I was conscious that I might struggle to incorporate both Maratha Hindus and Dalit Buddhists into my research without encountering opposition from both but, as the months wore on, no such problems became apparent to me, and, if anything, amusement was the main reaction. In addition to their own collective generosity, I suspect that it was specifically my foreignness as a white, British researcher with no identifiable affiliation to any specific Indian community that enabled me to interact so easily with both groups in the same neighbourhood.

Meanwhile, as a male, I believe I was far more readily accepted in all-male spaces, like the Jay Bhim Katta and the Gramastha Mandals, than a female researcher would have been, regardless of the extent to which she might otherwise be viewed an insider. There is a noticeable bias, in fact, towards men. It would be disingenuous to explain this bias solely as the inevitable outcome of a non-Indian male conducting research in a socially-conservative setting. I did meet women and strike up friendships with them and with more effort could have probably developed a much richer understanding of life as a woman in the BDD Chawls. Instead, however, I instinctively homed in on the settings where I felt most welcome, and most readily able to participate in conversations, gossip, debates and disputes: the Jay Bhim Katta and the Gramastha Mandals.[15]

Participant observation, indeed, formed the bulk of my research methodology. Famously described as 'deep hanging out' (Geertz, 1998), for me participation involved a great deal of sitting down – on benches, on floors, in teashops and sometimes in bars. I made notes on my mobile phone, for the most part openly and with explicit permission. Sometimes I even showed my companions what I had written and modified it at their suggestions, although at other times I did not try too hard to dispel the impression that I might be sending a text message. Although my working schedule varied, for much of the year I pursued a one day on, one day off model, whereby I would spend a day in the BDD Chawls, followed by a day of writing up notes, visiting the state archives, meeting other academics or simply relaxing. This meant that over a fortnightly cycle I got to experience the BDD Chawls on every day of the week, often until late at night, but also allowed myself time to reflect on what I had experienced and to identify gaps and further questions. In the later stages of fieldwork I conducted recorded interviews with 30 participants in order to gather documentary evidence and cross-check certain pieces of information.[16]

Throughout the research phase, I worried that I might be misleading people as to my intentions and spent a lot of time trying to explain my change of focus, a challenging task since I could not satisfactorily explain this to myself in English, let alone to anybody else in Hindi. I believe that in some cases I succeeded, but there are doubtless many in the BDD Chawls who remember me, if at all, as an aspiring but inept language student. I also reminded my interlocutors on a regular basis that I was not just a harmless friend, but something closer to an intellectual vampire, feeding off the scraps of information that they fed me. Humbled by the generosity with which – far from being shunned as a monstrous predator as might be expected – I was offered tea and food and, above all, time, I often agonised over what I could give in return. While I made some minor contributions in the form of occasional English classes, careers advice and small financial donations to a few social functions at which I tried my best to help out in whatever way I could, I have no illusions of anything but an enormous debt of gratitude.

Notes

1. Mumbai has a rich and confusing linguistic life. A plurality, rather than a majority (roughly 40–5 per cent) speak Marathi, the language of the surrounding state of Maharashtra, as a first language in the city. However, Marathi has not traditionally been associated with social prestige, although it is the language of political officialdom and its use has become heavily politicised as will be discussed further in Chapter 6. Economic and cultural capital remains disproportionately concentrated in the hands of a smaller mercantile population, many of whom (approximately one fifth of Mumbai's overall population) speak Gujarati. Despite this, the main lingua franca of the city is a distinctive local brand of Hindi, sometimes called Bambaiya. Hindi, in a variety of dialects, is also the mother tongue of slightly under 20 per cent of Mumbai residents. Smaller numbers speak other languages such as Tamil, Kannada, Telugu and Konkani. As in other parts of India, English is the language of the elite.
2. Bombay, the name given to the city by the British East India Company is a legacy of an earlier Portuguese presence and is believed to derive from *Bombaim* ('good little bay'). This in turn *may* be a folk etymology from the Marathi name Mumbai, referring to Mumbadevi, the patron goddess of the Koli fishing community that has been resident in the area for many centuries. For further details on the political salience of these names, and their use in the rest of the book, see 'When Bombay became Mumbai' in this chapter.
3. Unless explicitly stated, all names of individuals have been changed in order to protect the identity of my research participants.

4   Census data indicates that between 1881 and 1931, migrants from the coastal Ratnagiri District accounted for 16–22 per cent of Mumbai's population (Chandavarkar, 1994, p. 128), while the opening of the Bhor Ghat roadway in 1830 and the subsequent construction of the railways had begun to open up the regions due east and southeast of the city such as Kolhapur, Satara and Sangli Districts (Adarkar and Menon, 2004, p. 92).

5   A precursor to the BDD was the Bombay (City) Improvement Trust, established in 1898 following an outbreak of plague (Caru, 2019, p. 214). While the Trust's work was fairly limited in scope, it was the first state intervention in civic restructuring of its kind in colonial India, influenced by the 'Improvement Schemes' of nineteenth-century Britain (Kidambi, 2001, p. 57). The extent to which the colonial administration intervened in the issue of workers' housing in Bombay was 'significant and distinct', unmatched elsewhere in the British Empire, perhaps in part due to the limited housing provision by mill-owners themselves (Caru, 2019, p. 214). However, following Improvement Trust intervention, which included demolishing existing tenement blocks without providing alternative accommodation, housing and sanitary problems had actually increased by the early 1920s, and 'in belated recognition of its inadequacies as an agency of civic renewal, the Government of Bombay set up a new Development Directorate [the BDD] in 1920' (Kidambi, 2007, p. 113).

6   As with individuals, village names have been changed to further protect my interlocutors' identity.

7   I use the term 'community' in this book to refer to groups defined by an intersection of religion and caste, chiefly the Dalit Buddhists and Maratha Hindus. To avoid confusion, I do not apply the term to other overlapping groups such as the 'Maharashtrian community' or the 'BDD Chawls community', instead using the terms 'common identity' or 'shared belonging'. Moreover, I largely avoid using the term 'communal', which in a South Asian context usually refers to tensions between religious groups. Even within this framework possible ambiguities may arise. For example, at different points the term 'Dalit Buddhist community' is used to refer to the entire population of Dalit Buddhists in India, or to the Dalit Buddhists of the BDD Chawls or, most specifically, to my circle of friends and acquaintances who frequent the Jay Bhim Katta. In all cases my aim has been to provide sufficient context to ensure confusion is avoided. Although this concept of community is strictly an etic one, it has arisen in response to the close-knit social groups found in the BDD Chawls and the strong sense I detected among both Marathas and Dalit Buddhists of being part of a wider network of Marathas or Dalit Buddhists, sometimes referred to using terms such as *samaj* (society) or *jati* (caste) or often – even in a Hindi or Marathi context – the English word 'community'.

8   While most of the BDD Chawls Chambhars originate from the Konkan districts, there are Dalit Buddhists and Maratha families from both the Konkan and the Ghats.

9   *Varna* refers to the four broad social tiers set out in the *Manusmrti* (Laws of Manu), a Hindu law code dating from the first century CE. The four *varna*, from highest to lowest, are Brahman (priests; also spelled Brahmin, although this does not reflect the standard pronunciation in many Indian languages), Kshatriya (rulers, warriors), Vaishya (merchants) and Shudra (labourers), outside which sit the Ati-Shudras or untouchables (Dalits). Loosely grouped within this system is an enormous range of endogamous social groupings based on hereditary occupations and referred to as *jati*. Although the English term 'caste' is most often used to refer to *jati*, it is also used with reference to *varna* or to an amalgam of the two systems.

10 For further details on the passage and ultimate failure of this Bill, see 'Ek Maratha, Lakh Maratha' in Chapter 6.

11 In the years that followed, other colonial names were changed under the aegis of the Shiv Sena-led Maharashtra Legislative Assembly. Victoria Terminus was renamed Chhatrapati Shivaji Maharaj Terminus in 1996, and the Prince of Wales Museum became the Chhatrapati Shivaji Maharaj Vastu Sangrahalaya in 1998. At a similar time, Delisle Road, named after a one-time chief engineer of the Bombay Water Works, was renamed in favour of Narayan Malhar Joshi, co-founder of the All Indian Trade Union Congress.

12 In the BDD Chawls, the individual buildings are referred to by number (Chawl 1, Chawl 2, etc.) but to further protect the identity of my research participants I have replaced these numbers with letters. Alphabetical position does not correspond to number – that is, Chawl A does not refer to Chawl 1, and nor is Chawl 10 designated by Chawl J.

13 Palmié and Stewart have subsequently taken up the challenge themselves to launch an *Anthropology of History* book series that features, *inter alia,* studies of archival activism in post-Soviet Moscow, ghost tours in Chile and cosmology in the Papuan highlands. For further

details, see https://www.routledge.com/The-Anthropology-of-History/book-series/ANTHIST (accessed 23 February 2023).
14 See endnote 9 (this chapter) for further details on *varna* (caste), and on the orthography used in this book.
15 A fuller discussion of the implications of gender on my research can be found in Chapter 2 and a discussion on sexuality is included in 'An anthropologist's anxieties' in the Epilogue.
16 Informed consent, in adherence to SOAS's *Code of Practice for Use of Personal Data in Research* was obtained verbally and recorded in English at the beginning of each interview, after (where required) a more detailed explanation and discussion in Hindi or Marathi prior to the interview. Each interview was tailored to the individual, and my sample of 30 interviewees was neither random nor precisely engineered as a statistically-accurate simulacrum of my larger body of interlocutors. For example, my sample of 30 can be broken down by gender (26 men and four women), community (16 Marathas, 11 Dalit Buddhists, one Chambhar, one Catholic and one Muslim), living arrangement (eight current Gramastha Mandal residents, three former residents and 19 family residents) or mother tongue (28 Marathi, one Gujarati and one Konkani). Nineteen of the interviews were principally undertaken in Hindi, nine in English, and two in a mix Marathi and Hindi.

1
'Chawlness': a folk history of (un)locked doors

Away from Delisle Road and its soundscape of hoots and shouts and rumbling traffic, the BDD Chawls is a dell of calm. It is not an 'urban village' like Khotachiwadi, a warren of winding streets and Portuguese-style wooden bungalows that is a fixture on the heritage map. Nor is it a slum, that neighbourhood typology so indelibly linked to Mumbai through films and novels and breathless descriptions in travel guides. Even the archetypal chawl image – an external corridor with a wooden balustrade and saris hanging out to dry, as pictured on the front cover of Neera Adarkar's edited volume *The Chawls of Mumbai: Galleries of Life* – is not in evidence here.

The BDD Chawl buildings are more like barracks, with their uncompromising rectangular bulk and barred windows, but this effect is leavened by small irregularities and splashes of colour: the little ground-floor shops with bright signs and hanging crisp packets and plastic toys; the jerry-built extensions with blue plywood panels and tin roofs; the towels and clothes hanging in the windows, their billowing tendencies kept in check by the metal bars. Most enticing of all are the trees, dusty havens of shade and birdsong, some with concrete seating areas at their base.

The overriding first impression is one of homogeneity: 32 identical four-storey buildings with 20 small dwellings, little more than a single room, on each storey; and each building differing only in terms of orientation and colour – yellow, salmon pink, grey, light green. The grid-like structure of the streets makes it confusing for a first-time visitor, and well into my fieldwork I would still have moments of disorientation when I tried to remember which building was which, and how to get from one person's home to another's. Gradually, I developed an appreciation of the neighbourhood's diversity, which was after all why I had chosen it in the first place. Dalit-dominated buildings, I realised, featured prominent pictures of Ambedkar or Rohidas (a Chambhar saint), while Shivaji imagery was a fixture in the Maratha-majority chawls. Chawl P, with its large but dwindling number of Goan Catholic families, was readily identified by the Father Christmas murals at its entrance, while the ground floor corridor in Chawl A, known for the high socio-economic standing of its residents, was noticeably cleaner and brighter than those of other buildings.[1]

Less obviously visible is the history of Chawl E, once thought of as the 'Muslim chawl' until most of its Muslim families moved out after the 1992–3 religious riots that scarred the city. I would occasionally see women in black *chador* leaving or entering the building, but I never became acquainted with any of them. The only one of the few remaining Muslim residents I interacted with on a regular basis was a garrulous old man called Jafar who talked at length about the moral superiority of his native Lucknow over vice-ridden Mumbai. Chawls V1 and V2, meanwhile, are reserved for police constables and their families, as are several units in other buildings, and the N. M. Joshi Marg police station, a quaint old building with a wooden veranda and bright yellow walls, is situated at the southern edge of the BDD Chawls neighbourhood (Figure 1.1).

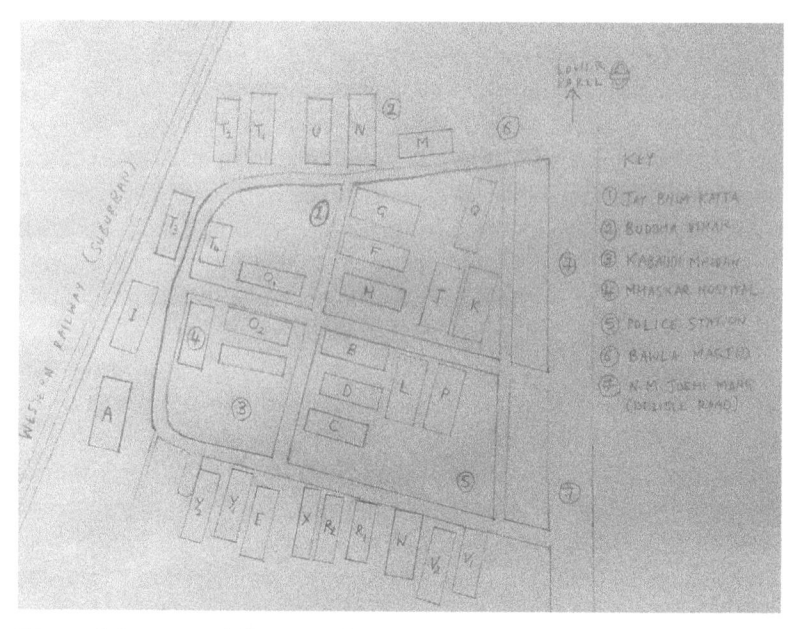

Figure 1.1 Map of the BDD Chawls neighbourhood. © Author.

Other modes of difference are even less legible: the loose building-wise segregation between families with roots in the coastal Konkan region and those who had come from the inland Ghat districts; the handful of Gujarati families in an otherwise Maharashtrian neighbourhood; and all the nuances of sub-caste that nestled within the broad divisions already sketched out. One highly significant axis of diversity only came to my attention months into the fieldwork. While most of the individual chawl dwellings are occupied by families, sometimes with three or more generations living in the same space, a substantial minority are given over to Gramastha Mandals, the dormitory rooms for male migrants from a particular village, such as the one Vikas lived in.

Difference is an organising theme in many of the ensuing chapters, in particular the divergent understandings different communities hold of the history of certain imagined geographies – villages, Mumbai, Maharashtra, and India itself. In this initial chapter, however, I introduce the BDD Chawls at a turning point in its own history to explore an extremely localised conception of history that is shared between communities. I call this shared neighbourhood history 'chawlness' and show how it underpins a common chawl identity that is both treasured by insiders but also legible to outsiders, albeit in a superficial manner that overlooks significant diversity.

Chawlness includes a commonly-told story that the chawls were originally built as prisons (the 'locked doors' of the chapter title) as well as a more general idea of belonging to a close-knit community that keeps its doors open ('*un*locked doors') and maintains social ties strong enough to subsume minor temporary disputes within a longer-term peace. Although this open-door culture is sometimes framed in opposition to the closed-door culture of middle-class flats, there is nevertheless a shared perception among many BDD Chawls residents that they themselves now belong to the middle class. I draw throughout on architect Neera Adarkar's (2011) *The Chawls of Mumbai,* an edited volume that brings together a wide range of voices to explore the social history of chawls, in addition to anthropologist Maura Finkelstein's (2019) *The Archive of Loss,* which features research conducted in the (Delisle Road) BDD Chawls, and historian Vanessa Caru's work on the Worli BDD Chawls (2011; 2019).

Breaking news

The first thing I knew about the BDD Chawls was that their days were numbered. Two days after an architect friend told me about the proposed redevelopment and recommended I visit the neighbourhood, my stumbling first entry was actually a coincidence. It was joining these dots later on that gave me the most powerful sense that this was, indubitably, the fieldsite for me. It surprised me that nobody seemed to share my sense of the BDD Chawls as a site living on borrowed time. In the first couple of months, none of my new friends said anything about living with the threat of eviction or with the enticing prospect of a new home. Any attempts I made to steer conversations towards the topic were brushed off with uninformative and distinctly unenthusiastic answers. Since debates around redeveloping the BDD Chawls had been raging for two decades or more, the residents may well have been bored of the subject, or perhaps they did not yet trust me enough to talk about it.

Back in October 1998, an article from the *Times of India* reported that a 40-member delegation met Maharashtra Industries Minister Ramrao Adik and urged the state government to 'demolish [the BDD Chawls] and construct new buildings in their place' (Times of India, 1988). Two years later, at Mantralaya (the headquarters of the Maharashtra Legislative Assembly), Mr Adik is recorded as having requested a report on BDD Chawl reconstruction by engineers and architects. The correspondent notes that the 'life of the buildings is almost over' (Times of India, 1990). Nearly a decade after that, at the tail end of the BJP-Shiv Sena cabinet that succeeded Adik's Congress government, the state government approved a proposal in which the four BDD Chawls sites would be demolished and redeveloped, housing existing residents free of charge in new 225 sq. ft. carpet-area tenements (Yeshwantrao, 1999a). The cost of this project would be funded by flats constructed elsewhere on the BDD Chawls sites 'to be sold at the present market rate and … expected to generate sizeable profits for the developer', according to one official (Yeshwantrao, 1999a). This proposal was criticised by a residents' association for the four sites, on the grounds that the new flats would scarcely be bigger than their existing 180 sq. ft. rooms, and the same size as those 'given to the illegal slum and pavement dwellers' in developments elsewhere in the city (Yeshwantrao, 1999b).

Seven years on, in 2007, the proposal had altered little, still featuring a mix of 225 sq. ft. flats for existing tenants, and 'swank apartments which would be sold in the open market' (Times of India, 2007). Due to internal disputes, the State Cabinet of Maharashtra, now back under the control of the Congress Party, remained unable to reach a decision on the proposal. By late 2015, 'news of the [BJP-led state government] initiating the chawl's redevelopment plan started doing the rounds' prompting a 'wave of jubilation' among residents who were 'oscillating between happiness and cynicism' at the prospect (Puranik,

2015). The terms offered to existing tenants were considerably more generous than in earlier proposals, with the promised free 500 sq. ft. flats described as 'the state's highest-ever compensation to be given in any redevelopment project in the city' (Phadke, 2016).

Despite the lack of interest I could elicit from my interlocutors, I kept a watchful eye on news reports throughout February and March 2017. At least part of my motivation was a self-interested concern that my fieldsite, so recently embraced, might disappear before my eyes, and with it my research project. A tender notice for the redevelopment of the BDD Chawls at Naigaon and N. M. Joshi Marg[2] had been published on 28 December 2016, a few weeks before my arrival in Mumbai. For the rehab portion of the N. M. Joshi Marg site it specified fourteen 22-storey towers with commercial space on the ground floor, alongside which four 47-storey residential towers were to be constructed for sales, two targeting middle-income groups and the other two targeting high-income groups. An 84-month time limit was specified for completion of the project.[3]

The initial 13 February tender response deadline came and went without a single bid being received (Gadgil, 2017) and even after a 15-day extension the minimum number of bids was not met, prompting a further extension (Hanwate, 2017). Reading these updates, I felt a churlish sense of relief. At this rate, I allowed myself to hope, the BDD Chawl buildings might remain intact for the duration of my study.

Shortly after this, a bout of heat exhaustion kept me at home for a few days. I was touched to receive a visit from Anish, who had become one of my closest associates in the BDD Chawls, and a few of his friends. They brought biscuits and solicitude and, it quickly emerged, news. Anish told me that I should start bringing my camera along to the BDD Chawls, as redevelopment was finally going to begin, perhaps by December. I felt a sinking feeling but also a thrill of excitement that sweeping change was on the horizon. '*Aaj ka breaking news*' (breaking news today) someone remarked, explaining that two developers' bids were now being considered by the Maharashtra Housing and Area Development Authority (MHADA). A few days later it was announced that the tender for the N.M. Joshi Marg redevelopment had been awarded to Shapoorji Pallonji (Phadke, 2016), a Mumbai-based multinational business conglomerate with particular expertise in engineering and construction.

Suddenly, it seemed, everybody wanted to talk about the redevelopment. Late one afternoon, a group of us left the Jay Bhim Katta (the seating area where Anish, Manish and my other Dalit Buddhist friends spent so much of their free time) and climbed up to the roof of Chawl G to enjoy the evening breeze and sunset views. I showed off my knowledge of

Mumbai's post-mill regeneration and pointed out the blue-glass Lodha Excelus residential tower that had been built on the former Apollo Mills site; the Peninsula Business Park complex that replaced Dawn Mills; the incomplete pink octagonal tower of Palais Royale on the old site of Shree Ram Mills, locked in a dispute between rival wings of a family construction business; and the blue-and-white One Avighna Park, supposedly destined to house wealthy Jain merchants, where New Islam Mills used to be.

Dinesh, a young man in his twenties, laughed and pointed to the Marathon Futurex building, on the former Mafatlal Mills site, and said that 'our houses will be this tall in future', prompting a general discussion on the redevelopment proposal. He told me that 3,000 flats would be built for sale on the site in addition to the free 500 sq. ft. flats for existing residents. I asked if the sales flats would be expensive and Anish said yes, given that this was the 'centre point' of Mumbai and that there are two stations nearby. Someone else – half-joking perhaps? – said that they would miss the common toilets as they are all so used to negotiating their morning ablutions under these constraints that it will actually be harder with one toilet per large family.

Many rumours were relayed to me at the Jay Bhim Katta in the days that followed. Somebody told me that Shapoorji Pallonji would give Rs 20,000 (c. £200) per month to each household to help them rent elsewhere while the redevelopment took place, while Anish at one point suggested that temporary accommodation (officially referred to as a 'transit camp') would be built in the park directly behind the Jay Bhim Katta. Someone else said that a new playground and school had been promised, and there was a general consensus that four 23-storey buildings would be constructed to house the existing residents for free.

But it quickly became clear that my friends looked on the redevelopment with more concern than excitement. Questions began to surface about the sincerity of MHADA's intentions to rehouse existing chawl residents, and about the pressure on space and infrastructure that would result from the rumoured 3,000 extra units that were being built for sale. Above all, they were worried about the effect that redevelopment would have on the social fabric of the BDD Chawls.

The impact of high-rise development on pre-existing modes of sociality is not a concern unique to Mumbai. In Cairo, Farha Ghannam (2002) describes the alienation and loss of old social networks as residents of a central neighbourhood are displaced into public housing on the outskirts of the city, echoing themes explored nearly 20 years earlier by Alice Coleman (1985) in the context of planned housing in east London. Meanwhile, Elisa Tamburo (2020), charting the experiences of

Taiwanese military veterans moving from urban villages to high-rise blocks, analyses the dissolution of 'warm social relationships' in terms of a specifically high-rise form of governmentality constituted by 'new technologies regulating access, new governance and authority implementing rules, and a new aesthetic of standardization'. In the following section, I sketch out the salient features of 'chawlness', the existing BDD Chawls sociality based on a shared chawl-dwelling identity and sense of local history.

Open doors and shared culture

In my initial months of hanging out at the Jay Bhim Katta I became preoccupied with the question of what I could possibly give my research participants in return for their continuing generosity and hospitality. I hit on the idea of offering English classes to help the young children in the neighbourhood improve their spoken command of the language. To my surprise, it was men of my age and older who were most eager to take advantage of the offer. Anish explained that he had several friends who are engineers, including a Brahman whose brother owns four colleges, and he feels 'guilty' around them when they speak English and he cannot join in.

Although I prepared plans and materials and sought permission to use a room in Chawl F for the lessons, the endeavour never really got off the ground. There were several expressions of interest but not many translated into actual attendance. The few sessions that I held took the form of rambling, trilingual conversations with Anish and Manish, and I reflected guiltily that, far from recompensing them for their time and information, these so-called English classes were simply taking up more of their time and extracting more information from them. After little more than a month of weekly classes the project fizzled out entirely.

During one class I floated another idea: making a website with video clips celebrating the history and contemporary life of the BDD Chawls. Anish appeared enthusiastic but cautioned me that some people might be sad to talk about the chawls given the spectre of demolition. 'We have been living here for more than 90 years,' he said in English, and this led into a characteristically forceful monologue in a mix of Marathi and Hindi. He talked about all the memories people have of the area. Of how, before water was piped into the rooms, women might fight in the early-morning queue to the taps but by the evening be friends again, chopping vegetables together. How men might fight and not talk for a few days, but then unite against a common outside enemy. How the rooms are small, and doors are always open. For example, he said gesturing to Manish's family's room, if Manish's mother is cooking chicken everybody in the corridor will get to try a bit. If anybody is in trouble, their neighbours will come to help them.

As with the English classes my plans for a website foundered, but as redevelopment discussions gathered pace in the months that followed, Anish declared his intention to immortalise the BDD Chawls in his own short film. For several weeks I would find him deep in conversations about 'out-focus shots' and how to portray critical events in the chawls' history. He described one of the scenes he was planning to shoot: a group of men, including Anish himself, brawling at the Jay Bhim Katta until somebody comes out to announce that Anish's father is having chest pains. The fighting ceases instantly, and all the men rally round to support Anish and his family. This, it seemed for Anish, was the crux of chawl life: minor quotidian squabbles erupting and then dissipating due to the strength of the bond between neighbours; petty disagreements rendered insignificant in the face of a common threat.

I began to think of this mode of life as 'chawlness', a term I used to signify all the minutiae of everyday life that defined the neighbourhood's present and past. Chawlness was the way men spent hours sitting outside on benches and chai stalls with their friends and neighbours. It was also the decades-old traditions of religious festivals that crowd the streets, and the stories people told of the textile mills that dominated life's rhythms for so long. Chawlness was the shouted question or cry of greeting that passed from the street to one of the windows in the building opposite, and the reply coming from a half-visible figure within. It was in the old friendships and older feuds that were explained to me by narrators I sometimes suspected of being unreliable, and the neighbourhood social clubs with proud histories of sports victories and philanthropic endeavour. It was there, too, in the building's imposing rectangular openings, some with attached seating areas that ensured all comings and goings were highly visible.

Above all, chawlness can be found in the doors that separate individual homes from the corridors. These doors are often left ajar, sometimes wide open and normally shut only at night or padlocked when nobody is home. They are crucial in the merging of domestic and common space, whereby the corridors (or 'galleries' as residents refer to them) hum with gossip and debate as residents sit on their doorsteps or loiter nearby and exchange pleasantries and news with their neighbours. The immediately surrounding portion of the corridor is claimed as an additional storage space: shoes are generally left there but sometimes so are other household items such as excess furniture or even certain foodstuffs.

Architectural theorist Kaiwan Mehta, noting how much of the action of classic chawl-based novels like Kiran Nagarkar's *Ravan and Eddie* occurs 'in spaces of the veranda, staircases and the shared courtyard', makes a similar observation that in chawls, 'the space of the family is overlapped with the space of the neighbours' (Mehta, 2011, p. 86). On occasions, such as a religious festival or a wedding, the BDD Chawls corridors transform into party venues, decorated and lined with plastic chairs. Snacks and soft drinks, sometimes even a full-blown meal, will be served to residents and guests alike before the corridor becomes a dance floor, complete with a DJ and speakers. I quite often found myself in a crush of sweating bodies at midnight, dancing to the strains of hit song Zingaat (from the 2016 Marathi film *Sairat*) and feeling chawlness at its most visceral (Figure 1.2).

Figure 1.2 (a) One end of the 'gallery' of Chawl F, afternoon. (b) The same gallery during a wedding party. © Author.

Open doors are a powerful symbol of chawl life for my interlocutors, and the feared shift to a 'closed door' culture in the new flats is a potent source of anxiety. Akshay, a Maratha friend from Chawl M described how the chawls had transformed over the last few decades from a working-class area to a middle-class area, but the open-door culture had persisted. 'I can walk into any room, any kitchen I like,' he told me, 'but after flats are developed, people's mentalities will change. You won't be able to go round to your neighbours at any time because doors will be closed.'

A motif I heard frequently was that if anybody experienced problems in their chawl room, all the neighbours would hear it and would come to help. The same thing would not occur behind the closed doors of an apartment block, friends told me. Anthropologist Maura Finkelstein, likewise, notes how the 'visibility and familiarity' of chawl life make these buildings 'bastions of safety in an otherwise dangerous city' (2019, p. 110). She also spent time in the BDD Chawls as part of her Mumbai-wide research and describes residents' fears of losing the open spaces of galleries and courtyards (Finkelstein, 2019, p. 114).

Anish seemed particularly hard hit by this prospect and, during one paean to chawl life, he started crying. Ebullient Anish, crying! Flustered, I put my arm around him. Prompted by a dim memory of reading about chawl residents moving to an apartment block and installing grille doors to aid cross-corridor gossip,[4] I suggested to Anish that surely this 'open door' culture would persist in the new buildings. He seemed doubtful. There was no guarantee that everybody would be able to stay together in a transit camp, so that staying in touch would take an effort, unlike the easy companionship found at the Jay Bhim Katta today. Besides, in the new buildings there would be fewer flats per storey, and since these flats would be larger than the current chawl rooms, and the open space smaller, people would have a tendency to shut the door behind them.

Beyond the ebb and flow of everyday chawlness, there seemed to be emergency-mode chawlness that could be deployed when the situation arose. In late May, a cricket tournament called the 'Nadeem Cup: BDD Premier League 2017', was held in the *kabaddi maidan,* the large neighbourhood sports ground occupying one quadrant of the neighbourhood grid (*kabaddi* is a popular Indian contact sport, and *maidan* refers to a public square or open space). Unlike the regular BDD Chawl-wide cricket competitions in which each building or pair of buildings put up a cricket team, this one featured six teams with names like 'Mumbai Stunners' and 'Shreya Eagles', each with players drawn from across the BDD Chawls. In itself an example of cross-chawl camaraderie, the Nadeem Cup had a history that struck me as chawlness at its most noble. According to Fawaz, a shopkeeper friend on Delisle Road, Nadeem was a Muslim from Chawl E: 'He was a good boy, popular in every BDD Chawl, a big champion in cricket, a good batsman and bowler.' Late in 2016, he travelled by car with friends to Shirdi to visit the shrine of popular saint Sai Baba. Tragically, the car crashed on the way back, and after two days in a coma Nadeem died, leaving behind a wife and a small child.

Several months after the tournament, Satyajit, a friend from Chawl D, introduced me to one of the young men who had been travelling with Nadeem and lost the sight in one eye in the crash. They told me that after the crash, residents from across the BDD Chawls had come together and contributed money for the victims' hospital care. Satyajit even lent his credit card for the purpose, and explained to me that 'If the boys in the BDD Chawls can't help each other, who can help them?'

Meanwhile, on 29 August 2017, Mumbai received the equivalent of 11 days' average monsoon rainfall on a single day, resulting in infrastructural chaos and multiple casualties (Warrier, 2017). Luckily, my own ground floor flat in Worli remained dry, but I received photo updates of ground floor chawl rooms knee-deep in water, and the street outside waterlogged. I reached the chawls as soon as I was able to the next morning, hoping to help out, but by then all the water had already been bailed out of the buildings and the streets had drained. Across the BDD Chawls, I heard the same story of the previous night's horrors: fridges and other bulky electronic goods from ground floor rooms had been stored on first floor corridors, and many of the ground floor residents had spent the night with friends or family or in common spaces in the upper storeys. At no point in my fieldwork year did I feel more simultaneously awestruck by the fellowship of the chawls, and ashamed of my own inability to help in any way.

Locked doors and shared memories

Ironically, closed doors – locked ones, even – are the basis for one of the most popular pieces of local history. Did you know, people would ask me when they found out I was a researcher, that the BDD Chawls had originally been built by the British as jails? Some even claimed that the 'B' in BDD stood for British rather than Bombay. It was not a stretch to imagine these buildings with their barred windows and fortress-like reinforced concrete exteriors as jails. Even the ground floor openings, notwithstanding their present function in softening the boundaries of indoor and outdoor life, gave the dark corridors beyond them a slightly menacing aspect.

I heard many different versions of this narrative. Some people said that the jails were converted into chawls after only five or six years, while others insisted they had remained jails until after Independence. In the most popular version of the story, the jails were specifically designated for freedom fighters, and one old man from Chawl J told me that when he was a child the prisoners used to throw rocks at the British soldiers outside. Since I had no reason to doubt these accounts, I accepted them at face value. Other than the elderly Chawl J resident's eyewitness account, the others were based on the apparently reliable hearsay of parents and grandparents but it did not occur to me to call into question the testimony, albeit second or third-hand, of so many people that was also repeated in several news articles (for example Chandran, 2017; Dhupkar, 2017).

Doubt only crept into my mind after several visits to the Maharashtra State Archives, during which I not only found no reference to the Delisle Road BDD Chawls having been used as jails, but also located the original 1922 tender for the construction of the '33 Reinforced Concrete Chawls at De Lisle Road & 10 R.C. Chawls on plot "A" at Naigaum' which specified that the chawls 'shall consist of self-contained blocks of 4 storeys and containing 80 rooms each' (Public Works Department, 1922). I also found a cache of letters between J.C. Gammon Ltd, the contractors who built most of the Delisle BDD Chawls, and the Development Department, demanding payment for their services (Public Works Department, 1925), and a similar correspondence between another contractor, Vali Hassan, and the Development Department requesting payment of Rs 1,36,408/10/1 for work done on 'certain chawls' at Delisle Road (Public Works Department, 1924).

None of these documents make reference to jails, and it is quite clear from the wording that the project under consideration is the construction of chawls to provide residential accommodation. A further file of papers dating from 1937–8 includes a memo outlining debates about whether the chawls should be rendered 'suitable for middle class people' or whether they should be 'altered for the comfort and convenience of the working class people for whom the chawls were originally intended' (Public Works Department, 1938). A table dated 28 January 1938 shows that 2,043 out of the 2,560 Delisle Road chawls were occupied at that time (Public Works Department, 1938).[5]

I was eager to share this newfound knowledge, but my initial attempts to cast doubt on the jails narrative were met with scepticism by my BDD Chawls acquaintances. 'Our fathers told us this when we were children, and their fathers told them too,' said Jackson, a Catholic from Chawl P, for whom remote archival evidence understandably meant little when compared to a truth he had grown up with. I wondered whether perhaps some of the chawls had been *used* as jails at some point in their history, even if that is not the purpose for which they were built. A conversation with Rohan, from Chawl K, lent some weight to this speculation. He told me that he had read a newspaper article claiming that the BDD Chawls in Worli were initially under-inhabited, as it was a poorly-developed area, so some of those buildings were used as jails. There was nothing in the article about the Delisle Road chawls, however, and he did not have copy he could share with me.

Historian Vanessa Caru corroborates Rohan's account. She describes how, in an attempt to utilise the Worli BDD Chawls that had become a 'white elephant' due to low occupancy, the government 'found numerous other ways to use the buildings', notably the 'conversion of certain chawls into a temporary prison, as a result of the overcrowding that prevailed at the central jail' (Caru, 2011, p. 30). Between 1929 and 1949, three chawls in Worli were kept aside as occasional jails, 'most notably for the detention of Congress activists during the Civil Disobedience and Quit India Movements' (Caru, 2011, p. 30).

For months I was intrigued by the question of whether and when any of the Delisle Road BDD Chawls had been also used as jails. Playing the historian in the dusty archives was a thrill at first, but my interlocutors' lukewarm responses to my findings brought me down to earth with a bump. Remembering that I was an anthropologist rather than a historian, I began to realise that I had been asking the wrong question all along. What was really interesting was not the nitty-gritty of archival history, but the history that is told in the galleries and the tea stalls. Like Finkelstein, in a different 'people versus archive' context, I realised the question I should have been asking was 'not whether these stories are *true* but instead what these stories *do*?' (2019, p. 144). In the face of manifold social divisions, the story of locked doors was something shared across communities, all of whom passed it down the generations as a treasured piece of BDD Chawls history and a badge of belonging.

The spaces in between: the *katta* and the Mitra Mandal

Anish was not alone in his fears of a future without chawlness. Dropping in on Dinesh many weeks after the Shapoorji Pallonji announcement, I found him in a pensive mood about the redevelopment. He told me he was worried that the spaces in between the buildings would be swallowed up by the new buildings and that the distinctive culture attached to these spaces would be lost. Between Chawl C and Chawl D, for example, is a large, paved space where children often play cricket. Across the road, backing onto the *kabaddi maidan* is a small shrine to Sai Baba and a seating area. At the far end of the same road is Chawl N, where Mahendra lives, to one side of which is a space separating it from Akshay's building, Chawl M. At the back of this space is a Buddhist temple. On the other side, in the space between Chawl M and Chawl N is a structure labelled (in *Devanagari* script, like most other signs in the neighbourhood) Sunil Sports Club. Back down the road, close to the central crossroads, the space between Mahesh's Chawl F and Chawl H has been encroached on by illegal extensions leaving a narrow, dirty passageway. Elsewhere, the gaps between, behind and in front of buildings are filled with small shops, tea stalls, benches, makeshift sports grounds and temples.

Dinesh's fears of imminent loss are echoed by journalist and author Naresh Fernandes: 'As Bombay soars higher, the shared spaces that make the city human … are shrinking' (2013, p. 9). Indeed, the in-between space is a feature of chawl life much loved by residents and theorists alike; space that 'makes the chawl a home' (Finkelstein, 2019, p. 114) and where 'children may play cricket, and you may set-up the pandal [shrine] for the Ganesh festival' (Mehta, 2011, p. 86). I was especially fascinated by the prevalence of structures like the Jay Bhim Katta – some form of seating, typically under a corrugated metal awning, sometimes with a collection of newspapers. The generic term in Marathi for these seating areas is *katta* and, in the BDD Chawls at least, these spaces occupy an indeterminate status that is by no means private but is not truly public.[6] I was often told that anybody is welcome to sit in the Jay Bhim Katta, regardless of caste or gender. While this was demonstrably true in theory, in practice it was usually dominated by a stable core of male Dalit Buddhist users, mostly from Chawls F and G.

Invariably these spaces included a written sign, such as 'Bandya Maruti Seva Mandal' (outside Chawl J) and 'Satyam Krida Mandal' (opposite Chawls C and D) and 'Jay Bhim Mitra Mandal' on the Jay Bhim Katta itself. *Mandal* is another Marathi word, literally meaning circle, which tends to refer to an association or society. A Seva Mandal implies a service or social welfare organisation, while a Krida Mandal refers to a sports club and a Mitra Mandal, often used as a generic term for any of these organisations, is a friends' association. The Mitra Mandal is a familiar feature of working-class Mumbai life and a significant site of 'cultural interaction, and slow integration of the newcomers' (Heuzé, 1995, p. 219).

Most of the BDD Chawls *kattas* are owned by the Mitra Mandals, which are generally tied (at least notionally) to one or a pair of buildings. The Bandya Maruti Seva Mandal, for example, is attached to Chawls J and

K while the Jay Bharat Krida Mandal is linked to Chawl B, although in both organisations the membership base extends beyond these buildings. The remit of the Mitra Mandal is often rather flexible. The Jay Bharat Krida Mandal was first explained to me as a *kabaddi* team although I later learnt it was also responsible for organising various religious functions.

The Bandya Maruti Seva Mandal also featured a *kabaddi* team, organised Divali festivities and, in the past at least, had run blood donation camps on the neighbourhood *kabaddi* ground. Beyond this, the Mandal's history is shrouded in uncertainty. Some members, particularly younger ones, insist that it was formed as a merger between two *kabaddi* teams, each named after their star players: Bandya (from Chawl J) and Maruti (from Chawl K). Others told me that Bandya refers to a group of fighters who were active in a time of local rioting between Hindus and Muslims in the 1940s, while Maruti refers to the Hanuman temple on the corner of Chawl J which is owned by the Mandal.

On a day-to-day level, Mitra Mandals and their *kattas* provide outlets for (mostly) young men to hang out and chat (cf. Hansen, 2001, p. 73). They are the most hyper-visible and hyper-masculine manifestations of chawlness, both welcoming and, for an outsider, a little intimidating.

Change, class and colliding worlds

Chawlness is my own term, but the social world it describes is treasured far and wide in Mumbai, and I encountered an enthusiasm for chawls in unexpected places. When I bought a copy of Adarkar's *The Chawls of Mumbai* in an upmarket mall bookshop, the old man behind the counter smiled fondly at it and told me he had happy memories of growing up in a chawl. An architect friend who now lives in a flat in the satellite town Dombivli, and who I had mentally classified as belonging to a different stratum of Mumbai society to that of my BDD Chawls friends, revealed that he had also grown up in a chawl in Sion (north of Lower Parel). He said he missed chawl life, because he used to know all his neighbours, whereas in his Dombivli apartment he does not interact with any of them.

For many outsiders, however, this perception of chawlness renders social diversity invisible and there is a tendency to conflate residents into an undifferentiated mass of 'chawl people'. Ample evidence of this came from my own rather disparate circle of Mumbai friends. There were those, like the architect, who romanticised the closely-woven sociality of chawl living. This is celebrated in films like Hrishikesh Mukherjee's *Asli-Naqli* as the *asli* (true, genuine) world of 'kind-hearted and caring' workers 'living together in a chawl, like one big family', as opposed to the *naqli* (fake) world of greed and untruth that characterises Mumbai's wealthy (Gangar, 2011, p. 91). Others regarded my research as an adventurous and even slightly dangerous foray into a world that they knew little or nothing about.

Underpinning these viewpoints was a perception of chawls as places of low social status which often seemed to elide the categories of caste and class and carried negative rather than exotic or romantic connotations. My dominant-caste landlady, after a dispute with Sujata, my Dalit Buddhist cleaner whom she regarded as 'arrogant', told me that since I spent my days in the BDD Chawls I should try to find a replacement cleaner from among my circle there since they would probably be grateful for the employment. Another dominant-caste friend, a doctor whom I had asked for some medical advice, cautioned me on the risk of contracting tuberculosis from chawls since they are dirty and densely inhabited. Having visited his *bouji* seafront apartment where he held drinks parties and cultural soirees, I was astonished to learn that he, too, had grown up in a chawl. This was admittedly in Girgaon, which is considered middle class in contrast to working-class Girangaon (cf. Adarkar, 2011).

When I explained my research to him over iced lattes in an air-conditioned café, he expressed his eagerness to visit the BDD Chawls with me as his guide. Since we were round the corner, I suggested we go right away, but he looked at me in horror and gestured at his expensive shirt and cufflinks. 'I'd stick out like a sore thumb!' he laughed. We never found our chance, but months later I did take another friend on a chawl tour, introducing her to some of the residents. A historian from a privileged background, she was full of curiosity and warmth for the neighbourhood, but when I asked whether any of her family members or childhood friends would visit such a place she was emphatic: 'Never! Never! They'd only come by if maybe one of their maids was getting married here. Otherwise absolutely never.'

It is this apparent gulf between the world of chawls and that of upmarket localities like Breach Candy and Pali Hill that has made the 'mill to mall' narrative[7] so potent, allowing Mumbai's policymakers to fixate on a dream of creating the next Shanghai or Singapore with scant regard for the working class. Sceptics of this dream point out how the wealthy, once noted philanthropists, now sequester themselves in air-conditioned fortresses 'gat[ing] themselves off as much as possible' due to their 'fear [of] the poor' (Appadurai, 2000, p. 628). In the specific context of Parel and Lalbaug, one geographer describes the elites, shuttling in air-conditioned vehicles from their luxurious residences to their similarly rarefied offices, as having 'deliberately looked to disassociate themselves from their industrial surroundings and the area's predominantly Marathi-speaking and working-class population' (Harris, 2008, p. 2421).

But is this gap truly as stark and absolute as is often implied? In 2002, D'Monte could write, doubtless quite accurately, that debates over the redevelopment of Girangaon do not 'evoke the same passions' as slum redevelopment debates, since the 'middle class' does not live or work in Girangaon and its members merely 'traverse' these areas 'on their way to work in south Mumbai' (2002, p. 13). Today, however, this middle class works in the converted mill sites of Peninsula Corporate Park or the Marathon Futurex building, shops in High Street Phoenix mall and parties in the rooftop bars of Kamala Mills. In the early months of fieldwork, I would sometimes linger on a bridge overlooking a footpath that led from Lower Parel station to Ganapatrao Kadam Marg, where several office blocks were located. Motivated by a vestigial desire to classify, perhaps the legacy of an early training in life sciences or a colonial hangover in my ethnographic training, I tried to determine who, in the human rivulets below, was a 'local' (from the Village of Mills) and who was a 'corporate' outsider (working and shopping in the City of Malls). I dwelt mostly on stereotypes of clothing and body language. A young woman in a blouse and black trousers hurrying towards the Peninsula Business Park would be filed away as corporate, while an old man shuffling along in an ill-fitting polyester shirt and baggy trousers was doubtless local.

While there was some validity to this categorisation – the old man quite possibly *did* live in the area, and the young woman might well have come from a different part of town – it was premised on the dubious assumption that I was observing entirely separate strands of Mumbai society, both using the same streets but never intermingling. With more careful observation, this assumption became untenable. In the early evenings, in fact, I would often see employees of Hindustan Petroleum, L'Oréal, and other Marathon Futurex-based companies snacking on bread-omelettes or *sev puri* at Delisle Road pavement stalls alongside people I knew from the BDD Chawls who were returning from their own offices. I later became aware of a trio of Zee TV employees who left their Marathon Futurex office every lunchtime for a stroll round the BDD Chawls, sometimes pausing at the Jay Bhim Katta to leaf through the newspapers and exchange pleasantries with Anish or Mahendra or whoever happened to be sitting there at the time. On a more intimate setting was Dinesh's relationship with a girl, from a wealthy family, who worked nearby in a swanky office. But even this case is not clear cut, as her grandmother used to live in one of the BDD Chawls and Dinesh had met her on one of her family visits.

The blurring between these worlds runs deeper than streetside commensality and the occasional romance, since chawl residents themselves now work in the malls and office complexes of the new Girangaon. Most fill low-paying, precarious roles such as drivers, security guards and waiters that perhaps belong in the 'local' category, but a sizeable minority work in corporate or creative jobs. In the following chapters we will meet civil engineers, IT managers, chartered accountants, graphic designers and even a DJ.

What, then, can we say about class in the BDD Chawls? Leela Fernandes has conceptualised a 'new Indian middle class' tied to economic liberalisation that 'largely encompasses English-speaking urban white-collar segments of the [existing] middle class who are benefitting from new employment opportunities' (2006, p. xviii). At first glance, this description best fits my upstairs neighbours in Worli, management graduates who worked for a sports advertising channel in a Lower Parel office and ate organic mangoes that they ordered online. But could it also apply to some residents of the BDD Chawls? Although Fernandes is clear that her 'new' middle class is primarily located within the traditional middle class (to which my neighbours, unlike my chawl friends, decidedly belong) she stresses that 'the heart of the construction of this social group rests on the assumption that ... [the] upwardly mobile working class can potentially join it' (2006, p. xviii).

Fernandes describes 'symbolic strategies of upwards mobility' such as English-medium education, MBAs and the purchase of branded goods (2006, p. xviii), all of which are becoming increasingly common among younger BBD Chawl residents. Dinesh's father Sayaji, a shop owner, school administrator and political activist, reflected on the material changes he had observed in the chawls rooms and told me that:

> Aisa nahin hai ki BDD Chawl mein bahut poor log rehte ... abhi aap jaoge toda gumenge to har ek ghar mein matlab just like flat banaya unhone. AC hai ... well-furnished room hai, bike hai ... BDD Chawl mein abhi achche log rehte.
>
> (Sayaji, interview, 1 September 2017)

> (It's not that really poor people live in the BDD Chawls ... if you go and look around, then you'll see every residence has been done up just like a flat. They've got AC ... the room is well furnished, they'll have a bike ... Nowadays good people live in the BDD Chawls).

These changes continued even as the spectre of redevelopment loomed. On a return visit in 2022, I saw that Manish's hitherto very simple room had been transformed into an elegant sanctuary with patterned tiles, an illuminated fish tank, an enormous wall-mounted television and an elaborately decorated door. Indeed doors, those symbolic gatekeepers of chawlness, can be read as markers of upward mobility. Some are simple slabs of wood, dull monochrome only relieved by a nameplate or number. Others feature delicate paintwork or even wooden carving and substantial marble doorsteps.

Akshay told me that, in contrast to the mill era when the neighbourhood had been very poor and plagued with gang fights and water shortages, it was now 'a middle-class and lower-middle-class area' with even a few 'upper-middle-class families'. Although I did not ask him, I suspect he would have placed himself firmly in the middle- or upper-middle-class bracket based on his corporate job and English-medium education. That said, he appeared nostalgic for his youth when, with fewer cars and motorbikes in the neighbourhood, kids would play everywhere: cricket, hide-and-seek and another game involving piles of seven stones. Young men were happy to use the local gym. Now only cricket is played, and there is less even of that, and his contemporaries use expensive branded gyms.

Akshay's lament for a lost chawlness rooted in working-class history is perhaps a function of his own relative levels of privilege in the BDD Chawls economy. It was certainly not a lament I heard often. During an English language role-play exercise, I asked Anish to act as a visitor making enquiries about Lower Parel with a view to moving there. Manish, as the designated local resident informed him that 'Rent is very high because Lower Parel is a corporate area, better than Andheri, Borivali, Churchgate. So many corporate people are staying here.' He also stressed that the area is 'very safe for living, food, safety'. Everything about the way he delivered this sales pitch suggested not resentment and alienation but pride and a sense of belonging in this new chapter in the neighbourhood's history.

A sense of difference

People asked me, both in Mumbai and back home in London, whether I lived in the BDD Chawls while conducting fieldwork. The question always filled me with shame, partly due to the unspoken assumption that a 'proper' anthropologist must surely live in the neighbourhood they studied; partly, also, due to my embarrassment at living alone in a flat over twice the size of a chawl unit and many times more expensive to rent. I was often evasive when my chawl friends quizzed me about the cost and sometimes lied outright. Most chastening of all, however, was the way my chosen living arrangements exposed my inability to handle chawlness full-time. My flat in Worli, actually rather modest by the standards of middle-class Mumbai, became my sanctuary. Sometimes I kept my door open and caught stray wafts of my neighbours' lives, but at other times I closed and bolted it and lost myself in cheap beer and Netflix.

These living arrangements presented clear methodological shortcomings. Even though I spent large chunks of time, day and night, in the BDD Chawls and made many friends and acquaintances there, I missed out on the chance to fully inhabit chawl life. One overnight stay excepted, I never experienced sleeping at night on floormats or narrow cots in rooms without air conditioning, or washing with cold water in the tiny *mori* (enclosed washing space) and queuing for the common toilets each morning. Without living this cheek-by-jowl lifestyle with its almost total lack of privacy on a daily basis, I cannot truly be said to have participated in chawlness. Taking up residence in one of the BDD Chawls tenements would probably have complicated the insider–outsider dynamic further and would have undoubtedly made for a richer ethnography, although at what cost to my ambivert's mental health I cannot say. However, tethering myself to a particular building may have compromised the 'everyman' outsider status that enabled me to flit between Dalit and Maratha communities with ease.

Before arriving in Mumbai, I worried that I would be judged for not having a real job, and for spending my days sitting around apparently doing nothing. Happily, the pace of life in the BDD Chawls provided the perfect setting for an anthropologist in pursuit of 'deep hanging out' (Geertz, 1998). In her rich and lyrical study, Finkelstein conceives of chawl residents as 'trailing behind Mumbai's conception of progress' and hence 'declared useless as productive citizens.' She argues that 'chawl time' is a kind of 'queer time' that operates through a 'tactic of remembering' at odds with the 'chrononormativity' of malls and skyscrapers, perhaps an act of resistance against 'a future that has no room for them' (Finkelstein, 2019, pp. 94–6). This analysis has a particular poignancy in the case of the BDD Chawls, where anxieties over having a living space in the future are quite literal, but it rigidifies the mill/mall boundary that I have shown to be porous and ambiguous. It also risks overlooking those chawl residents for whom nostalgia coexists with an eager embrace of the 'chrononormative' future – we shall meet them in Chapter 7.[8]

And this brings us back to difference. So far, I have explored shared narratives of chawlness, of open-door culture and locked-door jail folk history and resisted the urge to complicate the narrative with questions of caste and religion, or even gender. But as Doreen Massey, geographer and eminent theorist of place tells us in relation to Kilburn, the London neighbourhood she called home:

> while [it] may have a character of its own, it is absolutely not a seamless, coherent identity, a single sense of place which everyone shares. It could hardly be less so. People's routes through the place, their favourite haunts within it, the connections they make … between here and the rest of the world vary enormously. If it is now recognized that people have multiple identities then the same point can be made in relation to places.
>
> (Massey, 1991 p. 27)

Even the most apparently homogenous 'communities', she argues (using the hypothetical case of a small English mining village) have 'internal structures', such that:

> a woman's sense of place in a mining village – the spaces through which she normally moves, the meeting places, the connections outside – are different from a man's. Their 'senses of the place' will be different.
>
> (1991, p. 27)

Much of the rest of this book is concerned with looking beyond the homogeneity imposed on chawl life by the external gaze and understanding the *different* ways in which Dalit Buddhist and Maratha communities experience the BDD Chawls and the larger imagined territories of Mumbai, Maharashtra, certain villages and India as a whole.

Crucial to these different 'senses of place' are the varying conceptions of history that underpin them, ranging from the ancient to the contemporary. In the face of these historically-informed differences, chawlness will be revealed to be limited in its potential to unite the disparate groups living in the BDD Chawls. Emergencies notwithstanding, on an everyday level chawlness is most keenly felt in the corridors and *kattas* and Mitra Mandals and thereby serves to strengthen bonds *within* rather than *between* communities. The concept lurks, in its many and varied forms, behind the stories that follow, and in Chapter 7 we will return to chawlness more explicitly to ask whether it can bind the BDD Chawls together in the face of the redevelopment proposals.

Notes

1. Chawl A also houses the head office of the Bombay Mothers' and Children's Welfare Trust, which established the Mhaskar Hospital, initially a maternity ward but now a convalescent home for cancer patients from the nearby Tata Memorial Hospital, in the chawl building across the road. The hospital building is identical in shape and structure to the other 31 chawls, but is immediately identifiable from its white and green façade printed with logos of a mother cradling a baby. Its interior is pristine with white floor tiles in the corridors and washbasins in the bathrooms. It is the presence of the Mhaskar hospital which explains the otherwise surprising number of people from northeast India walking through the neighbourhood, since the patient base draws heavily from those regions.
2. In line with the official documentation under discussion here, I use the official name rather than the more familiar Delisle Road used in rest of the book.
3. For a copy of the tender, see Mumbai Housing and Area Development Board (2016) on the website of the Embassy of India in Caracas.
4. See Pendse et al. (2011, p. 8) for the account in question.
5. Far more extensive recently-published archival research conducted by historian Vanessa Caru has revealed that the Bombay Development Department received 21 petitions from its chawl tenants – not prisoners! – between 1924 and 1930, on subjects 'as varied as water supply to reductions in rent' (2019, p. 232).
6. Of her experience in the BDD Chawls, Maura Finkelstein recounts that 'Manda teaches me that "domestic space" leaks out of the units and courtyards of the chawls and bleeds into areas often misunderstood as "public space"'(2019, p. 110).
7. See also 'A rooftop interlude' in the Introduction.
8. Finkelstein goes on to clarify that she does 'not intend to reinscribe poorer communities as nonaspirational in relation to the engines driving modern capital forward' but rather to 'destabilize temporal narratives that naturalize unidirectional renderings of progress and participation' (2019, p. 96).

2
'Ganesh is a fake god': the ambiguous humanity of Dr Babasaheb Ambedkar

Halfway through my year of fieldwork Lord Ganesh came to town. If Rio de Janeiro is synonymous with carnival and New Orleans with Mardi Gras, Mumbai can make a similar claim to Ganesh Chaturthi, a Hindu festival that convulses the city for eleven days in August or September each year.[1] The festival honours the arrival on earth of the potbellied, elephant-headed god Ganesh, renowned as the remover of obstacles, whose blessing is routinely sought at the beginning of journeys, cultural events and new business ventures.

Throughout Mumbai, clay idols (*murti*) of Ganesh are installed in private homes, community spaces and grand public temporary structures called *pandals*. Family members and friends visit each other, recite devotional prayers and eat *modak,* a sweetmeat filled with coconut, jaggery and cardamom. On the final day, the idols are paraded down to the sea for a ritual immersion or *visarjan.* I visited large public *pandals* and smaller neighbourhood ones, but above all I experienced Ganesh Chaturthi as a household celebration in the BDD Chawls, joining in family prayers while attempting to fend off offers of *modak*.

By this stage I was familiar with the neighbourhood, and it came as no surprise to me that the residents participating in the festival were overwhelmingly Hindu. Few of my Dalit Buddhist friends took part and they seemed to look on my involvement with an amused indulgence. Sayaji, the shop owner and political activist we met in the previous chapter advised me to put the following questions to my Hindu friends: 'What is Ganesh's surname?' and 'What is his date of birth?' Without this information, he explained, there can be no proof Ganesh existed. He constantly questions Hindus on these matters and never gets a satisfactory answer because Ganesh is a 'fake' god, most likely invented by Brahmans in the seventeenth century. Any supposedly ancient carvings of Ganesh I might have seen would have originally been sculptures of elephants that had been modified by Brahmans to support their fraudulent cult – Hinduism.[2]

At the time, while familiar with the Dalit Buddhist rejection of theism, I found Sayaji's specific line of argument rather eccentric. Only later did it occur to me that I had perhaps missed an implied comparison: with a famous surname and a very publicly celebrated date of birth, Dr Babasaheb Ambedkar unquestionably *did* exist. As an *idea*, Ambedkar is the subject of widely reproduced imagery, daily greetings and ceremonial chants, and superficially, the celebrations in which Dalits honour Ambedkar's life have little to distinguish them from the religious festivals of their Hindu neighbours. Even the more humanistic *ideas* of Ambedkar, which undergird the social institutions through which Dalits organise their lives and participate in the nation, function like a form of doctrine. Indeed, Ambedkar is a central figure in the histories of social emancipation that my interlocutors tell, his role often elevated to a heroic status that, from the detached perspective of this British anthropologist, appears godlike, or at least rather more than human.

In contrast to the inevitable polarisation that characterises much public wrangling over history (the 'Was the British Empire a force for good or evil?' category of question we encountered in the Introduction) the central thread running through this chapter is the apparently comfortable coexistence of contradictory ideas. While psychological studies of cognitive dissonance are legion, anthropologist David Berliner recently called for fellow anthropologists to 'bring back ambivalent statements, contradictory attitudes, incompatible values, and emotional internal clashes as research objects' (Berliner, 2016, p. 5). In this chapter I explore the ambivalences and incompatibilities I encountered at the Jay Bhim Katta: Ambedkar as human alongside Ambedkar as superhuman; the narrative of Dalits as oppressed alongside the narrative of Dalits as emancipated. I conclude that such contradictions reflect the position Dalit Buddhists inhabit in twenty-first century Mumbai – as a matter of self-respect, my interlocutors emphasise the extent to which Dalits are now able to participate in the social, political and economic life of India, while never losing sight of the casteism, both subtle and violent, that remains a reality across the country.

A rather different and more difficult contradiction to interpret is the way the claim that gender equality is inherent to Ambedkarite Buddhism sits alongside a reality of stereotypical gender roles and a male-dominated public sphere. In the 'Interlude: gender trouble', I examine this phenomenon both as a material condition of Dalit Buddhist life that confounded my expectations, but also as a methodological limitation that has implications for the study as a whole.

History and nationhood at the Jay Bhim Katta

My first sustained encounter with Ambedkar occurred on 26 January 2017, India's Republic Day. I set out to the BDD Chawls in the morning to join my new friends Anish, Manish and Mahendra in their celebrations. Excited, since it felt like fieldwork was truly beginning, I was also filled with doubts. Had they genuinely meant to invite me or were they simply being polite? What if none of them were in sight when I arrived? I resolved to keep as low a profile as possible. As I rounded the corner into the street that separates Chawls F and G from the Jay Bhim Katta I saw a large crowd of men, women and children. Directly in between the two chawl buildings was a flagpole fronted by a waist-height concrete slab on which a framed photograph of Ambedkar had been placed amid rose petals and garlands of marigolds. A small knot of men was standing right next to the structure, and they seemed to be in charge of proceedings.

I was surprised to see Manish, who I had thought of as quiet and self-effacing, apparently compering the day's events with a microphone. As soon as he saw me, he beckoned me over and introduced me to the assembled crowd as *amcha mitra Jon* (our friend Jon) who would say *don shabd* (two words), while someone else stuck an Indian flag sticker onto my shirt. I stumbled my way through rather more than two Marathi words, thoughtlessly concluding with the Hindu greeting *namaskar,* which I hastily followed with 'Jay Bhim' on Anish's whispered instruction. I was later invited to help garland the picture of Ambedkar with further flowers, before hoisting the Indian flag with a retired army officer and joining the entire congregation in a rendition of the Indian national anthem.

Later, when there was time to mingle, a smiling lady in her forties came up and introduced herself as Tejaswini More. She explained that she lived in nearby Chawl O1 and was also a Buddhist and follower of Ambedkar, and that she and the three friends with her were all social workers. Before I had a chance to talk any more with them, Anish summoned me over to join a procession round the perimeter of the neighbourhood. I found myself walking next to the ex-army officer and, remembering Mahendra's comment of two days back that most of the people sitting at the Jay Bhim Katta were Buddhist, I asked him if the procession was a largely Buddhist affair. 'All, all', he said, using the English word and gesturing to the crowd marching behind us, although another man in the procession told me there were also a few Hindus present.

Once we were back at the Jay Bhim Katta, Anish and Manish took me to one side and asked whether I knew the meaning behind the celebration. They explained that for the Dalit Buddhist community, Republic Day commemorated Ambedkar's role as the chief author of the Constitution of India, which was why we had garlanded his image. Manish told me how Ambedkar had been the first Dalit to study abroad, at Columbia University and the London School of Economics, and they both emphasised how much their community had benefitted from the Constitution, which outlawed untouchability. Anish said that there had been seven people on the Constitution-drafting committee but the other six did nothing. He asked if I knew about Gandhi and made a balancing motion with his hands to suggest a contest for national greatness between Gandhi and Ambedkar, the latter clearly taking the upper hand.

In the weeks and months that followed the Republic Day celebrations, I began to get used to Ambedkar's spectral presence, and it grew apparent that in many ways it was through his work that my Dalit Buddhist interlocutors made sense of their own place in Indian society. As the author of the Constitution he was – far more than Gandhi to them – the father of the nation, and through his social reforms he had created the conditions whereby Dalits were able to stake a claim to being Indian and participate in national life. Not surprisingly, therefore, conversations frequently circled back to Ambedkar, no matter what the starting point, and it was clear that my new friends were anxious to impart to me the details of his life's work and highlight the importance they placed on them.

Many of these conversations took place at the Jay Bhim Katta which, for the residents of certain chawls (notably F and G), functions as a sort of outdoor common room and a highly visible manifestation of chawlness. *Katta,* as explained in the previous chapter, is a Marathi word referring to a seating area, while 'Jay Bhim' (Victory to Bhim) is a commonplace Dalit Buddhist utterance that functions both as a homage to Dr *Bhim*rao Ambedkar and an everyday greeting. In the mornings, chawl residents of all ages will come across from their buildings and sit on the benches. Some are on their way to work, or to some other engagement, or are killing time before a later shift. Some are retired and others are unemployed, or are engaged in some form of study. Some will pore over newspapers, others will chat with their friends and neighbours, but many will simply watch the passing fare on the small road that separates the *katta* from the chawl buildings, greeting acquaintances as they pass.

Throughout the day, friends from other chawls and other neighbourhoods will come and stay for a chat. Office workers from nearby businesses sometimes come and use the space on their lunchbreaks, and itinerant workers of one kind or another – social workers, sales representatives, peripatetic health workers – might pause on a bench and look through their files. In the afternoon, one or two benches at least will be occupied by men taking a postprandial snooze. Throughout the morning and afternoon, in fact, the *katta* crowd is almost exclusively male, but in the evenings it is not unusual to see a few women and some more children on the benches.

Where the *katta*'s supporting poles meet the corrugated roof, a long banner runs across the front of the structure and bears the label Jay Bhim Mitra Mandal, referring to one of the associations that organises the social and political life of the community (Figure 2.1). Either side of this label are four portraits, including one of Ambedkar himself alongside Jyotirao 'Mahatma' Phule, a nineteeth-century Maharashtrian educationalist and anti-caste reformer, and the wives of each man: Ramabai Ambedkar and Savitribai Phule, both noted reformers in their own right. At the back, behind the benches, is a larger printed screen that displays a triptych of figures. On the left is Chhatrapati Shivaji, the seventeenth-century Maratha ruler, whose inclusion initially puzzled me given his prominence as a Maratha and Hindu figurehead (his important

Figure 2.1 The Jay Bhim Katta. © Author.

role as a national hero in Dalit Buddhist life and thoughts will be explored further in Chapter 6). The middle figure is a seated golden Buddha, surrounded by a small group of *bhikkhus*, or Buddhist monks. To his right is Ambedkar, dressed in white and holding a staff, a much less familiar representation than the portrait of a blue-suited bureaucrat on the front banner, a peculiarity that is explained by the mound-like white structure pictured behind him. This is the Dikshabhoomi, or 'initiation ground', a monument constructed in Nagpur, modelled on the Buddhist *stupa* (monument) of Sanchi, to commemorate the site of the mass conversion (*diksha*) to Buddhism that Ambedkar led there in 1956.

This imagery is replicated in Dalit Buddhist homes, which almost invariably display at least one framed picture of Ambedkar on the wall, often next to an image of the Buddha and sometimes Phule and Shivaji. Similar images can be found in many of the chawl corridors, or in other public spaces such as the local Buddhist temple where Ambedkar is displayed next to a large Buddha image and a smaller Shivaji. Importantly, as we shall see further in Chapters 4 and 6, these figures (especially Ambedkar) are not simply considered heroes of the Dalit Buddhist community but architects of India's nationhood. Their inclusion is thus a statement of Indianness as well as one of Dalitness.

Ambedkar's constant presence is maintained in other, less material ways, too. For example, when a team of cricketers from Chawls F and G won a BDD Chawl-wide cricket contest, they paraded back to the flagpole opposite the Jay Bhim Katta where a team member raised up the trophy and roared '*Dr Babasaheb Ambedkarancha*', to which the crowd responded '*Vijay Aso!*' Meaning 'Triumph be to Dr Babasaheb Ambedkar', it was a formula I would hear frequently during the year, suggesting that any triumph the community experienced was directly attributable to Ambedkar himself.

The idea of Ambedkar: man or Messiah?

In such ubiquitous imagery and quasi-devotional chanting, and in the quotidian homage-greeting Jay Bhim (which sometimes reminded me of the everyday greeting 'Ram Ram' by which I had, years previously, heard Rajasthani farmers invoking Lord Ram, one of the incarnations of Vishnu)[3] it is hard not to see a challenge to the idea of Ambedkar as strictly human. Even one of his more vitriolic detractors, journalist and politician Arun Shourie, acknowledges this challenge albeit derisively in his 1997 book *Worshipping False Gods: Ambedkar, and facts which have been erased*.[4] More sympathetically, historian Anupama Rao has described the 'process of sacralization' through which the Dalit Buddhist community has 'invested Ambedkar ... with affective energy' and developed an associated set of symbols, including a new ritual calendar, *krantiparva* ('Revolutionary Days'), organised around Ambedkar's life (2009, p. 184).

Born to a military family on 14 April 1891, Bhimrao[5] Ramji Ambedkar, studied at Elphinstone College in Bombay and later at Columbia University and the London School of Economics, a highly unusual education for a member of the Mahar caste. The career that followed transcended disciplinary boundaries and Ambedkar is variously referred to as a lawmaker, politician, social reformer, writer and economist. On Republic Day (26 January), as we have seen, Dalit Buddhist celebrations place a distinctive emphasis on Ambedkar's role as lead author of the Constitution. In March, his 1927 campaign for untouchables to be allowed to use a public water tank in Mahad village is commemorated with a pilgrimage to the site of the tank, known as Krantibhoomi, or Land of Revolution. On 14 April, Dalit-dominated neighbourhoods like the BDD Chawls erupt with speeches and raucous processions to mark Ambedkar Jayanti, his birthday. The 1956 Buddhist conversion is celebrated in October, as Dhammachakra Pravartan Din (Religious Conversion Day), with lectures and cultural programmes, and on 6 December, Dalit groups from all over the country converge on Mumbai to honour Ambedkar's death anniversary at Chaityabhoomi, the site of his cremation in Dadar.

'*Unhone gutter se nikala*', Anish once remarked to me: he dragged [us] up from the gutter. I quickly realised that even among such avid admirers of Ambedkar, Anish stood out as particularly fervent. In his mid-thirties, stocky and conversationally dominant, I admit I initially misread Anish as something between a buffoon and a zealot. Although I liked him from the outset – it would have been difficult not to respond to his generosity and I was always grateful for the enthusiastic welcome he gave me at the Jay Bhim Katta – respect came a little later, and at first I found it difficult to connect with what I perceived to be his pious and uncritical reverence. On occasions, I grew impatient at the inevitable trajectory of our discussions, such as when Anish saw in a newspaper article about maternity leave provisions a tenuous (or so I thought) opportunity to expound on Ambedkar's good works. It was with some remorse that I later learned that Anish was entirely accurate, since Ambedkar had in fact supported and defended the Bombay Presidency Maternity Benefit Bill in 1928 (Ambedkar, 1982a).

It was in Anish's relationship with Ambedkar that I saw the starkest ambiguity as to his hero's status. Despite telling me many times that

Buddhism is a scientific religion in which god-worship has no place (see also Omvedt, 2003, pp. 139–42), at times he referred to Ambedkar in unambiguously religious terms. Once, he explained to me that 'we only worship Ambedkar and Gautam Buddha – no other gods' and that for the Mahars, Ambedkar is a *masih* (Messiah). Even on Republic Day, when elaborating on the differences between Ambedkar and Gandhi, he finished by saying that Ambedkar is like a god, a mother and a father to him. Anish was not alone in this. Sujata, the Dalit Buddhist lady who came to clean my flat, once noticed I was reading a book with a picture of Ambedkar on the front cover and exclaimed that '*ve hamare god hain!*' (he is our god). Meanwhile, at a musical concert to commemorate the 1956 mass conversion to Buddhism, the formula '*Bhagwan Buddha, Bodhisattva Ambedkar*' was often used in the songs, labelling Buddha as a god, and Ambedkar as a *bodhisattva*, an enlightened being on the path to becoming a Buddha himself.

I felt Ambedkar's superhuman status most strongly during the Ambedkar Jayanti celebrations on 14 April. The celebration has a special importance in the BDD Chawls, since it was here that the first public celebrations of Ambedkar's birthday were held in 1933, organised by communist leader R.B. More, who held classes on Marxism in the chawls (Shaikh, 2011, p. 71). Ambedkar himself was critical of these celebrations that were lavish even in his lifetime, and on his fiftieth birthday in 1941 asked his followers to stop them (Beltz, 2005, p. 177). Since then, there has been an ongoing debate in the wider Dalit Buddhist community over whether and how Ambedkar Jayanti should be celebrated, and calls have been made to curb expenditure and religious undertones (Beltz, 2005, pp. 177–8). The noise and light and crowds that surged across Mumbai for several days in April 2017 suggest that those urging moderation remain on the losing end of this debate.

The crux of the celebrations at the BDD Chawls featured a procession round the neighbourhood which, just like many Hindu festivals, seemed to combine the pomp of a religious function with the effervescence of a college club night. One of Anish's friends referred to the celebration as 'our Divali' and, despite the disparaging terms with which many of my Buddhist friends referred to Hindu ritual, there were few obvious differences in mood between this procession and the neighbourhood processions I attended with my Maratha friends during Ganesh Chaturthi. When I made this observation to Anish, however, he made the point that while Hindus wait in long queues for *darshan* (sighting) of Ganesh in order to request something of their deity, Buddhists form queues on

Mahaparinirvan Divas (Ambedkar's death anniversary) simply to pay homage to their leader at his memorial, and to give thanks.[6]

A study of Dalit folk songs from eastern Maharashtra in the 1980s concludes that many Mahars regard Ambedkar as the *avatar* (incarnation) of a supreme deity, and that elevating him to such a status was a way of filling the void left after the rejection of the Hindu pantheon (Junghare, 1988). While the latter argument provides a plausible explanation of Ambedkar's early deification, nothing in my Dalit Buddhist friends' conversations gave any indication they conceived Ambedkar's story as one of incarnation.[7]

Meanwhile, religions scholar Timothy Fitzgerald acknowledges that 'there is no doubt that many Buddhists conceive of Buddha and Ambedkar ... as supernatural beings who can bring benefits' but that 'this is completely at variance with Ambedkar's own philosophy' (2004, p. 269). Educated Buddhists, he claims are 'explicitly against the idea that Ambedkar is a supernatural being' and celebrate 'his potential as a human being, not in a transcendental way' (Fitzgerald, 2004, pp. 269–70). I do not recognise Fitzgerald's clear-cut supernatural/human binary in the discourse of my mostly well-educated interlocutors, for whom the modes of humanistic admiration and quasi-religious devotion appear to coexist without obvious tension.

The ideas of Ambedkar: political economy and civil society

These coexisting ideas of Ambedkar shape the organised social life of the BDD Chawls Buddhists which is tied both to the memory of a godlike Ambedkar but also to his humanistic legacy of political and social philosophy. Anish and his friends often used the English words 'thinking' and 'thoughts' to refer to a set of Ambedkarite values that were never comprehensively elucidated to me, but included the privileging of reason and equality over religious superstition and hierarchy. These values underpin the major political and social structures that loom large over neighbourhood life.

One of these was the Republican Party of India (Athawale) or RPI(A). For several weeks leading up to the Ambedkar Jayanti festivities, Anish spent some of his evenings collecting contributions from the 13 chawl buildings in which Dalits lived. The capacity in which he made this collection was that of a member of the local ward-level RPI(A) committee. The original Republican Party of India was established by Ambedkar in the 1950s, as a successor to his earlier Scheduled Caste Federation. It was founded on the principles of liberty, equality and fraternity and these ideas, generalised as a rational, egalitarian opposition to caste oppression and religious superstition, are guiding principles for the RPI which remains thoroughly steeped in Ambedkarite symbolism.

Although Ambedkar envisaged it as a political party that would speak for all of India's 'dispossessed', the RPI has been 'largely confined to the Mahars' throughout its history (Zelliot, 1996b, p. 114). Despite this apparent unity of purpose, however, the party has suffered from factional splits and there are currently several independently operating RPI outfits of which the RPI(A), headed by the eponymous Ramdas Athawale, now a member of the Rajya Sabha (parliamentary upper house), is one of the most prominent. Most of these parties use a version of the same flag, a white Ashoka Chakra (the Buddhist 24-spoke wheel symbol that is also printed at the centre of India's national flag) against a background of dark blue, the colour of the wider Ambedkar movement.

In the BDD Chawls, the RPI(A) is the party of choice for the majority of the Dalit Buddhists. In addition to Anish, the slightly older Pradeep and several others are actively involved in the ward-level committee which uses one of the tenements in Chawl F as a small office. Mid-50s Sayaji, meanwhile, occupies a position of power in the general South Mumbai RPI(A) branch, and enjoys a close relationship with Ramdas Athawale himself. There is also a separate RPI(A) ladies' committee, of which activist Tejaswini More is a prominent member, describing her role as coordinating with the 'Gents' committee in organising festival and functions.

On 21 February, municipal elections to appoint new ward-level representatives (Corporators) to the BMC,[8] were held across Mumbai. In the preceding weeks, a group of men from the Jay Bhim Katta, including Anish, Pradeep and Sayaji, but also Manish who has a position in the Mumbai-wide RPI(A) Employment Wing, and several other enthusiastic supporters, set out on door-to-door campaigning expeditions on behalf of the Ward 198 RPI(A) candidate, a young Dalit Buddhist man with an impressive air of gravitas from Chawl G.

I was surprised to discover that this RPI(A) candidate was in fact representing a Mumbai-wide alliance between his party and various others including the right-wing Bharatiya Janata Party (BJP), incumbent in the national government. Crudely translated into British political terms, this struck me as just as implausible as an alliance between the Green Party and the Conservatives, and I asked Anish how it had come about. He grimaced and said that he did not support the BJP given its Hindu nationalist stance, but that Athawale had decided on this alliance and he therefore had to accept it. In fact, this kind of alliance is not at all unusual in Indian politics, and nor is it uncharacteristic of the RPI(A) or other RPI factions which have joined forces in the past with the Congress Party and the Shiv Sena (Rao, 2009, pp. 199–205). In the event, the RPI(A), even allied to the BJP, was no match for the Shiv Sena, whose Dalit Hindu candidate Snehal Ambekar, previously mayor of Mumbai, won the seat with a heavy majority.

Despite its lack of elected representation in Mumbai, the RPI(A) is a significant organisational force in the social life of the BDD Chawls, in charge of coordinating neighbourhood-wide functions to mark Ambedkar's birth and death. In a sombre counterpoint to the exuberant Ambedkar Jayanti procession, Mahaparinirvan Divas (Ambedkar's death anniversary) is commemorated at midnight on the 5–6 December with a candle march following a similar route around the neighbourhood. Anish acted as master of ceremonies for the 2018 festivities, leading the preliminary Pali prayers in the local Buddhist temple and the march that followed. This culminated in further prayers at a temporary memorial structure labelled 'Republican Party of India, Ward No. 198' where Sayaji was invited to lay a wreath on behalf of the South Mumbai branch of the RPI(A).

The following day, a large group of us set out from the Jay Bhim Katta, in a truck labelled Republican Party of India (Athawale) and loaded with vats of vegetable *bhaji* and chapatti, to Shivaji Park in nearby Dadar neighbourhood. On 6 December Shivaji Park heaves with Dalit visitors from far-flung corners of Maharashtra and beyond, many dressed in white with splashes of Ambedkarite blue, who come to pay respects at Chaityabhoomi, a memorial erected at the site of Ambedkar's cremation. The streets surrounding Shivaji park are also thronged with people, and food trucks, each branded with the name of a political party or civil organisation, distribute free food such as *pulao* (a rice dish), *puri* or biscuits to long lines of pilgrims. Once our RPI(A)-branded truck was parked, Pradeep's wife Sunita and a lady from Chawl H started ladling out *bhaji* onto paper plates.

The park itself plays host to stalls selling Ambedkar memorabilia of all kinds – framed pictures, key chains, blue turbans and waistcoats – as well as stands offering free healthcare services. But more than a site of pilgrimage-related charity and consumption, Shivaji Park is a critical node in the circulation of Ambedkarite ideas. Most numerous of all the stalls are those selling books by Ambedkar, books about Ambedkar and a host of other books on broadly related subjects including social justice, Buddhism and Indian history. On my visit I was lucky enough to be introduced to J. V. Pawar, one of cofounders of the Dalit Panther activist movement that flourished in the 1970s. He and his wife were running their own stall, and I bought a copy of his autobiography in its English translation *Dalit Panthers: An authoritative history* (Pawar, 2017).

For many of my interlocutors, moreover, these bookstalls had long been a major site of their engagement with Ambedkarite thought. Anish was a prolific reader and he told me he often spent part of his evenings reading 'books related to our movement', many of which he had picked up from the Shivaji Park bookstalls, including a Marathi translation of Ambedkar's English-language *The Buddha and His Dhamma,* which is often thought of as a sacred text for Ambedkarite Buddhists (Beltz, 2005, p. 191). Manish also patronised these stalls, and on a separate occasion took me to the Nehru Centre Library in Worli, which he recommended as a great source of information for my research.

But learning about Ambedkar is by no means a purely independent, solitary endeavour. Almost everybody I asked referred to their parents' formative role in exposing them to the life and thoughts of Ambedkar. Public lectures on Ambedkar, Buddhism and Dalit history are also an important part of the BDD Chawls social calendar, often hosted by one of the Mitra Mandals, or neighbourhood social clubs, linked to the Dalit Buddhist-majority buildings including Chawls F and G. The Yuvak Kranti Seva Mandal, literally the 'Youth Revolution Service Association', is linked to Chawl F, and according to Manish, who acts as the Mandal's secretary, its membership and its 'thinking' is essentially identical to that of the Jay Bhim Mitra Mandal, linked to Chawl G.

The Yuvak Kranti Seva Mandal and Jay Bhim Mitra Mandal also organise festivals, sports competitions and social welfare activities such as cleaning the area around the buildings and holding educational events. The Jay Bhim Katta was in fact established by the Jay Bhim Mitra Mandal, both as a seating place and *sarvajanik vartamanpatr vachanalaya* (public newspaper library). As with many other Mitra Mandals, the newspaper library is maintained by individuals who each subscribe to a different paper, in this case a range of Marathi dailies and the English-language *Times of India.*

In addition to the RPI(A) and the Mitra Mandals, there is a managing committee attached to the Buddha Vihar (Buddhist temple). This committee was responsible for organising a three-day programme of music and lectures to commemorate the Dhamma Chakra Pravartan Din (Religious Conversion Day) in 2017. Indeed, social life in the BDD Chawls is characterised by a complex web of civil, political and religious organisations with a significant degree of overlap both in terms of general membership and committee membership. For example, the President of the Jay Bhim Mitra Mandal is also the Treasurer of the Ward 198 RPI(A) branch committee, while Tejaswini sits both on the RPI(A) ladies' wing and on a local Dakshata Samiti (vigilance committee) that coordinates with the N. M. Joshi Marg police station in tackling crime against women.

The line between the political and the civil is not a rigid one. Gérard Heuzé, noted for his studies of the Shiv Sena, points out that while some Mitra Mandals are 'strictly committed to sports, leisure or community service', others have a direct connection to a political movement such as the Congress Party, the Dalit Movement or, most often, the Shiv Sena (1995, p. 219). Somewhere on most of the BDD Chawls *kattas* can be found the name and often headshot of either the current or previous MLA,[9] from the right-wing Shiv Sena and centre-left Nationalist Congress Party (NCP) respectively, who have made donations to the associated Mitra Mandal. This does not necessarily imply political alignment: the Jay Bhim Mitra Mandal, deeply enmeshed with the RPI(A) as it is, received funding from the former MLA from the NCP.[10]

Perhaps just as important as these formal organisational structures are the informal, unlabelled social networks produced by chawlness, this cheek-by-jowl lifestyle of shared spaces and (in many cases) abundant free time. Pradeep's wife Sunita once told me about a flat in Dadar that her grandfather had been entitled to, due to his government job, but had given up. She did not know why he had done so but said that she was glad they had stayed in the demographically-mixed BDD Chawls rather than moving to the Brahman-dominated location of the flat, since the chawls provided a good environment for studying and discussing the life of Ambedkar and the Buddha. *'Har ek chiz samajh mein aye chawl system mein rehke'* (living in the chawl system we understand everything), she added. In particular, the Jay Bhim Katta, used every day by a relatively stable group, provides a forum for naturally-dominating individuals like Mahendra, Sayaji and Anish to influence the discourse and bind the community together in a common identity.

Oppression and emancipation: parallel histories

If I have given the impression of confident individuals within a politically assertive community, it is because this is the impression I myself received. This is not to say that my friends did not regularly remind me of the oppressions faced by Dalits, but what I saw every day in Anish and Sayaji and Tejaswini was not self-pity but rather a deep sense of self-worth. Even Manish, despite his serious and somewhat introspective demeanour, struck me as very confident in his manner of navigating Mumbai life. One afternoon I accompanied him to a Chartered Accountants' office where he had some business, and we later had coffee in the air-conditioned lobby of the building. Here he appeared entirely at ease, surrounded by a well-dressed professional crowd, many speaking English and exuding in a multiplicity of subtler ways their belonging to a class that probably did not live in chawls. Later, he remonstrated angrily with a taxi driver to get him to take us to back to Delisle Road.

It dawned on me that I was being told two distinct versions of Dalit history: one a *longue durée* account of caste-based oppression that persists today, the other a story of emancipation and new assertiveness following the social upliftment work of Ambedkar. In this section I firstly consider the latter type of history, with reference to employment and clothing, both areas in which many Dalit Buddhists have experienced a measure of social uplift, and examine the way these changes are often attributed with almost mythological force to Ambedkar. I then turn to accounts of anti-Dalit oppression and reflect on how both these types of accounts were important in the way my interlocutors presented themselves and their community's history to me.

Employment is one of the most obvious spheres in which recent historical changes have been observed, and one that was a clear source of pride to many Dalits I knew. There are many examples across India of formerly oppressed castes, including the Ad-Dharmis in Punjab and the Jatavs in Uttar Pradesh, distancing themselves from their traditional caste occupations (Gupta, 2005, p. 754). The Mahars' traditional roles were, by definition, village-based and comprised 'necessary duties' such as 'watchmen, wall-menders, messengers, removers of cattle carcasses' (Zelliot, 1996a, p. 34). Naturally, these duties played no part in the urban lives of my friends at the Jay Bhim Katta, but neither did the menial roles of sweeper, cleaner and peon (office boy) often associated with the urban Dalit experience in literature and in the media. My core group of Dalit Buddhist acquaintances covered a wide range of professions between them and included a real estate broker (Anish), a chartered accountant (Manish), a children's tutor (Tejaswini), a journalist (Vinod), a charity worker (Pradeep) and a school administrator (Sayaji, who also owned a small shop). Other regulars at the Jay Bhim Katta included a retired Merchant Navy officer, a lab technician, a sous-chef, an electrician, an Uber driver and a member of a fraud-detection unit in a major bank. In addition to all these, creative professions were well represented, and my acquaintances included a dance teacher, a choreographer, a playwright, a DJ, a singer and a tabla player.

In Anish's view, and that of many of his friends, the fact that all these jobs were open to their community was a direct result of Ambedkar's intervention. In particular, they emphasised the importance of reservations, or quotas, for Dalits and other non-dominant castes in government, the public sector and certain higher education institutions. This implicit presentation of Ambedkar as the sole source of India's reservations policy and of improved job prospects for Dalits is slightly misleading. By Ambedkar's time the Mahar community had begun to experience significant changes. A population surplus, particularly after 'many village occupations were removed from local control' under the British, meant that in the later nineteenth century Mahars began to enter or non-traditional occupations and a general 'upward thrust' of the community was observed by commentators (Zelliot, 1996a, p. 35). Meanwhile, reservations policies were already in place in the late nineteenth century in a number of the Princely States that existed alongside British-ruled India.

Ambedkar was subsequently instrumental in developing a nationwide reservations policy in independent India and provisions were made in the Constitution for reservations in the legislature and in public services for Scheduled Castes and Scheduled Tribes (SC/ST). The SC category is essentially the same as that of Dalit, although it was only in 1990 that Buddhists were included in this category (Das, 2000, p. 3833).[11] In other words, the accounts I received papered over some of this history and instead exceptionalised and amplified Ambedkar's role. Despite this teleological story of progress, workforce discrimination against Mahars did not end either with the British or with Ambedkar, as evidence of recruitment bias in the textile mills attests (see Adarkar and Menon, 2004, pp. 112–13; Upadhyay, 2004, p. 32).

A second example of Mahar social uplift is that of clothing. I was struck by how many of the Dalit Buddhist men I knew were for the most part formally attired in pressed shirts and trousers, especially if they were going outside the BDD Chawls on business. Some of the younger members, girls included, wore a t-shirt and jeans or shorts while at leisure, but the older women tended to wear a salwar kameez or sari at all times. During a conversation about shopping malls, Anish told me a story about visiting Mumbai's first mall back in 2000 wearing what he called 'simple footwear' and being denied entry by the security guard. It was only after getting his shoes fixed by a cobbler that he was allowed into the mall. In those days, he explained switching to English, 'we used to wear simple clothes'.

'Before and after' stories of Dalit clothing are common in academic literature and news media. Anthropologist Nicolas Jaoul describes the 'assertive attitudes' of a 'new generation of Dalits' emerging in Uttar Pradesh villages in the 1970s 'who openly defied caste hierarchies' by rejecting the degrading *jutha* system whereby they were offered old clothes and leftover food in return for traditional (and highly demeaning) services rendered, opting instead to wear 'neat shirts and trousers' (Jaoul, 2006, pp. 191–2). Elsewhere, there are accounts of Dalits earlier being required to wear old, dirty clothes in order not to anger the upper castes (see Mungekar, 2007, p. 132) even sprinkling dirty water on new clothes to make them appropriately dirty (Masoodi, 2017).

What interested me most about Anish's story, however, was that he attributed this sartorial shift – which apparently occurred in his own lifetime – to Ambedkar, who died nearly three decades before he was born. As with the accounts of reservations, this appears to be another (modestly) distorted and simplified narrative that positions Ambedkar as the singular benefactor. In this case, the connection between Ambedkar and Dalit clothing is a logical one given his near ubiquitous portrayal in a blue three-piece suit, including on the front banner of the Jay Bhim Katta. This representation has been interpreted as a way in which Dalits celebrate 'his successful storming of an upper caste citadel', since by 'the canons of tradition and history this man was not supposed to wear a suit, blue or otherwise' (Guha, 2002). Indeed, many elite non-Dalit detractors criticise Ambedkar's blue suit as symptomatic of his anti-Indian 'Western alienation', at odds with the way many Dalits 'take pride in Ambedkar's dress as symbolic of his excellence in education and statesmanship' (Jaoul, 2006, p. 183).[12]

In contrast to the celebratory tone of these, and other, accounts of progress were the bleak reminders I received from Anish and his circle that Dalits are still marginalised and discriminated against today. Sometimes, as we shall see in later chapters, these reminders referred to specific incidents in the BDD Chawls that revealed the highhandedness of the Marathas, especially those living in Chawl M. At others, the reminders were placed in a more general historical context, with particular reference made to the Peshwa, a Brahman dynasty that ruled the Maratha Empire for much of the eighteenth century after assuming the mantle of power from Shivaji's descendants. Descriptions of the Peshwa as caste oppressors whose treatment of their Mahar subjects was brutal and degrading often echoed Ambedkar's own account in his 1936 *The Annihilation of Caste*:

> [T]he untouchable was required to carry, strung from his waist, a broom to sweep away from behind the dust he [trod] on lest a Hindu walking on the same should be polluted … [and] an earthen pot, strung from his neck wherever he went, for holding his spit lest his spit falling on earth should pollute a Hindu who might unknowingly happen to tread on it.
>
> (Ambedkar, 2013, p. 18)

More recent examples of casteism and atrocities against Dalits were also recounted to me. Most notorious of these was the 2006 violence against the Dalit Bhotmange family in Khairlanji, also in Maharashtra, in which the mother and daughter were 'paraded naked to the village centre [and] the genitals of the boys [were] crushed with stones' while two other women were gang raped and murdered, their corpses 'callously thrown into the canal' (Teltumbde, 2007, p. 1019).

Beyond specific incidents, however, my interlocutors conveyed a more general sense that, despite the vast strides made by Ambedkar and his followers, Dalits were still discriminated against in public life. This is a familiar theme in Dalit scholarship – Anand Teltumbde, himself a Mahar academic and activist, argues that the Khairlanji massacre explodes the 'myths' that 'economic development does away with casteism', that 'there exists a significant progressive section of non-dalits that is against the caste system' or 'that dalits placed in the bureaucracy can orient the administration to do justice to dalits' (2007, p. 1019).

In a parallel to the way accounts of racism, gender discrimination and homophobia are widely documented and shared by activists and others in the UK (and elsewhere in the 'West') to illustrate how far we still are from equality despite gains in certain areas, these narratives of Dalit marginalisation seem to be saying: 'Just because we work good jobs and wear nice clothes, don't be fooled into thinking casteism is finished.' If this was an important message to ensure that the foreign researcher took away with him, equally so was the assertive message of emancipation that was, like so much else in Dalit Buddhist life, intimately wrapped up in the legacy of Ambedkar. It is entirely understandable that, as a matter of self-respect, Anish and his friends wanted me to be clear that much progress had, in fact, been made in their community and to ensure that Ambedkar was squarely at heart of this progress. Far from contradicting each other, these two messages draw honestly from the same histories but are framed differently to produce different, and equally necessary, effects.

Interlude: gender trouble

If there was one area, more than any other, in which I struggled to square my observations of my interlocutors' reality with the Ambedkarite 'thinking' they propounded, it was that of gender relations. Bahujan[13] scholar Kancha Ilaiah argues that gender relations among Dalits and Bahujans are fundamentally different from those among the dominant castes, since the 'domains of man and woman are not completely bifurcated at home and in the field' (1996, p. 46). Traditional strategies of Dalit social mobility, indeed, such as those reported in a Chamar community in Uttar Pradesh (Cohn, 1955), have often been rooted in an attempt to emulate dominant-caste practices by lowering marriage age, strengthening paternal authority and increasing the seclusion of wives. Mahar social mobility, in contrast, has long been premised on a rhetoric of women's rights championed by Ambedkar as well as nineteenth-century marginalised-caste reformers Jyotirao and Savitribai Phule.

Using what has since become a well-known aphorism, Ambedkar informed 3,000 women in a 1927 speech that 'I measure the progress of a community by the degree of progress which women have achieved' (quoted in Ramteke, 2018, p. 100). In a 1951 article, 'The rise and fall of the Hindu woman', he argued that Brahmanical Hinduism was responsible for the subjugation of women in Indian society, and that this was intensified in reaction to the Buddha's teaching which 'endeavoured to ennoble the woman' and 'raise her to the level of man' (Ambedkar, 2014c, p. 129). In the same year, he resigned from Nehru's cabinet following the failure of the Hindu Code Bill 1951 that he championed in an 'attempt to strike legally against Hindu patriarchy' (Jaoul, 2016, p. 49). This Bill would have modified traditional Hindu inheritance laws in favour of daughters and widows, in addition to sanctioning divorce (Williams, 2006, p. 103).

The Ambedkarite movement has a rich tradition of honouring Dalit and other Bahujan women, most notably Savitribai Phule, renowned as an anti-caste activist and pioneer of girl's education in the nineteenth century. Ambedkar's own emphasis on the importance of education for Dalit women has been cited by a leading female Dalit academic as one of the major inspirations behind the emergence of a body of Dalit feminist writing and autobiography in the later twentieth century (Kumar, 2015). Meanwhile, the importance of Buddhism for gender equality is also emphasised by many Dalit women, such as writer-activist Meenakshi Moon who told anthropologist Johannes Beltz that 'All the progress we have made is a result of our conversion to Buddhism. Nowadays, girls can become doctors, engineers and teachers. They have the same opportunities as boys' (Beltz, 2005, p. 134).

Back on the benches of the Jay Bhim Katta, however, I became increasingly aware of and somewhat uncomfortable with the almost total absence of women. One afternoon in March, the conversation turned to a forthcoming visit from my parents, and Mahendra insisted I must bring them to the BDD Chawls. I asked him whether there would be any problem with my mother sitting at the Jay Bhim Katta, since at that stage I had only ever seen men sitting there. He looked slightly indignant and said that of course it would be fine, and that everybody is welcome to sit, since Buddhism is the only religion to give complete equality to women. I couldn't resist a barb: if everybody is welcome, why are none of them sitting here? Most of them are too busy to come out here, he said, since they will be preparing the evening meal and looking after their children. Anish hastily intervened at this point and told me that women tend to sit out at the Jay Bhim Katta later on in the evening, often coming with their children on the way back from classes.

These are hardly novel observations. In her autobiography *I want to destroy myself*, the poet Malika Amar Shaikh, who was raised without any religion by her Muslim father (the singer Amar Shaikh) and dominant-caste mother, recounts in visceral detail the physical and mental abuse she faced at the hands of her husband, fellow poet and Dalit Panther cofounder Namdeo Dhasal. She rails against the expectation that she and her mother-in-law would be always on hand to feed and entertain a constant stream of visitors from the movement (Shaikh, 2016, pp. 91–4) and ridicules an Ambedkarite Buddhist associate of Dhasal's who claimed to be 'progressive' while citing Hindu scripture to justify his expectation that women should remain housewives (p. 126). Unlike Meenakshi Moon, she is sceptical that Buddhist conversion 'has brought much change in Dalit society' (p. 154).

I never became privy to such inner worlds of any female members of the Dalit Buddhist community, but I struck up a number of more casual friendships. Towards the middle of the year, for example, I got to know Anish's cousin Gunjan who sold biscuits, eggs and soap and other general provisions at a small stall on the corner of Chawl G. She was extremely shortsighted and also used a walking stick, and had managed to get herself enrolled on a training programme specifically designed for people with mobility challenges at a company that manufactured water purifiers. Since she was struggling with written English, I took to spending half an hour or so, several days a week, helping her improve her spelling. The more time I spent with her, the more I felt her apparent marginalisation within the community. She was generally addressed in a rather impatient tone, especially by men, and she rarely participated in any of the festivals that brought the rest of the community together so frequently. Other than her mother, her closest associates appeared to be a few young children who often sat with her in her shop, and a couple of young men with whom she had a teasing relationship. Mortifyingly, as a result of their English-medium schooling, the children spoke far better English than she did.

I once asked Gunjan if she ever sat at the Jay Bhim Katta, to which she laughed impatiently.

'*Sirf gents rehte*' (only men stay there). Why not ladies, I asked.

'*Aise…*' (it's like that) she said with a shrug.

'Except at Ambedkar Jayanti,' said one of the girls. 'Then all ladies come.'

We had a similar conversation about the Yuvak Kranti Seva Mandal which she explained she was not part of.

'*Hamare bhai log yahan pe rehte. Aurat nahin*' (Our brothers are there. Not women).

'*Kyon?*' (why?) I asked.

'*Aise …*' (Because …)

Although Gunjan appeared to occupy an unusually marginalised position in relation to the male-dominated world of the Jay Bhim Katta, perhaps in part due to her disabilities, nothing I observed in over a year of fieldwork contradicted her observation that women only join in with the Mandal for social functions. Even these social functions invariably featured a spatial separation based on gender, quite unlike the free mixing I observed within private Dalit homes. When wedding parties turned whole corridors into dance floors, for example, one half would be taken up by men, the other by women, although these halves tended to merge as the night wore on.

Sunita was often to be found dancing at the line of segregation, and she and I developed a jokey rapport, gradually becoming friends. There was never a suggestion of impropriety when I went to visit her and her young son Pravin, even if Pradeep was out, whereas in many other women in the BDD Chawls I detected a palpable sense that I was seen as their husband's or son's associate. If I went to visit Manish, for example, his mother was unfailingly generous in offering me a large plate of biscuits and black tea. We would greet each other cordially, but beyond that conversations between us were rather stilted: I did not really know how to talk to her and vice versa (or so it seemed), meaning I felt more than usually like an imposition. I experienced something similar with Anish's aunt and Sayaji's wife. While I grew fond of all three and was always grateful for their hospitality, visits were typically brief and ended, as far as I can guess, with relief on their side as much as on mine.

A notable exception was Tejaswini, the social worker from Chawl 01, whose active involvement in the RPI(A) and various other local committees was the subject of long conversations between us. I was shown numerous photographs of community events in which she was apparently playing a prominent role. The potted life story she relayed to me on a number of occasions was one of achievement in the face of considerable adversity. She described her farmer father as *kamchor* (lazy), which meant she had to 'earn and learn' from an early age, ultimately receiving a BA from the locally prestigious Shivaji University in Kolhapur. She came to Mumbai to work as a teacher, and now continues to run her own tuition classes in Maths, Science and English within the BDD Chawls. She also organises skills training for rural women, including jewellery making, and during the time I knew her was reading a law book so as to better explain to other women what their rights are in a marital dispute.

But even Tejaswini's daunting range of social activity seems predicated on a fundamental separation between men and women in public. Her educational activity, other than children's teaching, is aimed at women, and her political activity is through a separate ladies' wing of the local RPI(A) branch. It only occurred to me with hindsight to question the compatibility of gender-segregated RPI(A) committees with a belief in gender equality, and to draw uncomfortable parallels with the so-called 'separate but equal doctrine' that originally referred to race relations in Jim-Crow-era America, but has since been applied to contexts of gender segregation such as religious schooling in the UK (McCann, 2017) and the workplace in the US (McGrew, 2016).

Of course, none of this is unusual in India, where male-dominated public spaces are a common sight, even in famously 'liberal' Mumbai,[14] and Mahila Mandals (women's committees) of one kind or another are part of daily life across the country. Moreover, all my observations above could be applied equally to the Hindu communities of the BDD Chawls. But they sit awkwardly alongside the claims, made overwhelmingly by men in my own experience, that the Ambedkarite Buddhist community provides absolute gender equality. Theoretical commitments to equality are apparently insufficient to disrupt gender norms shaped over centuries. Indeed, a glance at some of the questions that currently dog gender relations in the global North – the gender pay gap, trans rights issues, sexual harassment and institutional gender-based violence – would attest to this.

The most significant practical implication this has had on my own research is that of a heavy bias towards male participants. In retrospect, of course, I wish that I had spent more time and made more effort in trying to forge deeper relationships with female members of the community, but I tended to gravitate towards the all-male public spaces where I felt most welcome and least intrusive. My conclusions on gender relations among the BDD Chawls Dalit Buddhists have therefore been made overwhelmingly from the vantage point of its male-dominated spaces, and it is entirely possible that a researcher who had spent more time in the company of Dalit women might have reached rather different conclusions.

Beyond this, I am almost certainly guilty of applying a Eurocentric liberal-feminist lens to my fieldwork, and this has shaped my own expectations of what gender relations in a politically 'progressive' community (to borrow Malika Amar Shaikh's term) might look like.[15] In truth, I simply have no idea how Tejaswini would regard an imagined future in which she spent her afternoons debating in the Jay Bhim Katta with fellow members of a mixed-gender RPI(A) committee while her husband prepared dinner – it may well not present a particularly desirable prospect. That said, Shaikh herself is emphatic that her story is not unique and that women are almost universally oppressed by men (2016, pp. 156–7), as a result of which she is 'now of the firm opinion that women must exploit their own husbands' (p. 189). Quite possibly, unbeknownst to me, this is what the Dalit women of the BDD Chawls have been doing all along.

Comfortably ambiguous? The necessity of slippery stories

A few weeks after the pandemonium of Ganesh Chaturthi had abated, Sayaji informed me in an offhand way that he had in fact attended a prayer function at the home of his Hindu father-in-law. I smiled inwardly at the contradiction, as I had often wondered how such a staunch critic of Hinduism navigated family life after having married a Hindu. I asked him if he had taken the opportunity to enquire as to Ganesh's surname and date of birth, but he simply laughed and squeezed my shoulder.

Aptly, we were sitting at the Jay Bhim Katta next to the picture of Ambedkar. As we have seen, his image is ubiquitous in the Dalit-majority BDD Chawl buildings where he is referred to as the father of the nation, the emancipator of Dalits, a Messiah, a *bodhisattva,* and sometimes explicitly a god, while his writings have a status similar to sacred scripture and his name is incorporated into ritualistic chants and everyday greetings. This comfortably ambiguous adulation bordering on deification is not unusual in India, where newspaper headlines revel in stories of temples erected to film stars, politicians and even the cricketer Sachin Tendulkar (Mishra, 2013). Indeed, communist politician Govind Pansare observed that it 'does not take too long in our country and traditions for humans to become Gods' (2015, p. 88). However, there is something less comfortable about it when it occurs in a community that places such an emphasis on Ambedkarite thought that encompasses humanistic rationalism and the rejection of god-worship.

Ambedkar himself admonished a group of Dalits who celebrated him in an address in 1933, cautioning them that:

> These ideas of hero-worship will bring ruin on you if you do not nip them in the bud. By deifying an individual, you repose faith for your safety and salvation in one single individual with the result that you get into the habit of dependence and grow indifferent to your duty.
> (Ambedkar, 2014d, p. 88)

He went on to add that it was precisely this combination of 'hero-worship, deification and neglect of duty' that has 'ruined Hindu Society and [is] responsible for the degradation of our country' (2014d, p. 88). Nevertheless, despite my occasional irritation and not infrequent cynicism where my interlocutors' adulation for Ambedkar was concerned, I generally got a far stronger impression of Ambedkar as a galvanising inspiration than as a cause of neglect of duty or a source of degradation.

When Sayaji told me that Ganesh was simply a Brahmanic fabrication, he asked me 'bhagwan kaun hai?' (who is God?) before swiftly answering his own question: 'insan bhagwan hai!' (man is God!). The Buddha, he explained, taught us that humans are the real gods because they can actually help people. Years later, it is recalling this exchange that convinces me that obsessing over Ambedkar's humanity is ultimately fruitless. Rather, it is the very coexistence of these slippery, contradictory notions that reveals most about Dalit Buddhist life in twenty-first century Mumbai.

The annual Ambedkar Jayanti processions provide a useful illustration here. It would be easy enough to criticise the celebrations as over the top and hypocritical in the face of Ambedkar's own cautions and the Dalit Buddhist community's disdain for lavish Hindu festivals. But for a community that has been so consistently marginalised and excluded from public life over centuries, perhaps the only viable way to lay claim to the public sphere is with a quasi-religious fervour that effectively elevates Ambedkar to a heroic, superhuman or even godlike status and warrants comparisons with Divali.[16] Crucially, when Dalit Buddhists parade the neighbourhood on Ambedkar Jayanti, they follow the same route and take up space on the same streets as Hindus do when they take their Ganesh idols for ritual immersion at the end of Ganesh Chaturthi. In the BDD Chawls this is already a long-established tradition (Shaikh, 2011, p. 71), but in its earliest incarnations it would have been a bold new act of transgression, similar to that of a marginalised-caste religious procession deviating from its time-honoured route into upper-caste territory as described by Diana Mines in the context of a Tamil village (2005, pp. 192–4).

The importance of the BDD Chawls as a physical space is no coincidence and this can also be seen in my interlocutors' coexisting narratives of oppression and emancipation. Dalit Buddhists and dominant-caste Hindus live in close proximity to each other in identical dwelling types with the same amenities and infrastructure. This place-derived equality is only partial at best, and there are still dominant-caste Hindus who resent living at such close quarters and on such apparently egalitarian terms with Dalits. Moreover, since there is a loose building-wise separation between demographic groups (Dalits and non-Dalits in particular), the BDD Chawls do not throw communities together in the same way that more mixed buildings can. This loose segregation has resulted in and been perpetuated by the formation of organisational structures and spaces that are closely tied to a particular community. In the Dalit Buddhist-led Mitra Mandals this tie is reinforced by political links to RPI(A) and the everyday circulation of ideas at the Jay Bhim Katta, which serves to intensify group identity under the totemic images of the community's heroes: Buddha, Shivaji, Phule and, above all, Ambedkar.

Nevertheless, the situation is quite unlike the spatial segregation encountered in villages where Mahars traditionally lived in a separate 'Maharwada' in poor-quality dwellings compared to those of the dominant castes (Rao, 2009, p. 230). It is therefore understandable that my Dalit friends were not only anxious to impress on me that caste-based inequality, discrimination and violence remain very real phenomena in contemporary India, but also keen for me to appreciate how far removed their urban lives are from their rural Mahar past, and the outsized role of their *masih*, or *bodhisattva*, Dr Babasaheb Ambedkar in effecting this transformation.

Notes

1. *Chaturthi* is the Sanskrit word for fourth, and the festival begins on the fourth day of the Hindu month Bhadrapada.
2. Beltz (2005, pp. 152–9) outlines a number of analogous cases of Hindu sites that are claimed by Buddhists, including the image of the deity Vithoba at a famous Hindu temple in Pandharpur which Ambedkar himself declared to be that of the Buddha 'in spite of the absence of scientific validity' (2005, p. 156; see also Pawar, 2017, p. 78).
3. My interlocutors, I fear, may wince at this comparison, and it is important to draw a distinction between 'Ram Ram' and the more overtly political slogan 'Jai Shri Ram'. It should also be noted that Ambedkar himself wrote scathingly about the merits of the mythological Lord Ram both as a king and as an object of worship (1987b, p. 343).
4. Shourie's (1997) core argument that Ambedkar played no part in the Indian Independence struggle will be considered further in Chapter 4.
5. Except in the context of the expression 'Jay Bhim', Ambedkar is rarely referred to by this name, and the honorific Babasaheb ('respected father') is much more commonly used, as in 'Dr Babasaheb Ambedkar'.
6. Beltz quotes a Buddhist college principal who says he pays homage to Ambedkar and shows his respect to Buddha, 'but I do not ask for any gifts. If a Hindu goes to a temple, he expects something in return.' This is described as *vandana* (homage, salutation) rather than *prarthana* (prayer, request) (2005, p. 177 and 187).

7. The 22 vows that Ambedkar administered for all new Buddhist converts includes an emphatic rejection of any belief of incarnation.
8. The Bombay Municipal Corporation (BMC), now renamed with a clever sleight of hand to Brihanmumbai Municipal Corporation (BMC) or Municipal Corporation of Greater Mumbai (MCGM). At the municipal level, Mumbai is divided into over 200 numbered wards (for example Ward 198 to which the BDD Chawls belongs), each of which elects a Corporator to the BMC. Meanwhile, for the purposes of electing representatives to the Maharashtra Legislative Assembly (state government), Mumbai is divided into larger alphabetically-named wards (A-T), each of which has a Member of the Legislative Assembly (MLA) representing it.
9. Member of the Legislative Assembly – see note 8.
10. I was intrigued to discover that Mahendra, usually so prominent at Dalit Buddhist events, was not part of the RPI(A) but rather an active member of the NCP, traditionally considered a 'party of the Marathas' (Deshpande and Palshikar, 2017, p. 80). I never heard this political difference remarked upon, and the few times I raised the issue it was downplayed. Whether this was because it was genuinely considered unimportant or because it was not something my research participants wished to discuss with me, I never found out.
11. In 1992, following the recommendations of the Mandal Commission, reservations were further extended to incorporate the so-called Other Backward Classes (OBC), those castes considered disadvantaged but not included in the original SC/ST designation. Despite this, Teltumbde points out, since reservations were never extended to privately-funded education institutes, or the 'far bigger' private employment sector, it is 'glaringly' evident that there remains a 'poor representation of dalits in higher education and in the higher echelons of employment' (2009, p. 16). Teltumbde also argues that reservations are 'disproportionately cornered by a single sub-caste in every state', and proposes a solution whereby 'reservation[s] should be prioritised to the families that have not availed of it so far' (Teltumbde, 2009, pp. 16–17).
12. Anthropologist Emma Tarlo interprets Ambedkar's adoption of European dress, and by extension the 'shiny, synthetic rayons' worn by her Harijan interlocutors, as antithetical to Gandhi's strategy of adopting homespun (*kadhi*) as a way of asserting Indian values and 'identify[ing] with the plight of the poorest villager' (1996, pp. 283 and 321).
13. *Bahujan*, a Pali term literally meaning 'the many', has been used by analysts of caste (including Ambedkar and Phule) to refer to communities outside the dominant castes, such as Scheduled Castes (Dalits), Scheduled Tribes and OBC (Other Backward Classes).
14. This is compellingly illustrated in *Why Loiter,* a manifesto by Mumbai-based Shilpa Phadke, Sameera Khan and Shilpa Ranade (2011) urging women to take up space in Indian cities.
15. A huge and growing body of academic and activist literature challenges the universalising epistemologies of first- and second-wave (and predominantly white, heterosexual, cisgender, middle-class and able-bodied) feminism. In particular there is a well-established canon of Black American feminist scholar-activists including Audre Lorde, bell hooks and Kimberlé Crenshaw; Muslim feminists such as amina wadud and Leila Ahmed; and of course Dalit feminists, notably Rajni Tilak, Babytai Kamble, Gogu Shyamala and Joopaka Subhadra. Recent interventions into these debates include Françoise Vergès 2019 *Un Féminisme Décolonial* (see Vergès, 2021 for an English translation) and Rafia Zakaria's (2021) *Against White Feminism.*
16. It is worth noting that Ganesh Chaturthi was itself revived as a public festival in the late nineteenth century (after a century or more of predominantly domestic celebration) to galvanise Hindu civic consciousness in the same way that *muharram* processions (commemorating the martyrdom of the Prophet's grandson) did for Shia Islam.

3
Adrift in history? Living between village and city

Tukaram's room

At the beginning of April I met Tukaram. I had just had my hair cut at Maruti's shop, where I had by now become a regular, and was making small talk with a group of young men who were standing outside. As usual, they wanted to know who I was, where I had come from and what I was doing. Tukaram's good looks and obvious attention to his physical appearance – close fitting clothes, neatly trimmed beard and a pair of headphones round his neck – marked him out slightly from the group, as did the fact that, unlike the others, he was not an engineer but was studying animation at a college in nearby Dadar. In other circumstances I might have read him as a hipster; in the setting of the BDD Chawls he simply had a slight apartness that aroused my curiosity.

I quickly learnt that his friends were in fact his relatives. They told me they all lived together in a chawl room that had been bought by their grandfathers who had lived there years ago. They were from a village called Katkarwadi and had come to Mumbai to work, as had their fathers and grandfathers, now living back in the village. One of the older cousins had already been living in Mumbai for a decade, while Tukaram, aged 22, had arrived a couple of years previously. The ice now broken, I would often meet them for chai and after the third or fourth meeting I was invited into their room.

The same size as any other BDD Chawl room I had visited, it immediately reminded me more of the room in which my language-exchange friend Vikas lived with his fellow villagers than it did of the rooms occupied by families. Little natural light penetrates the gloom, and usually a number of young men will be stretched out on bed sheets, either asleep or watching videos on their smartphones. Just as in Vikas' room, the plaster wall is largely obscured by clothes – t-shirts, shirts, jeans and formal trousers – hanging from a row of hooks running around three sides of the room (Figure 3.1). Directly ahead is a pink wooden balustrade fronting a small gallery piled with boxes and bags. It is called a *potmala* ('sub-floor') and is used as a space for sleeping, storage and, in some cases, study.

Below this, the far end of the tiny room is divided into two parts. A narrow portion on the right leads past an alcove, stuffed with multiple rolls of bedding, to an open window enclosed by chicken wire. On the left is a larger square portion lined with off-white tiles. This is the *mori*, a space for washing clothes, dishes and bodies. As with other chawl rooms, there is no internal toilet, and residents use the common toilets at the end of the corridor. In the *mori* is a large blue plastic drum full of water, surrounded by smaller metal buckets and earthenware pitchers, and in the corner four small shelves are crammed with soap dishes.

Everything in the room signifies multiple occupancy. Immediately to the right of the door is a five-shelf shoe rack stuffed with around 15 pairs of footwear including black office shoes, trainers, sandals and flip-flops. Overhead, a similar number of towels hangs from a series of poles

Figure 3.1 Katkarwadi Gramastha Mandal room, BDD Chawl K, Delisle Road. © Author.

and wires crossing the room. Above the rows of hanging clothes round the side is a wooden ledge piled up with trunks and suitcases. Other details emerge: to the left, at chest height, a small wooden shrine with images of Hindu deities; on the balustrade, a clock and a mirror next to a framed picture of Sai Baba of Shirdi, a famous Maharashtrian saint; a number of stainless steel tiffin boxes on the shelf above the rolled bedding, next to a tangle of phone chargers.

Despite my earlier exposure to Vikas' living arrangements, I was slow on the uptake when it came to Tukaram's room. It took me weeks to notice that there was a sign on the door that read 'Katkarwadi Gramastha Mandal' and to connect this to the name 'Amrutwadi Gramastha Mandal' that Vikas used to refer to his own room. Eventually, I realised that Tukaram's room was not simply the private property of the boys' grandfathers but a more formal, village-wide arrangement overseen by the Katkarwadi Gramastha Mandal.

Gramastha is a Sanskrit-origin word meaning 'belonging to a village', but equally translatable as rustic, villager or simply village. *Mandal,* also from Sanskrit, literally means disc or circle but in Marathi is used to refer to a committee or association like the Mitra Mandals or chawl-wide social clubs discussed in Chapter 1. A Gramastha Mandal is therefore a villagers' association, and Katkarwadi Gramastha Mandal is specifically an association for residents of Tukaram's village Katkarwadi, in the Ajara *taluka* (municipality) of Kolhapur District, a few hundred miles southeast of Mumbai.

There are over 40 Gramastha Mandals in the BDD Chawls alone, their rooms located in the same buildings and corridors as those of the families. Of these 40, I interacted with 18, in some cases meeting multiple members and spending a lot of time with them, in others meeting only one member on a couple of occasions. The physical layout of the rooms is strikingly uniform, and all operate under a similar model: the village committee rent or buys one or more chawl rooms and then sublets out bedspace to male migrants from their village at a low rate, usually between Rs 100 and Rs 500 (c. £1–£5) per month. Many have been operating for 50 years or more and are now housing a third generation of migrants. Some, like Gaowadi Gramastha Mandal (for migrants from Gaowadi village, also in Kolhapur District near Katkarwadi) only own a single room, while many others, including Katkarwadi Gramastha Mandal own five or more. Management committees are elected by residents and are sometimes run by ex-residents now living with their own families in other parts of the city.

Most rooms house between 10 and 20 residents. They are exclusively male, many in their late teens or twenties, a few much older. The vast majority of these Gramastha Mandals are linked to villages in the Kolhapur District[1] and members speak Marathi as their mother tongue. Most are Hindu and of these many belong to the Maratha community with a sizeable minority of OBCs[2] and a few Dalits, but there are also some (Dalit) Buddhist residents who we shall meet in Chapter 5.

This is a well-established system across Mumbai's chawls, as attested by Neera Adarkar's description of 'rooms taken on rent by the ... village committees and converted into dormitories for the single migrants from that village' (2011, p. 19) and Gyan Prakash's observations of a 'single chawl room packed tight' with 'male workers from the same village' who 'grouped together to rent a room' (2011, pp. 64 and 67). Throughout Mumbai, in fact, Gramastha Mandal rooms can be found in chawls and other apartment blocks, although they are most densely concentrated in the heart of the former mill district. While the subject of glancing references in social histories and the occasional newspaper article, the Gramastha Mandal system has not been given the academic attention (in English, at least) it deserves as a manifestation of rural–urban migration. One notable, but now rather dated, exception is Hemlata Dandekar's *Men to Bombay, Woman at Home*, an ethnographic study of migration from Sugao village in Satara District[3] to a shared room in Mumbai (Dandekar, 1986).

For me, the Gramastha Mandal system was a thrilling discovery, enhanced by the realisation that so little had been written about it. It was this sense of discovery that led me to spend so much time hanging around in Gramastha Mandal rooms. Another researcher might have been drawn to an entirely different segment of chawl life, and it is not inevitable that a book about the BDD Chawls should devote so much space to Gramastha Mandals. In the sections that follow I reflect on the circular migration patterns that keep ties between Gramastha Mandal and village so strong, before building up a picture of everyday life in the contemporary Gramastha Mandals of the BDD Chawls.

The subsequent sections explore the disjuncture between Gramastha Mandal life and the wider chawl life of the families living next door, and the differences in the neighbourhood histories these two groups (bachelor migrants and families) recount. I understand this disjuncture as a result of 'autochthony' (Yuval-Davis, 2012), the 'I was here before you' sense with which groups of more established migrants reject more recent arrivals. What makes this case unusual, however, is that, unlike the more familiar story of ethnic or religious differences between migrants and host communities or other migrant communities, these neighbouring families frequently belong to same communities (mostly Maratha Hindu) as the Gramastha Mandal migrants and maintain ancestral connections with the same villages. After several generations in Mumbai, however, the families have developed their own networks of more settled urban belonging, notably in the form of Mitra Mandals (chawl social clubs). While Mitra Mandal members tell stories about their clubs' proud histories of sporting achievements and social service, the Gramastha Mandal members complain of being excluded from these clubs which they perceive as being for permanent resident families only, despite their own fathers and grandfathers (now back in the village) sometimes having been founder members. Trapped in tedious jobs and repetitive social lives, nostalgic for their childhoods and frozen out of the social institutions of their ancestors, the Gramastha Mandal population of today sometimes feels like a faintly awkward relic, drifting in a sidestream while the main current of history flows by. Throughout the chapter I complicate this picture and in the closing section offer some alternative perspectives.

Belonging to two places

At almost any given time, at least one member of each Gramastha Mandal is visiting their village. Perhaps there is a family wedding to attend, or a religious festival. Maybe a change of air is required, or an escape from the sweltering city heat in May. Some go to spend time working in the family fields, or for some other kind of informal labour. The village is also a place to return when ill, the comfort of the family home and a familiar doctor apparently outweighing the advantages of city healthcare.[4] For a major village festival the entire room might empty out, its residents heading back en masse to join the celebrations. The Gram Panchayat (village council) elections every five years exert a similar pull, and some Gramastha Mandals charter a minibus to assist members in exercising their democratic right.

This back-and-forth movement is a kind of circular migration. Such migration, which Deshingkar and Farrington define as 'a temporary move from, followed by a return to, the normal place of residence, for purposes of employment' (2009, p. 1), is often conceptualised in terms of a separation between 'home' (usually a village) and the place of temporary employment (frequently a city). Echanove and Srivastava, following the lives of Mumbai families with roots in the Konkan region, have developed the somewhat different concept of *circulatory urbanism* which shifts the centre of gravity to the city as both source of employment and place of long-term residence, from which links to the village remain 'very much alive through frequent family visits, financial investments, and institutional linkages' (Echanove and Srivastava, 2014, p. 2).

Neither conceptualisation quite captures the circular migration of the Gramastha Mandal migrants, which plays out over multiple, nested timescales. There is the life-cycle circularity of coming to the city for work at a young age, and (traditionally, at least) retiring after several decades to the village, but within this arc are the short-term, frequently-repeated seasonal circulations – the week or fortnight-long trips to visit the family, attend a wedding, cast a vote or pitch in at harvest time.

A visit to southern Kolhapur district will usually begin with an overnight coach journey, the tedium sometimes leavened with a bag of snacks and small bottle of whisky. A Gramastha Mandal traveller will often bring sweets for his family and sometimes other items such as tea powder or soap, which are expensive to buy in the village, or even electronics and new clothes.[5] The flow of goods is not unidirectional. When the visit is over, mothers ensure their sons are ready to return to city life by plying with them with eatables: peanuts, cashew nuts, sweets and perhaps *bhakri* (rice-flour rotis) or sugar cane. But without fail the traveller will bring back a snack made from puffed rice called *bhadang*. Indeed, my own impression was of a constant flow of *bhadang* from the villages of Kolhapur District into the BDD Chawls, such that in most Gramastha Mandal rooms I could count on a recently-returned resident reaching for a plastic bag to offer me what he would invariably describe as the best *bhadang* in Maharashtra. This struck me as not only a sense of hospitality towards a guest, but also a genuine desire to ensure that I tasted the produce of his village and family. When I visited Chincholi Gramastha Mandal, *bhadang* was pressed on me with an insistent '*Try karo, taste karo. Dukan se nahin hai, ghar se banaya gaya!*' (Try it, taste it. It's homemade, not from a shop!).

This village-wards orientation that characterises the lives of many Gramastha Mandal migrants also extends to politics. Few of my migrant interlocutors had registered to vote in Mumbai, some citing the difficulties of providing sufficient proof of address that came with their living arrangement. Others told me that they considered the village-level Gram Panchayat elections more important than national and state elections, since their vote carries greater proportional weight, and the Gram Panchayat is the most tangible manifestation of the state that they actually encounter. In October 2017, an organisation linked to Bhandewadi Gramastha Mandal chartered three minibuses for Mumbai-based Bhandewadikars to return to vote in the village elections and in many cases express their dissatisfaction with the current Gram Panchayat's approach to water and electricity management. The same organisation has previously helped to finance a new village school and a new Hindu temple.[6]

Gramastha Mandal life in the twenty-first century

Mills, malls and MBAs: work and remittances

Back in Mumbai, the day starts early for most. Water is supplied by the municipal corporation (BMC) directly to the *mori* through a length of orange rubber tubing between around 5 a.m. and 7 a.m. and then again in the afternoon. Since in most rooms water demand outstrips storage capacity, residents take their baths – a bucket of cold water and a bar of soap – while water is flowing through the pipe. By 7 a.m. knots of Gramastha Mandal residents can be found outside drinking chai or eating *poha* (a popular dish made from flattened rice) at nearby stalls before, in many cases, heading off to work.

Traditionally, the rhythm of Gramastha Mandal life was dictated by the three eight-hour shifts of the cotton mills (Adarkar and Menon, 2004, pp. 93–5). Sushil, a self-styled local historian from Chawl B, suggested that it was the shift-wise nature of mill work that made the Gramastha Mandal model economically viable in the first place – a large pool of rent payers was needed, and it was easy to accommodate 30 or more in a small chawl room if only a third of them needed to sleep at any given point (see also Chandavarkar, 2004, pp. 21–2).[7]

Datta, a former Katkarwadi Gramastha Mandal resident, told me that when he arrived in Mumbai in 1972, aged twelve, there were 30 people living in the room working in three shifts. During holidays, people had to sleep on the roof terrace or outside. His own father had come from Katkarwadi to work in Shree Ram Mills and lived in the same room during Datta's village childhood. He died when Datta was twelve, at which point Datta came to Mumbai to seek employment to support his family. At first, he worked as a compounder for a doctor, but the pay was low so he sought work in small eating houses. In 1978, aged 18, he joined Shree Ram Mills where he worked as a winder for the next 18 years, with a brief interruption during the mill strike of 1982–3, when he worked with a carpenter. When Shree Ram Mills closed in 1996, he joined Dawn Mills as a winder for a few years until that mill also closed. Since then, he has worked as a packer for Conscious Foods, a pioneer of the organic movement that caters to Mumbai's ethically-minded middle class.

Unlike Datta, many of his roommates lost their mill jobs immediately after the strike and returned to Katkarwadi. The population of the room halved to 15 and since then has dwindled even more, a story I heard replicated in almost every Gramastha Mandal I visited. One of the Katkarwadi Gramastha Mandal rooms has so few members now that it has started renting out spaces to outsiders from other villages, while many Gramastha Mandals rent out or even sell some of their rooms to families.

Nevertheless, there is still a steady stream of migration from the villages, and among today's Gramastha Mandal residents the range of jobs is much more diverse, encompassing blue- and white-collar professions, although mostly at the lower-paid end. Among the members of Katkarwadi Gramastha Mandal can be found drivers, security guards, office boys, shop assistants, waiters, carpenters, IT support staff and several web designers as well as a graphic designer, glasswork designer and civil engineer. In some other Gramastha Mandals the range is noticeably narrower. Almost all the residents of the Shiravali Gramastha Mandal room (in Chawl J) work as security guards, and one told me that low levels of education mean that security is one of the few options open to them. Likewise in Kingaon Gramastha Mandal, various room members work as couriers, while in Manewadi Gramastha Mandal there is a preponderance of hospital workers. Several other Gramastha Mandal residents run nearby tea or snack stalls.

In general, I found myself reticent to probe too deeply into financial matters, partly due to a British reluctance to talk about money, but also an uncomfortable awareness of the disparity in our respective economic means. From what I could glean, however, wages vary considerably and the highest figure I heard of was Rs 20,000 (c. £200) per month, commanded by a switchboard operator (from Kingaon), a web designer and an IT support worker in a bank (both from Katkarwadi).

Clearly, employment prospects are not the same for all Gramastha Mandals or individuals within a Gramastha Mandal. Caste and class play a role here[8] as do the material conditions of the villages themselves. Personal recommendations are also an important mechanism for established migrants to help their newly arrived roommates from the village to find work (cf. Chandavarkar, 1994, p. 187; Dandekar, 1986, p. 226). In Manewadi Gramastha Mandal, for example, Vinit's access to a radiography training course was supported by a personal recommendation from a roommate who is a politically well-connected hospital accountant.

Meanwhile, Datta's new role as a packer for Conscious Foods is no aberration, and many migrants now work on the margins of the gleaming new world of malls and corporate offices and fancy restaurants that have replaced the old mill sites. In addition to needing security guards, these building complexes employ an army of office boys, drivers, parking attendants and housekeeping staff. Other migrants find customer-facing roles as shop assistants and waiters, including Upendra who worked in an upmarket café and wine bar in the Raghuvanshi Mills Compound. Watching him eating *bhadang* on the floor of his Gaowadi Gramastha Mandal room while expounding on his preference for Chilean Merlot, I mentally removed yet another brick from the impenetrable wall separating 'mill' from 'mall'.

Indeed, some Gramastha Mandal residents have penetrated far beyond the periphery of this new world and have joined the ranks of India's white-collar workforce. Abhinav, from Jhambe Gramastha Mandal, was studying for an MBA in finance while working full time as an Assistant Manager in IT process in the trading arm of a bank. Numerous others have studied at least to bachelor's degree level, many at Shivaji University in Kolhapur. Sandesh, from Katkarwadi, was studying for his BA in English literature during my fieldwork year and has subsequently completed an MA from Mumbai University on maritime history. On a return visit in 2022 I found him in the room sitting on a folding study chair, poring over a textbook with the help of a small solar-powered lamp. He confided that, despite his parents' lack of support and his roommates' frequent bullying, he was planning to apply for a PhD in a British or American university.

When Tukaram first came to Mumbai aged 19 he started a long-distance BA Economics course from a college in Kolhapur District while working in a Café Coffee Day, India's homegrown answer to Starbucks. He completed two years of the BA but skipped the third in favour of starting a one-year diploma in animation in Mumbai. For this, he depended on his family, assuring me that the income from his father's civil-engineering job and the family cashew fields – in the region of Rs 50,000 (c. £500) per month – was ample. Nevertheless, his mother was urging him to get a new job, and a few months after I met him he started work as a graphic designer for a marketing company that worked for fashion brands. He sometimes indicated that he would be expected to send money to his parents once he started earning, although his older brother did not regularly send home a cut from his web designer's salary and to the best of my knowledge neither did Tukaram.

This was rather unusual, since around two-thirds of those I asked told me they sent money back to their families in the village. For some this was a monthly bank transfer in the order of Rs 3,000–4,000 (around £30–£40, and in most cases between 20 and 50 per cent of the month's wages). For others, money was sent on a more ad hoc basis, often in the form of cash handed over directly or a via a roommate who happened to be visiting the village.[9] In Maharashtra, flows of money from Mumbai to its rural hinterland are a long-established component of the political economy (e.g. Chandavarkar, 1994, pp. 139–40), which Adarkar and Menon describe as a 'money order economy' (2004, p. 92).

This money order economy has been conceptualised as a way in which families split across sites work towards the 'common goal' of 'portfolio diversification and risk spreading' (Deshingkar and Farrington, 2009, p. 27) which can help make sense of the economic relationships between Gramastha Mandal migrants and their families. The pattern of parents in the village funding their sons' education in the city, as in Tukaram's case, appears to be a long-term family investment strategy. In earlier decades, the majority of migrants to Mumbai had no choice but to start earning and remitting immediately, and the cotton mills were often the most obvious source of income. In the more precarious post-mill economy it makes sense for those families who have amassed sufficient capital (from the land, from remittances or most likely from a combination of sources) to invest in their children's futures through education and training to ensure a more resilient source of support for the family in future.

Much debate exists over the relative importance of family-level *strategy* and migrant-level *agency*. Regarding Indian migration to Bahrain, Andrew Gardner describes the household-level strategies that may result in one child leaving education to enter the local workforce in order to finance another's trip to Bahrain, the 'well-being of the extended family' superseding the interests or desires of the children themselves (2010, p. 61). While internal migration from within India to Mumbai incurs a much lower upfront cost, and hence risk, than migration from India to the Gulf, evidence suggests that this is also usually a family decision (Rowe, 1973, p. 226). Conversely, Alpa Shah's study of brick-kiln workers in Jharkand reveals that in certain cases migration does not make any obvious economic sense but provides an escape from parental control and a chance for sexual exploration and other kinds of fun in a different environment (Shah, 2009). I am reminded of one young Katkarwadikar who told me that although he could make much more on the family chicken farm than he was currently earning in Mumbai, he had come to the city to be closer to his girlfriend.

A mix of strategy and agency seems to have guided two of Tukaram's cousins, with Vipin coming to work in Mumbai while his brother Nitesh remained in Katkarwadi running the family cashew business. Nitesh explained that in Mumbai he could earn Rs 20,000–25,000 (c. £200–£250) per month whereas the cashew processing factory earns him Rs 50,000 (c. £500). Vipin, meanwhile, was quite explicit that he needed to live in Mumbai to get ahead and make money. When I asked him whether he would eventually want to return to live in Katkarwadi he replied with an emphatic negative. 'I'm living out,' he said, suggesting that this afforded 'many freedoms' and 'more comfort than living in.' Nitesh, on the other hand, claimed to detest Mumbai and had no aspirations to leave the village.

Boredom, beer and bhajans: eating and recreation

From 8 p.m. onwards, the roads that criss-cross the BDD chawls fill with young men carrying stacked cylinders of stainless-steel tiffins. They are heading towards what they call a 'mess', a small-scale catering business typically run out of a family-owned chawl room by a woman known as a *khanavalwali*. For around Rs 2,000 (c. £20) every month, the *khanavalwali* will provide her clients, many from Gramastha Mandals, with two meals a day – lunch, often taken to work, and dinner. Food is mostly vegetarian but on Sundays and occasionally during the week 'non-veg', normally egg but sometimes chicken or mutton, is provided as a treat.

I took to joining some of my friends from Katkarwadi on their visits to a mess run by Kanchan, the wife of a fellow Katkarwadikar who had left the Gramastha Mandal room and was now renting a room in Chawl A with his family. There is no requirement to use a mess run by a family from your village, but there is typically a preference for food from the same general area. Gramastha Mandal bachelors from villages in Kolhapur district told me that there were nearby messes run by Konkani women, but the food was not to their taste.[10] We would walk over at around 8.30 p.m. and, greetings exchanged, hand over our tiffin boxes to Kanchan to fill with rice, a vegetable dish, dal and rotis wrapped in newspaper. Others usually dropped in at a similar time, so often a group of boys would hang out there for a while, chatting and playing with Kanchan's toddler or watching the television before taking the tiffin away with them. Back in the rooms, sheets of newspaper are spread on the floor and tiffins are opened. Roti and bhaji are always eaten first, following which rice and dal are mixed in the empty containers. Afterwards newspapers are thrown into the bin, the floor is swept and then wiped with a cloth, and people take it in turns to wash their tiffins in the *mori*.

Like chawls themselves, the mess is a much-recounted piece of Mumbai folk history in which kindly, entrepreneurial local matriarchs, realising the migrant millworkers next door had nowhere to eat, would cook extra and invite them over for a small fee. Over time, these *khanavalwalis* became like a family to the bachelors they cooked for, sharing their triumphs and listening to their problems. By the end of the twentieth century, however, the system had become more 'more business-like' (Adarkar and Menon, 2004, pp. 97–8). In the BDD Chawls, at least, average mess costs have quadrupled within two decades and represent the most significant monthly expenditure for most Gramastha Mandal residents. An even bigger change is the shift from a dine-in model to a takeaway service. Datta suggested that this change occurred after 1982, the year of the mill strike; perhaps this was precipitated by the change from standard mill shift timings to the more varied and unpredictable working hours of today's workforce.

Not all Gramastha Mandal residents take their meals from a mess. Several ate with a sister or aunt who lived in the neighbourhood, while Abhinav managed to strike up a friendship with the family living in the opposite room and ate with them free of cost. Six members of Borgaon Gramastha Mandal left their mess due to frequent stomach problems and set up a two-hob stove and gas canister in the room so they could cook for themselves, each asking their mothers to teach them some recipes. Those who do stick with mess food often complain that the food is boring, and frequent changes of mess are not unusual.[11] Tukaram changed mess three times in the two years since arriving from Katkarwadi, and by the time I left the field he was already tired of his fourth mess and would sometimes skip it in favour of Chinese fast food.

Boredom, indeed, seems to be a constant backdrop to Gramastha Mandal life, especially on weekends. One Sunday evening at 6 p.m. I met Sunil, from Kingaon Gramastha Mandal, for tea and asked him how he had spent the day. He took lunch from his mess, he said, then slept for a few hours before washing his clothes when the water came mid-afternoon. Then he slept a bit more before coming outside to drink tea and play a game on his phone. Sunil appeared to face this routine with equanimity, but Tukaram often complained on Sundays that *kantala ala* ('boredom has come'). His preferred diversion was to go clothes shopping, and with monthly expenses adding up to no more than Rs 3,000 (c. £30), his graphic-design salary of Rs 10,000 (c. £100) left him with a considerable disposable income even if he put some aside in savings. He would regularly visit High Street Phoenix mall, spending hours with his friends trying on stylish new clothes. Sometimes he actually bought the clothes, but more often they were just a vehicle for a selfie that might briefly end up as his WhatsApp 'DP' (Display Profile). This he changed with bewildering rapidity and he often berated me for not doing likewise with my own.

Tukaram's love of fashion was matched by a penchant for gadgets which was shared by many of his friends and roommates who would occasionally show off their new acquisitions such as cameras and headphones. Above all, the smartphone is the fulcrum around which their free time turns. Boys sit outside in the evenings talking to friends, relatives or girlfriends, and many maintain a constellation of relationships over multiple social networking sites. I was flummoxed watching the ease with which Amrut, from Katkarwadi, flicked between WhatsApp, Instagram, Hike Messenger and other platforms. Towards the end of my fieldwork year, Tukaram downloaded Tinder and I spent a couple of evenings watching him swipe compulsively through girls' profiles, but I did not get a sense of whether dating apps were in general use among Gramastha Mandal residents. When I decided to buy a new phone myself, I received a barrage of advice on the relative merits of various models and my eventual, relatively inexpensive, choice was met with derision.

A few of the rooms had their own internet connections but as far as I could tell this was not typical, and most residents relied either on data bundles they purchased themselves, or WiFi connections at their workplaces and elsewhere. Some Gramastha Mandal residents owned laptops, although this was not very common. In Tukaram's case this was the cause of conflict as one of the older members objected to his using it in the room, but the member moved out shortly afterwards and henceforth I would often be met with the sight of Katkarwadi boys browsing, applying for jobs or even coding on their laptops. Some Gramastha Mandal rooms had televisions, purchased collectively and often playing during mealtimes, but in some others, televisions were strictly banned, and residents used YouTube on their phones to watch films individually.

Alcohol is another way to alleviate boredom. The cheap, noisy bars along Delisle Road fill up with Gramastha Mandal bachelors, especially on a Saturday night, and an all-male clientele orders pegs of domestic whisky or 650ml bottles of Kingfisher or Tuborg beer and snacks of boiled chickpeas and *chakli*, deep-fried wheat snacks served with Szechuan sauce. Others opt to buy from the local wine shops and drink in the ruins of nearby Apollo Mills. Either way, drunkenness is common and arguments often ensue. Vikas, whose English continued to improve as my Marathi plateaued, described the fallout from these jaunts with the verbal flourishes that he knew would delight and amuse me:

> On weekends ... most of the people they have a habit of, you know, to get to the beer bar, or somewhere, get drunk, and come home in a stuporous position ... Then the intoxication makes them say something unconventional, they say some curse word, they put, er, unnecessary things on other people ... Most of altercation happens because of this.
>
> (Vikas, interview in English, 3 November 2017)

Drinking sometimes takes place in the rooms themselves. In the Gaowadi Gramastha Mandal, for example, room parties are a mainstay of weekend life, and slurred speech, spilled beer and complaints from neighbours are the norm. In addition to beer and whisky, these occasions might feature *bhadang* and Kolhapur-style chicken stew cooked by the room members themselves. However messy the occasion, the subsequent cleaning up is meticulous.

A more structured form of recreation associated with Gramastha Mandal life is the Bhajan Mandal, a group of musicians specialising in Hindu devotional songs called *bhajans* (see also Adarkar and Menon, 2004, p. 100). I only once encountered evidence of these in the form of a lone harmonium player practising on the *potmala* of one of the Manewadi Gramastha Mandal rooms. The harmonium had 'Manewadi Bhajani Mandal, Mumbai' inscribed on it in Devanagari script, and the boy practising told me that this was an organisation of musicians from Manewadi who lived all over Mumbai. He was self-taught, and only started learning after he arrived in Mumbai. Other Gramastha Mandals used to have such music groups, he said, but they are less common now as children rarely learn musical instruments and other music styles have become popular.

Parallel lives, parallel histories

If chawls themselves are capsules of 'queer time' set against a tide of high-rise 'chrononormativity' (Finkelstein, 2019, pp. 94–6), then are Gramastha Mandals capsules within capsules, self-contained bastions of 'village time' operating within a wider framework of chawlness, the term I introduced in Chapter 1 to describe the fraught conviviality that emerges from the close-knit life of a chawl? A young man joining a Gramastha Mandal will usually end up sharing a living space with friends that he grew up with in the village, often including an older brother or cousin and sometimes even his father. He will eat, socialise and in many cases work with these familiar figures. His food will most likely be prepared by a lady from his part of Kolhapur district, supplemented by a steady supply of village snacks brought back by roommates. After dinner he might talk on the phone to family for over an hour. Even the room next door might be owned by his Gramastha Mandal, or one linked to a nearby village.

His participation in the life of the chawl around him, particularly that of the resident families, is in most cases extremely limited. This is particularly true of the Mitra Mandals, the social clubs we encountered in Chapter 1 that are tied to particular chawl buildings or pairs of buildings. The Bandya Maruti Seva Mandal, for example, is run by Chawls J and K, and owns a small *kabaddi* practice ground for its team. In front of this is a *katta* that, like the Jay Bhim Katta, has its own crowd of male regulars mostly drawn from the families in these buildings. Since I hardly ever saw any Gramastha Mandal residents sitting at this *katta,* I started asking them whether they were members of the Bandya Maruti Seva Mandal. One boy looked at me incredulously before shaking his head and saying *'Ham log nahin'* (not us lot), while Vaibhav from Borgaon Gramastha Mandal simply said of the Bandya Maruti Seva Mandal members that 'they are different people'. Vikas explained that the Mandal does not accept 'non-native people', meaning those born outside the BDD Chawls, and that 'they don't show any interest' in people like him.

Tukaram was characteristically withering in his appraisal of the Bandya Maruti Seva Mandal and chided me for my interest in it, but he became unusually shy around Mandal members at the local chai stands. During Dahi Handi, the celebration of Krishna's birth in which teams of young people speed round Mumbai on motorbikes to take part in pyramid-building competitions, I watched the Bandya Maruti Seva Mandal boys form a pyramid outside Chawl J (Figure 3.2). Tukaram and Vipin hung around awkwardly beside me, very much spectators rather than participants. Later in the year, when the Mandal held a Divali *garba* (dance) in the space between Chawls J and K, I was hard-pressed to persuade any of my Katkarwadi Gramastha Mandal friends to attend, and it was only after an hour of dithering on the sidelines that a trio of them joined in.

I asked Ram, an 18-year-old Bandya Maruti Seva Mandal stalwart who lived with his grandparents in the room opposite Tukaram's, why so few Gramastha Mandal members got involved with the organisation. He replied that they sometimes 'feel shy to come with us … We do welcome them but they like to stay separate. We don't know the reason.' His friend speculated that the Gramastha Mandal bachelors feel awkward around the families, asking themselves *'Kaise bat karte hai?'* (how can we talk [with them]?). Similarly, residents of Jhambe Gramastha Mandal in Chawl C insisted that the Satyam Krida Mandal (tied to Chawls C and D) was only for people who were 'yahan se proper' (properly from here). They would feel uncomfortable joining the Mandal, they said, as families tend to take a dim view of bachelors.

This was a commonly-voiced opinion on both sides. A feature of the parties I attended in the Gaowadi Gramastha Mandal was Upendra's frequent injunction to his friends to keep the noise down and close the door, for fear of creating a bad impression in front of their neighbours. Likewise, Vikas ventured the opinion that the 'natives', as he referred to long-term family residents, think of Gramastha Mandal bachelors as noisy, drunken nuisances. 'They tolerate us,' he said, 'but they do not entertain us.' A middle-aged man I spoke to in Chawl L told me there were no Gramastha Mandals in his building: 'We don't allow. We don't like it.

Figure 3.2 Bandya Maruti Seva Mandal's Dahi Handi pyramid, BDD Chawls, Delisle Road. © Author.

They keep the room dirty, chewing tobacco.' As Satyajit, who lives in Chawl D with his wife and parents, explains:

> [Families] will not that much mix up with the Gramastha Mandal because there are too many people living in the single room ... so that's a kind of, you know, the restriction, or boundary.
> (Satyajit, interview in English, 4 November 2017)

Is there anything unusual in all this? Dandekar describes the 'tenacious hold' of Sugao village over its Mumbai migrants, who remain 'psychologically and socially very much a part of village society' (1986, p. 255) while Rowe specifically notes that the North Indian migrants he studied have 'relatively little contact' with Mumbai's voluntary organisations (1973, pp. 232–5). This propensity of migrants to carve out a home from home, while sometimes making only limited connections in their new location, is by no means unique to the Maharashtrian experience. British investigative journalist Ben Judah (2016) has written vividly of the networks of Eastern European migrants who come to work in London and often live in social bubbles in crowded shared accommodation with workers from the same regions of Romania, Poland or Lithuania. The Osellas, meanwhile, have documented the experiences of Keralan migrants to the Gulf for whom daily life is, 'to a large extent, an extension of village life' (Osella and Osella, 2000, p. 120).

Unlike the situation described by Rowe, however, and even less like those described by Judah or the Osellas, there is little difference between Gramastha Mandal migrants and their neighbour families where most demographic categories are concerned. They speak the same language (Marathi), mostly belong to the same religion (Hindu) and community (Maratha) and in many cases have roots in the same villages. Ram's mother's family, for example, comes from Borgaon village, next to Katkarwadi, and on his corridor there are multiple Gramastha Mandal rooms linked to both villages. Moreover, the Mitra Mandals tend to be dominated by young men of a similar age to many Gramastha Mandal residents, meaning that even age and gender are not a source of difference there.

Class is a slightly more useful analytic here. When I asked a boy from a family in Chawl P whether there were any Gramastha Mandals in his building, he told me: 'We don't allow it – we're a medium class [sic] people.' Among those BDD Chawl residents with the clearest tendencies towards the 'new middle class' (Fernandes, 2006) described in Chapter 1, such as white-collar jobs, designer clothes and the linguistic proficiency that results from English-medium education, there is certainly a weighting towards family members over Gramastha Mandal migrants. However, this distinction is blurred rather than clear-cut. Migrants Rohan and Abhinav, for example, speak better English and work in better-paying professions (civil engineer and IT manager respectively) than many of the Mitra Mandal members of a similar age from their chawls.

The lack of interaction, while no doubt partly arising from differences in lifestyle between families and bachelors, is best understood as the product of different histories and timescales. Yuval-Davis (2012) has used the concept of 'autochthony' to denote the 'I was here before you' sense with which groups of more established migrants reject more recent arrivals. Although the examples she gives tend to also involve other more tangible kinds of difference (seen, for example, in the 'enmity' between Afro-Caribbean 'autochthones' and newer Kurdish refugees in Dalston, east London) the sense of a prior claim to an area can also be seen in the BDD Chawls situation. Many of the ('autochthonous') young men in the Mitra Mandals have parents, and sometimes grandparents, who were also born in the BDD Chawls, often in the same room that they live in now. While they may also have a deep loyalty towards their ancestral villages, it is the urban identity, bound up in part with a strong sense of belonging and ownership to Mitra Mandal and chawl, that is likely to be most salient day-to-day. Common spaces, like *kattas* and *kabaddi* grounds, reinforce this sense by bringing together family members from different villages, often in building-wide or even neighbourhood-wide endeavours such as sports practice or preparing for a festival.

Gramastha Mandal migrants, on the other hand, have typically been born and raised in the village and are thus, in Vikas' words, seen as 'newbies' and 'non-native' outsiders in Mumbai. Even if their fathers and grandfathers have spent time living in the same chawl room that they live in now, the lack of a continuous presence militates against the formation of deep social ties with chawl families (*khanavalwalis* aside) and of a correspondingly deep sense of belonging to the BDD Chawls, let alone the city beyond. Indeed, their experience of living in the BDD Chawls is mediated by the very structure that continually reinforces their connection to the village: the Gramastha Mandal.

The histories each group (Gramastha Mandal members and Mitra Mandal members) tell of the Mitra Mandals differ too. Members of Bandya Maruti Seva Mandal mythologise the organisation for its legendary *kabaddi* team and they also claim to have engineered the first six-tier human pyramid in the history of the Dahi Handi festival. Meanwhile, one of Tukaram's older roommates commented that a couple of decades ago, the Bandya Maruti Seva Mandal had actually been run by the Gramastha Mandal bachelors, and it was only more recently that the families started to dominate it. Datta also told me that when he lived in the Katkarwadi Gramastha Mandal he used to play *kabaddi* with the Bandya Maruti Seva Mandal and joined them for Dahi Handi. In a joint interview with Vipin, Tukaram suggested that:

> Us ke bad family members barh gaye, [Chawl J and K] mein … family members unhone room le liye aur unke members zyada ho gaye. OK, in Bandya Maruti members mein, jo group tha un mein family members add ho gaye, zyada ho gaye actually.
>
> (Tukaram, interview, 22 August 2017)

> (After [the initial period of Gramastha Mandal dominance], family members bought more rooms in Chawl J and K, and their numbers increased. And so in Bandya Maruti [Mitra Mandal] the number of family members kept increasing actually).

Vipin added that this shift in membership was the cause of fighting between the family members and the Gramastha Mandal members, though neither could elaborate further on this. 'That's why we're not interested in these things, Jon,' was Tukaram's way of closing down the topic.

It was Sushil, the self-appointed local historian from Chawl B, who gave the most detailed explanation of these parallel histories. He listed the easy availability of rooms in the mid-twentieth century and the shift-wise nature of mill work as the conditions that allowed Gramastha Mandals to come into being in the first place. But once 30-odd men were housed in these spaces by virtue of phased sleeping schedules, they found there was nothing much to do. Slowly they clubbed together with their neighbours, usually migrants from nearby villages to form 'organisations where they can gather together, play sports, educate each other, singing, dancing,' In some cases, the founding members of these Mitra Mandals did not move back to their villages but instead bought rooms in the same chawls that had housed their Gramastha Mandals and moved their families in to live with them there. Growing older, they have proved unwilling to let go the reins of the Mitra Mandals, according to Sushil, and often hand over responsibility directly to their children, many of whom were born in the BDD Chawls. In this way, organisations like the Bandya Maruti Seva Mandal and Satyam Krida Mandal have become dominated by the chawl-based families of former Gramastha Mandal migrants, leaving newer Gramastha Mandal arrivals feeling left out.

However, the era of Gramastha Mandal dominance has left a legacy in the form of annual festivals held by some of the Gramastha Mandals in the BDD Chawls. Some are transplanted versions of village religious festivals, while others mark national holidays and affirm a specifically Hindu vision of Indian nationhood by featuring a *satyanarayan puja*, a lengthy ritual prayer to Vishnu. Amrutwadi Gramastha Mandal holds its *puja* on 15 August to celebrate India's Independence Day, while Manewadi Gramastha Mandal holds a similar function on 26 January (Republic Day). Like so many other chawl festivities, these functions take place in the corridor, which are decorated with fairly lights, bunting and flowers and lined with red plastic chairs. Guests, many of them former residents of the Gramastha Mandal hosting the function, will be served crisps and sweets on paper plates, and sherbet or perhaps turmeric milk in plastic cups. For one day at least, the Gramastha Mandal migrants officially take up space in their chawls.

Gramastha Mandals are perhaps best thought of not as isolated capsules but as nodes in social networks that operate in parallel with the more dominant networks of family-led chawlness. Strong threads connect these nodes back to their villages, and these threads are constantly reinforced by back-and-forth travel and new arrivals. Connections exist between some of these nodes, as friendships flourish between members of different Gramastha Mandals, especially if they are in the same chawl corridor or if they come from neighbouring villages. Some connections exist between Gramastha Mandal and chawl families in the form of the mess system and other more ad-hoc arrangements, and also ties extend beyond the BDD Chawl neighbourhood into workplaces and family connections living elsewhere in Mumbai. But the flows from Gramastha Mandals to Mitra Mandals, so foundational to chawlness, have largely been staunched.

'A place to earn, not learn'

Hemmed in by everyday monotony and marginalised within the wider social life of the neighbourhood, many Gramastha Mandal migrants share Nitesh's deep attachment to the village and vocal dislike of the city. Again and again, my interlocutors extolled the virtues of the calm village life over the noisy urban rush; the quality of village food compared to the inferior produce available in Mumbai; the fresh, cooling air of the countryside as opposed to the heat and dirt of the city. The Katkarwadikars showed me pictures of rural life on their phones and described the pleasures of swimming in the local river, while elsewhere Sameer from Gaowadi shared video clips of village festivals and weddings that in his view surpassed any entertainment on offer in Mumbai. Sometimes, the village was specifically framed as a place of good health (cf. Dandekar, 1986, p. 226). After a bout of malaria, one Katkarwadi resident told me he was going back to the village for an 'air change', and when Tukaram caught typhoid he went back home to convalesce. Shortly after turning down an invitation to accompany Sameer to Gaowadi for Ganesh Chaturthi, I caught dengue fever. He later told me that I should have gone with him, as I would not have caught dengue in the village.

I was curious to see these villages, to breathe their cool, clean air and feast on their authentic chickens. Invitations came my way touchingly often, but time constraints and anxieties at the prospect of overnight bus journeys with limited toilet access made me selective and, to my shame, I only managed to visit Katkarwadi. Nevertheless, this short trip acquired a somewhat legendary status, and since many of the Gramastha Mandal villages are within an hour's journey of Katkarwadi, members of other villages were able to stake their own claim on some of the local landmarks I had visited. Despite this, people often rebuked me for not having visited their own villages and Sameer, in particular, was dismissive of Katkarwadi. With exaggerated arm gestures he would show me how much bigger than Katkarwadi his own village was, and therefore how much more interesting it would be for my research.

As a city-loving migrant myself, I was surprised by how few complaints of boredom I heard about village life. I asked Pratik, a *chaiwala* recently returned from a month in his village, how it felt being back Mumbai and he said that he missed the village. Didn't he find it boring, I asked, to which he replied that '*Do-tin din bor ata hai aur phir barobar lagta hai*' (For 2–3 days I get bored but then it seems just right).

In contrast, the few favourable comments I heard about Mumbai framed the city as an essential source of livelihood rather than celebrating any inherently likeable quality it might have. For example Datta, living in Mumbai since 1972, explained that the only way he could have supported his family in Katkarwadi was by working in the city: '*Is ke liye, mere liye Bombay bahut barya hai*' (For this reason, Bombay is great for me). Meanwhile, despite his appetite for malls and technology, Tukaram never referred to his Mumbai life in enthusiastic terms. Granted it is a good place to study, but otherwise it is too crowded and dirty, and train travel is a nuisance. He was scathing about conditions in the BDD Chawls which he referred to as 'dirty living', a sentiment I later heard echoed by Yashwant, recently arrived from Kingaon. With a common toilet at the end of a corridor it feels like living in a village, Tukaram said, although his living space here is far more cramped than his parents' house in Katkarwadi.[12]

Of course it often occurred to me that this was, at least in part, an expression of homesickness. I began to wonder whether, Pratik's claims notwithstanding, urban nostalgia for village life translated into actual enjoyment during a visit home. In a study of migration to a central Indian steel town, Parry questions the 'migrant's visceral "commitment" to "home"', observing how quickly returning migrants' 'village as a pastoral idyll' narrative sours into one of 'the village as a rural prison' (2003, pp. 237–8). This was not a pattern I detected in my own trip to Katkarwadi, but during the three days Ramesh, who I had travelled with, grew a little distant and offhand with me. At the time, I assumed this was a natural reaction to our being thrown together for a longer period than usual, and I worried that my presence was diminishing his pleasure at coming home. I now wonder whether this was a result of the claustrophobic nature of village life that Ramesh could never openly acknowledge.

Indeed, Dandekar suggests that compared to their village counterparts, Mumbai migrants 'are more inclined to talk freely about personal problems and about the larger political and social world of the village and the city' (1986, p. 255). I suspect that Vipin, who once told me that he found living in the BDD Chawls interesting due to the range of people and mindsets you encounter, would agree with this description. This was not a perspective I encountered often, and generally accusations of claustrophobia were levied at chawl life, not village life. This was particularly true of Tukaram who, despite his popularity, sometimes got into fights with roommates and would spend hours sitting outside on the phone to college friends, an escape valve from the close-knit Gramastha Mandal society against which he seemed to be continually straining. Two people told me the effect of living in a Gramastha Mandal is that residents are unable to 'develop their minds' (both used this English expression). One of these men had lived in a Gramastha Mandal room for 16 years before leaving, utterly frustrated by living among *bachche log* (children) who were trapped in a never-ending cycle of getting up, washing, working, eating, working, tea drinking, eating and sleeping. A third, Yogesh, said of his Amrutwadi Gramastha Mandal that it was a place to 'earn not learn', a claim somewhat undermined by the collection of history books he showed me.

Adrift in history?

Encountering a Gramastha Mandal in a Mumbai chawl, Maura Finkelstein marvelled at how 'very little has changed here, aside from the industries fuelling this migration' (2011, p. 52). I concur that the wide range of jobs being undertaken is a reflection of Mumbai's post-mill economy. At one end, as evinced by the number of couriers, security guards and *chaiwalas*, this suggests an increased casualisation and precariousness (cf. Mhaskar, 2013, pp. 152–3), although it should be remembered that for many, particularly of marginalised-caste status, work in the mills was itself often precarious (for example Chandavarkar, 2004, p. 13). At the other end, there are a smaller number of highly-educated migrants who are thriving in white-collar professions, like civil engineer Rohan and Abhinav, the IT Manager also studying for an MBA. Much else has also changed, however. The mess has become a takeaway service, weakening the bonds between migrants and resident families. Mobile phones and cheap internet access have reconfigured migrant social life, meaning that my interlocutors are more likely to be found watching Bollywood movies or playing *Angry Birds 2* than participating in a *bhajan* contest. The rooms themselves are less crowded than they used to be, and some have dwindled to the point of extinction, or their membership diluted with members of other villages.

The bachelor residents' emotional lives remain bound up in the village, which is where they expend much of their economic, social and political capital through remittances, family visits and vote-casting. Many of them claim to detest Mumbai and appear to spurn the social life of the BDD Chawls, a state of affairs that seems poignant in light of the Gramastha Mandals' original role in creating this social life. If they regard the families next door as straight-laced and rather dull, the families themselves apparently see the migrants as dirty, chain-smoking drunkards who make far too much noise. It is hardly surprising that the bachelors are thrown back again and again onto the companionship of the Gramastha Mandal where, eating, socialising and sleeping in such close quarters, they recreate a young, male approximation of village life in Mumbai.

What sets this case apart from the wealth of global examples of migrants being shunned by host residents due to differences in language, religion, ethnicity or other demographic categories (for example see Judah, 2016; Osella and Osella, 2000; Rowe, 1973; cited in 'Parallel lives, parallel histories', earlier in the chapter) is the degree of similarity between these Maratha Hindu migrants from Kolhapur District and the Maratha Hindu families, also with roots in Kolhapur District. Ultimately, it is the difference in lifestyle between bachelors and families, and particularly the differences in timescales and personal understandings of local history between 'autochthonous' family members (cf. Yuval-Davis, 2012) and Gramastha Mandal newcomers that are enough to create a disjuncture between the groups.

Is there any way to tell this story that does not fetishise the Gramastha Mandal migrants as adrift in history, living unfulfilled lives in declining institutions, homesick for their village childhoods and excluded from the organisations their ancestors helped to create? I offer three chinks of light in this gloomy picture. First, at least some migrants have chosen to come to Mumbai in search of freedom and even romance, not simply as an unthinking cog in the wheel of the family economy. Second, migrants *do* take up space in the chai stalls and sometimes even the *kattas,* and, on special occasions assert their rights to entire corridors in displays of religious or nationalist fervour. Third, as we shall see in Chapter 5, return to the village is not the only route out of Gramastha Mandal life, and many ex-residents have carved out new futures for themselves and their families in far-flung suburbs of the city.

Notes

1. The only exception I encountered was a room linked to a village in the neighbouring district of Sangli.
2. Other Backward Classes (see 'When Bombay became Mumbai' in the Introduction).
3. Just north of Kolhapur and Sangli.
4. Pendse et al. argue that this pattern arose because millworkers and other industrialists 'assumed no responsibility for the health' of the working class, so an 'ill millworker was expected to the leave the city, go back to the village, and recuperate there' (2011, p. 4).
5. Although this appeared a benign phenomenon to me, Dandekar concludes from her study of Sugao village that 'the tastes and preferences of the city are transmitted directly to the villages, and the market for locally produced goods gradually erodes in favour of the city product' (1986, p. 228).
6. Outside the BDD Chawls, a member of Pimpalgaon Gaonkari Mandal told Neera Adarkar and Meena Menon that 'Our mandal also did a lot of good work for the village. It organized water, lighting and the installation of the idol of a goddess. We built two temples there' (Maruti Gyandeo Satkar in Adarkar and Menon, 2004, p. 100).
7. Despite the strong association with the textile industry, not all Gramastha Mandal migrants worked in the mills before they closed in the decades following the year-long strike in 1982–3. I heard of some who, in the 1970s, worked in the BMC, or as civil engineers or in one case managing a beer company. Dandekar's research actually reveals a drop in the proportion of Sugao village migrants working in the textile mills between 1942 and 1977 and an increase in those working in factories, the police and other clerical and service professions (1986, pp. 234 and 295).
8. The implications of caste and religion will be discussed further in 'Gaon bhai in the city?' in Chapter 5.
9. I did not ask questions about the specific use to which this money is put, but existing research from across India indicates that the major uses of remittance payments include inputs for farming as well as non-farm enterprises, school fees, healthcare, the cost of weddings and other social functions, and debt repayment (Deshingkar and Farrington, 2009, pp. 13–14).
10. Adarkar, in her description of Mumbai chawl life in the pre-1980s mill era, likewise notes that the 'khanavals [messes] were separate for Ghatis and Konkanis in order to cater to their specific food cultures and habits' (Adarkar, 2011, p. 20).
11. Back in the 1980s, Dandekar's Sugao interlocutors made similar complaints of the 'monotony and tastelessness' of mess food (1986, p. 249).
12. Dandekar met with similarly disparaging comments about the crowds and smells and bad food of Mumbai compared to the open fields, fresh breeze and home cooking of the village (1986, p. 220).

4
'We are Indians, firstly and lastly': Buddhist nationalism and the true history of India

An incident at the Buddha Vihar

> Little boy hanging around Maruti's barbershop wearing a t-shirt with an Ambedkar photo and the message 'We are Indians, firstly and lastly' on the back.
> (extract from fieldnotes, 31 January 2017)

What, I wondered at the time, was the significance of this message? And why would a picture of Ambedkar be associated with such an apparently jingoistic statement? The first hint at an answer came a few months later when, walking round the BDD Chawls one afternoon, I came across a large group of Dalit Buddhist acquaintances outside the police station. Sayaji, hands flying and face in a characteristic grimace of frustration, was in the middle of an angry exchange with a police officer. I did not linger, but over the next few days I pieced together the following story.

The space between Maratha-dominated Chawl M and the more mixed Chawl N in which Mahendra lived, was historically used as a ground for playing *kabaddi*. At the back, where the BDD Chawls abuts the former Mafatlal Mill site, is the Buddha Vihar (temple), a shed-like structure with a tin roof, owned and managed by a BDD Chawl-wide committee of Dalit Buddhists and used for prayers and cultural programmes. It is also rented out to a local school which holds classes throughout the day.

Some years ago, the Buddha Vihar committee declared its intention of laying a tiled footpath from the street to the *vihar*, to facilitate access. Although the area it would cross had long since fallen out of use as a *kabaddi* ground, certain residents of Chawl M raised objections to the proposed footpath, stating that they wished to revive the space's sporting function. This escalated into a dispute between Chawl M members and the users of the Buddha Vihar, which was eventually brought to the local police station, who ruled in March 2017 that tiles could be laid since the *vihar* is registered with the Public Works Department (PWD). The police also requested that when Chawl M residents organise cultural programmes in the space, the Dalit Buddhists should support them, and vice versa when Buddhist functions are held. The issue did not flare up again, to my knowledge, and on my brief return in late 2018 I saw that the tiles had been laid.

My Dalit Buddhist interlocutors explained that it was because the Marathas in Chawl M considered themselves superior in caste terms that they felt empowered to disregard the Buddhists' claim to the space. At the time I wished I could have spoken to residents of Chawl M to hear their perspective on the matter, but I knew no-one in that building. A few months later, having struck up some casual Chawl M acquaintances, my tentative attempts to broach the topic were firmly brushed aside and I felt powerless to pursue it further.

In a conversation shortly afterwards, I asked Manish to tell me more about the demographic composition of different chawls. He told me that several buildings were exclusively occupied by Marathas, or at least dominant-caste Hindus, and that the residents maintained an informal embargo on renting or selling rooms to Dalits. He gave Chawl M as an example and attributed their behaviour over the Buddha Vihar paving stones to the fact that 'They do not believe that "We are Indians, firstly and lastly". *Jati* [caste] is more important to them.'

He explained that the t-shirts I had seen featuring this message were left over from the 2015 Ambedkar Jayanti celebrations organised by the neighbourhood RPI(A) branch (Figure 4.1). The aphorism is popularly attributed to Ambedkar, and appears to have originated in a 1938 Bombay Legislative Assembly debate, 'On the creation of a separate Karnatak province', in which he argued that the 'dismemberment' of India into states organised on linguistic lines would undermine his ideal of 'want[ing] all people to be *Indian first, Indian last and nothing else but Indians*' (Ambedkar, 1982b, pp. 194–5, my emphasis). He reused the expression elsewhere, and, as 'We are Indians, firstly and lastly', it is now frequently used, devoid of context, in online Republic Day and Independence Day greetings.

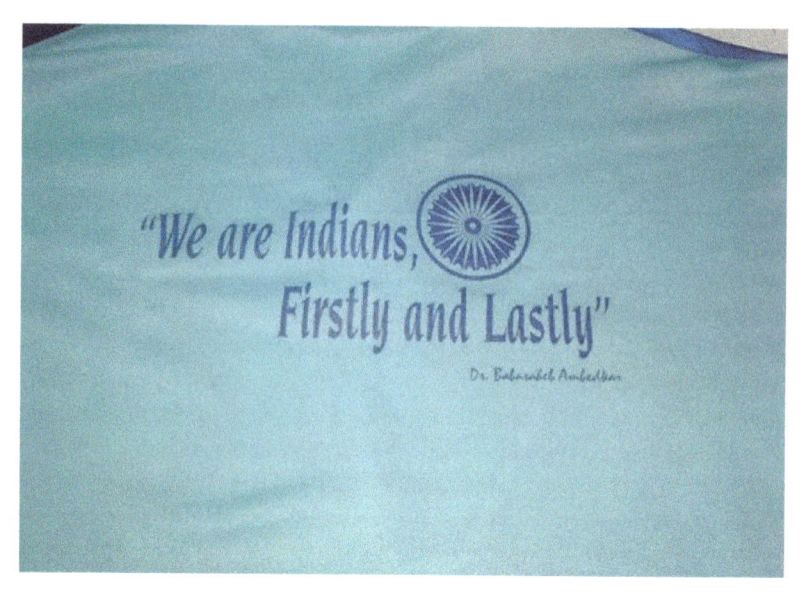

Figure 4.1 Back of a custom-made t-shirt produced by the BDD Chawls RPI(A) Ambedkar Jayanti committee for Ambedkar Jayanti 2015 celebrations. © Author.

Manish, however, appeared to use the formula to convey an *egalitarian* loyalty to India, in contrast to the hierarchical caste affiliations he perceived among his Hindu neighbours. In subsequent conversations he went further and explicitly described himself as a nationalist, sometimes using the English word, sometimes the Marathi *rashtrawadi*. Anish, Pradeep, Mahendra and others also referred to themselves as nationalists in our discussions, and sometimes invoked the idea of being Indians, firstly and lastly. This surprised and disconcerted me, coming from a community that had experienced centuries of suffering in India, including at the hands of those with the most vocal claim to Indian nationalism in the present day: the right-wing Hindu nationalist forces of the BJP and its paramilitary parent organisation, the Rashtriya Swayamsevak Sangh (RSS).

This surprise, I shall argue, takes us to the central motifs of the book: how do people talk about history and how does this shape their lives? Why do they sometimes think in ways that others might not expect? So many disputes over history are in fact embedded in arguments about nationhood and nationalism: Vladimir Putin's rhetorical (and in places quite literal) erasure of Ukrainian history in service of an imperial conception of Russian nationalism (Kasianov, 2022); Conservative British politicians' appeals to the idea of a pristine Merrie England of warm beer, tolerance, no migration and a global civilising mission, as opposed to the Labour Party's experiments with a so-called 'progressive patriotism' that draws on historic examples of British radicalism as a blueprint for present-day reform (Robinson, 2016). Much Hindu nationalist rhetoric, like that of Amit Shah,[1] is steeped in ideas of an ancient India that was fundamentally and eternally Hindu, ideas roundly challenged by many prominent historians in India, including Ambedkar himself, and outside (also see, for example, Anthony, 2007; Doniger, 2009; Thapar, 2005).

But so often, less prominent individuals' conceptions and experiences of nationalism are overlooked unless they fit into clearly understood categories such as majoritarian nationalism or minority separatism. This chapter explores how 'Dalit Buddhist nationalism' – or being Indians, firstly and lastly – sits uncomfortably outside these more familiar moulds but underpins my interlocutors' political and cultural engagement with wider Indian society. En route, I consider the inclusionary form of nationalism championed by Jawaharlal Nehru before analysing the role Ambedkar's Constitution plays in Dalit Buddhists' lives. By this stage, a reckoning with the broader question of what nationalism actually *is* becomes inevitable, and I draw on foundational theorists Ernest Gellner, Benedict Anderson and Partha Chatterjee, placing them in dialogue with Dalit scholar G. Aloysius and the organic intellectuals of the BDD Chawls. Readers anticipating a singular new definition of nationalism to emerge at this point will be disappointed. Instead, concluding that the question is misplaced, I am led to a rather different question: how is Indian history a site of contestation in which competing nationalisms play out?

In the second half of the chapter, I show that my Dalit Buddhist friends' understanding of themselves as Indians, firstly and lastly, is premised on an understanding of history that casts Dalits as original inhabitants in an ancient Buddhist India characterised by egalitarian rationalism, and subsequently destroyed by the imposition of inegalitarian Hinduism by 'Aryan' invaders. In Buddhism lies the solution to India's present-day problems, but the Hindus of Chawl M do not accept their position on the Buddhist side of the Aryan–Buddhist divide, and they remain the neighbourhood caste oppressors in an ambivalent everyday dynamic characterised more by microaggressions and surprisingly close bonds than by open hostility.

I conclude that 'We are Indians, firstly and lastly' is best understood as a claim to space in the discursive imagination of the nation, a claim that rejects the paths of separatism and globalism and critiques majoritarian Hindu nationalism. It is an appeal for both redistribution of power and opportunity while also demanding recognition as a minority and simultaneously espousing a politics of universalism ('We are *all* Indians, firstly and lastly') and a politics of difference ('We *alone* are Indians, firstly and lastly'). Given the Dalit Buddhists' special connection to the Constitution through Ambedkar, and to ancient India through Buddhism, they are readily able to frame these appeals as nationalism.

Nationalisms in India

Should I have been disconcerted by my friends' declarations of nationalism? After all, such declarations had been visible since our earliest encounters, when Mahendra told me that nationalism was more important than religion, and invited me to join the Republic Day celebrations to witness the hoisting of the Indian flag. For India to become a superpower, he explained some weeks later, every building needs to display the flag and people need to respect the national anthem. But today, he continued, only Dalit Buddhists celebrate national holidays such as Republic Day and Independence Day, while other communities waste their time on religious festivals. By then, I was used to the sight of boys and men (but almost never women) in t-shirts which informed me that 'We are Indians, firstly and lastly', but Mahendra's claim seemed far-fetched to me when I thought of the government's official Republic Day parade in Delhi with its vast crowds of all castes and religions, and when I recalled that news reports typically emphasise protest over participation when covering Dalit activity on national holidays (for example TNN, 2017).

Moreover, all around me – in conversations, in newspapers, in academic papers, on social media – a different kind of Indian nationalism, noisier, angrier and more forceful, was on display. In April, Gujarat tightened its state legislation against the slaughter of cows, sacred in Hinduism, while across the country vigilante mobs attacked traders (mostly Muslims) transporting, or suspected of transporting, cattle for beef. A few weeks earlier, a Hindu monk called Yogi Adityanath with a reputation for scapegoating Muslims and exhorting Hindus to take matters in their own hands (Jeelani, 2017) had been elected as Chief Minister of Uttar Pradesh state. By this time, the first term of Narendra Modi's premiership was well underway and, by placing 'ultra-nationalists' into mainstream political posts and abetting the 'militant cultural policing' of non-state vigilantes, his BJP-led government had lifted Hindu-majoritarian populism and minority scapegoating from the fringes to a position of 'unfettered social articulation and acceptability' (Chatterji et al., 2019).

In short, in early 2017 I unquestioningly identified nationalism in a contemporary Indian context with the BJP's brand of Hindu nationalism. I was hardly alone in this. In the same year, political historian Irfan Habib brought out a volume excavating the varied thoughts on nationalism of numerous influential Indians since the nineteenth century, noting in the introduction that in 'current usage' nationalism has become a 'crude jingoism fed by a populist majoritarian exclusivism' (Habib, 2017, p. 6). The wider academic world was, and remains, awash with studies of Hindu nationalist ideology, many foregrounding the deliberate and painstaking organisation that underpinned its late twentieth-century ascendancy, through militancy (Jaffrelot, 1996), control of public culture (Hansen, 1999) and state education (Bénéï, 2008).

Modi's rule is frequently placed in a wider constellation of global right-wing nationalism, spearheaded by leaders who espouse a comparable ideology of majoritarianism and/or authoritarian populism, including Putin, Erdoğan and Trump (see Gudavarthy, 2018; Habib, 2017 p. 6; Kaul, 2017). Although it is widely accepted that nationalism comes in numerous varieties, this is the strain with the greatest share in the current global imagination, which has only bolstered a long-held sense in sections of liberal- and left-leaning academic scholarship that nationalism is a 'dark, unpredictable' (Chatterjee, 1993, p. 4) and 'negative' force (Ranjan, 2020); simply put, a 'dirty word' (Doran, 2017).

A particular bone of contention is that majoritarian nationalism is inherently violent towards minorities, prominent examples including the former Trump administration's scapegoating of migrants in the US and the Erdoğan administration's treatment of religious and linguistic minorities in Turkey (Rothberg, 2019). Hindu nationalism, likewise, frequently manifests as an anti-Muslim and anti-Christian ideology, the seeds of which can be detected in its earlier codification by Vinayak Damodar Savarkar. It was Savarkar who popularised the notion of *Hindutva* (Hindu-ness) which elides 'Hindu' and 'Indian' and in *Hindutva: who is a Hindu?* (originally published in 1923), he emphatically asserted the 'foreign origin' of Islam and Christianity 'far off in Arabia or Palestine' (Savarkar, 1949, p. 92).[2]

Today, in populist discourse, anybody suspected of not fully embracing the Hindu nationalist dogma risks attracting the slur 'antinational', which is notably applied to leftist intellectuals and Muslims but also frequently to Dalits (see Beltz, 2005, pp. 102–6; Guru, 2016; Hansen, 1999, p. 228). In the lead-up to the tragic suicide of PhD student and Ambedkarite activist Rohith Vemula at Hyderabad University in 2016, for example, local MP Bandaru Dattatreya linked the university's Ambedkar

Students Association to 'extremist and anti-national' activity (JanMohamed, 2019, p. 245).

Where minorities worldwide *are* linked to nationalism, it is generally in the context of a campaign for a separate nation such as Kurdistan, Catalonia or Scotland. In India, the label 'minority nationalism' has been applied to secessionist movements including tribal insurgencies in the northeast of the country (Nag, 2009) and the Khalistan movement for an independent Sikh state (Shani, 2008). Such movements more often attract the labels 'separatism', 'resistance' and 'freedom struggle' and, in some cases, elicit greater sympathy or at least less opprobrium in academia than do majoritarian nationalist movements. This is especially true of the quest for autonomy in Kashmir, in the far north, something of a *cause célèbre* among left-leaning Indian students and academics. While calls have been made in several quarters for an independent 'Dalitstan',[3] this was never a feature of conversations with my interlocutors, none of whom (in my hearing, at least) showed the slightest interest in secession.

For all these reasons – an academic field flooded with critiques of Hindu nationalism, a personal understanding of 'minority nationalism' as a demand for independence, and, more nebulously, a widespread academic queasiness about the very idea of nationalism – I struggled to picture Manish, Mahendra, Anish and their friends as nationalists. But in fact Mahendra had already given me a cipher of sorts. While telling me that nationalism should take precedence over religion he recommended I read Nehru's *The Discovery of India*. This is a sweeping account spanning thousands of years from the Indus Valley Civilisation to the last years of colonial rule and was written in the early 1940s, while its author was incarcerated by the British in Ahmednagar Fort. Of all India's nationalist ideologues, Jawaharlal Nehru, at the forefront of the freedom struggle and at the helm of the country's first independent government for 17 years, has cast perhaps the longest shadow. Quite unlike the proponents of *Hindutva* today, Nehru is associated with a 'secular, tolerant, inclusive and non-discriminatory' nationalism (Habib, 2017, p. 25) that dominated Indian politics and society in the decades following independence. In *The Discovery of India*, he refers to India's 'intense nationalistic fervour' as a 'natural and healthy growth' that must nevertheless be maintained in equilibrium with the 'other ideals' of internationalism and proletarianism (Nehru, 2004, p. 44–5).

Despite this, it would be a stretch to describe the nationalism on display at the Jay Bhim Katta as Nehruvian nationalism. Beyond Mahendra's reading recommendation, Nehru barely featured in conversations in the BDD Chawls and he was never incorporated into ritual chants or visual displays alongside Ambedkar, Shivaji, Phule and other figures of historical significance. Alongside *The Discovery of India,* Mahendra told me I must read Ambedkar's *Manav Vansh Shastra* (anthropology), only much later clarifying that this was a general 'topic' rather than the title of a book. The juxtaposition was revealing: if Dalit Buddhist nationalism is inflected with a Nehruvian legacy, this needs to be understood in the broader context of Ambedkar's approach to nationalism and his turbulent relationship with Nehru's government and wider national project.

Ambedkar, father of the nation

On Ambedkar Jayanti 2017, an enormous banner was displayed outside Chawl G featuring a reproduction of Ambedkar's signature from the Constitution of India, next to the words 'Signature that changed millions of lives'. Several months later the street between Chawl G and the Jay Bhim Katta was taken over by a programme of concerts and lectures organised by the Buddha Vihar committee to commemorate the 1956 conversion to Buddhism. One song compared Ambedkar and Shivaji, framing them both as great Maharashtrian heroes who had helped to build the nation. While 'Shivrao' relied on his sword, the singer explained, 'Bhimrao' (Ambedkar) changed India with a pen. As the performance reached its climax, the singer paused before declaiming that *'Bhimrao Bharat ka baap hai'* (Bhimrao is the father of India) which was met with a barrage of cheers and applause from the audience.

Given that both occasions were largely Dalit Buddhist affairs and unconnected to any national holiday, the emphasis on Ambedkar's nation-building role rather than his more specifically pro-Dalit activism is perhaps not an obvious one. In academic circles, Ambedkar has received 'strikingly little attention' as a nationalist intellectual, his legacy having predominantly been 'examined … within the context of dalit emancipation' (Tejani, 2013, p. 111). Meanwhile Ambedkar's support for the creation of Pakistan, premised on his understanding of the Muslim community as a nation unto themselves, was 'seen by many as a betrayal of the nationalist cause' (Tejani, 2013, p. 115), one controversial biographer even claiming that there is 'not one instance … in which Ambedkar participated in any activity connected with the struggle to free the country' (Shourie, 1997, p. 3).

Manish and his friends, on the other hand, consistently talked about Ambedkar as a national benefactor who authored the Constitution for the good of India as a whole. By uplifting the marginalised sections of society through, among other things, the instrument of reservations (quotas for marginalised communities in government, education and public sector jobs) the Constitution enables the country to function properly. After all, Mahendra asked me irritably when I relayed to him the argument a Hindu friend of mine had made for discontinuing reservations, how can a country walk properly if one leg is drastically shorter than the other?

During one of the English classes I ran in the initial weeks of fieldwork Manish, elaborating on his activities as a social worker, told me a story about Rane, a friend of a friend who had come to him seeking help regarding a Rs 70,000 (£700) medical bill. After an abortive visit to the Dean of the Hospital, Manish went to meet a local member of the BJP and, introducing himself as a representative of the Mumbai Branch of RPI(A), managed to persuade the politician to fund the operation.

'Did you receive any money for this?' I asked

'No, it is my passion, my hobbies,' Manish replied.

'Was Rane a Buddhist?'

'No, he is a Maratha. I help all people because I follow the Constitution.'

For Manish and Mahendra, then, the Constitution is not only a means to achieve social upliftment for their community, but a blueprint for the betterment of society as a whole, albeit one that imperfectly followed in wider Indian society. Early on in our friendship, at the Republic Day parade, Anish claimed that discrimination against Dalits had come to an end due to the adoption of the Constitution. Since Republic Day honours the anniversary of this adoption, Anish's optimism is understandable, especially in front of a foreign guest who was little more than a stranger at the time. Not many days elapsed before he began to contradict this by enumerating recent and widespread atrocities against Dalits and simultaneously accusing the BJP of ignoring the Constitution and stirring up unrest between communities. The parallel narratives of emancipation and oppression recounted in Chapter 2 can therefore be seen as illustrating both the fruits of following the Constitution (education, better jobs, good clothes) and the ugly realities of pre-constitutional India that will continue to resurface if the Constitution is not followed (violence, rape, murder).

Such mobilisation of the Constitution is not new. From its adoption in 1950 it has been used by marginalised segments of Indian society, such as sex workers and Muslim butchers, as a tool to litigate for their rights (De, 2018, p. 222). More recently, commentators have noted the way the Constitution has been used as a symbol of protest against the actions of the state, or envisaged as 'endangered by the state and therefore requiring the protection of the nation' (Rao, 2020a, p. 21).[4] Inextricably entwined as it is with the legacy of Ambedkar, however, the Constitution has a very particular significance to Dalit Buddhists as a backdrop against which their quest for social recognition and justice can rest.

Anish often told me about arguments he got into with dominant-caste friends about Ambedkar's exact relationship to the Constitution. Was he, as Anish claimed, the sole author sitting on a drafting committee otherwise comprising white elephants, or did he (as his friends provocatively argued) simply play a rubber-stamping role? Ambedkar himself professed to be a 'hack' who authored the Constitution 'much against [his] will' (Keer, 1971, p. 444) and famously declared his readiness to burn the Constitution that 'does not suit anybody' in a parliamentary debate (Parliament of India, 1953). It has even been suggested that Ambedkar's appointment as chairman of the Constitution Drafting Committee was a strategic ploy on Gandhi's part to 'make the lowest strata of Indian society emotionally attach itself to the Constitution' (Yengde, 2018, p. 92).

I do not propose to enter the fray here, but rather to note that Ambedkar's relationship with the wider Nehruvian project was far from smooth, before and after independence. In the 1930–2 Round Table Conferences, a series of legislative reforms through which the British government extended limited voting rights to Indians, Ambedkar vigorously campaigned for separate electorates for the 'Depressed Classes' (a category broadly similar to today's Dalits) as had already been granted to Muslims. He was eventually forced to compromise with Gandhi, who threatened to fast to death, and separate seats were allocated for the Depressed Classes but within a common Hindu electorate (Beltz, 2005, p. 49).

In 1947 Ambedkar was appointed Minister for Law and Justice in independent India's first cabinet under Nehru. He resigned from this position in September 1951 with an excoriating speech in which he expressed his disappointment that Scheduled Castes (Dalits) were facing the 'same old tyranny' as before Independence, in stark contrast to the 'care and attention' afforded to Muslims (Ambedkar, 2014b, p. 1320). He explained that he was ultimately resigning due to the failure to bring about caste reform through the Hindu Code Bill, since attempting to resolve economic problems while leaving 'inequality between class and class, between sex and sex ... untouched' is like building a 'palace on a dung heap' and makes a 'farce' of the Constitution (2014b, p. 1326).

Whatever undertones of Nehruvian inclusiveness might be found in Dalit Buddhist discourse, such discourse draws on an intellectual heritage within which the legacy of Nehru is deeply conflicted. Nehru's legacy is similarly conflicted across India more generally but, in the febrile atmosphere of BJP rule, liberal commentators sometimes call for a return to Nehruvian values (such as Ranjan, 2020). However, it has been suggested that, in light of contemporary political language, the 'non-exclusionary nationalism' Nehru articulated is 'no longer classifiable as nationalism' (Zachariah, 2011, p. 206). Where, then, does this leave my interlocutors' nationalism?

But is it really nationalism?

I am sometimes asked whether I think 'Dalit Buddhist nationalism' is really nationalism at all. In response, I usually quote anthropologist Anna Tsing, who exhorts ethnographers to 'take our objects of study seriously even as we examine them critically' (2000, p. 351), meaning I take the line that 'since they tell me it's nationalism, I shall treat it as nationalism.' That said, I found it surprising that the word typically used, in English and Hindi/Marathi, was nationalism (*rashtrawad*) rather than patriotism (*desh bhakti* or *desh prem*). If, as discussed, nationalism has a bad reputation in much left-leaning academia, patriotism is more often considered benign, if perhaps rather small-minded and unfashionable, although the difference between the two is hardly clear cut. *Desh prem* literally translates to 'country love' and, like *desh bhakti* (country devotion) recalls Orwell's famous distinction between patriotism as a protective devotion to place and nationalism as inseparable from the desire for power (Orwell, 1945).

One of the most influential definitions of nationalism is found in the opening of Ernest Gellner's *Nations and Nationalism,* where he declares that nationalism 'is primarily a political principle, which holds that the political and the national unit should be congruent' and that this 'requires that ethnic boundaries should not cut across political ones' and 'should not separate the power-holders from the rest' (1983, p. 1). In essence, this means that a nation should be composed of a single, homogenous 'culture' which in practice can only be achieved by the 'general imposition of a high culture on society' through means including education, bureaucracy and technology (1983, p. 57). This resonates with Benedict Anderson's theory of the nation as an 'imagined community' whose members harbour an 'image of their communion' despite 'never know[ing] most of their fellow-members' (1991, p. 6). Such communion does not arise organically but needs to be fashioned by the 'policy levers of official nationalism' which include state-controlled education and media (1991, p. 100). Both Gellner and Anderson understand nationalism as a modern European-American ideology that has spread worldwide through colonialism.

There was little recognisably Gellnerian about the rhetoric I heard at the Jay Bhim Katta. More saliently, Dalit scholar G. Aloysius takes on Gellner's core proposition of nationalism as political-national congruence to argue that postcolonial nationalism requires *both* the transfer of power from an outside colonial culture to an independent nation, *and* the equitable distribution of power across society in the new nation (Aloysius, 1997, pp. 14 and 54). The independence movement of Gandhi, Nehru and others, Aloysius explains, was dominated by a caste elite preoccupied only by the transference of external power while maintaining traditional social hierarchies, thus precluding the possibility of forming a viable nation (Aloysius, 1997, p. 226). Ambedkar himself was adamant that the political reform of independence would not be possible without the parallel social reform of caste abolition (2013, pp. 16–24), that caste is inimical to nationalism (1987a, p. 304) and that by 'settl[ing] power upon an aggressive Hindu majority' the British 'would not be ending imperialism ... [but] creating another imperialism' (1990b, p. 9).

Elsewhere in India, other Dalit intellectuals made similar arguments, such as Kusuma Dharmanna and Vagiri Amosu, in the Telugu-speaking region of south India, who both maintained that without being accorded rights and respect from dominant castes, independence from British rule would mean nothing to Dalits (Gundimeda, 2015, pp. 165–6). Partha Chatterjee documents 'numerous fragmented resistances to [the] normalising project' of 'hegemonic' nationalism (1993 p. 13), and Aloysius argues that the mainstream independence movement regarded such resistances as attempts to undermine their nationalist project that were 'inspired and abetted by the colonial rulers' and thus inherently anti-national (1997, p. 92; see also Guru, 2016, p. 240). The political historiography of twentieth-century India has therefore tended to erase these local movements in favour of a straightforward narrative of decolonisation (Aloysius, 1997, p. 54), exemplifying Anderson's axiom that 'official rewriting of history' is one of the key 'policy levers of official nationalism' (1991, p. 100).

For nationalist struggles, indeed, history is one of the most significant sites of contestation.[5] Partha Chatterjee disputes Anderson's conception that postcolonial states simply 'choose their imagined community from certain "modular" forms already made available to them by Europe and the Americas' (1993, pp. 5–6). Instead, he argues, anticolonial nationalism divides the social/institutional world into material and spiritual domains, imitating the West in the former, while declaring the latter 'its sovereign territory', an inner, essential domain of cultural identity from which colonial interference must be precluded

(Chatterjee, 1993, pp. 5–6). The telling of one's own history belongs to this spiritual domain, and Chatterjee provides examples of Bengali historians such as Bankim Chandra and Tarinicharan Chattopadhyay laying claim to a 'true' history of Bengal, or of India as a whole (1993, pp. 76–7 and 95). To me, therefore, the question of whether my interlocutors' claim to be Indians, firstly and lastly, conforms to any accepted definition of nationalism is rather less interesting than the question of how they invoke a very specific understanding of Indian history to bolster this claim.

Buddhism and false history

When Mahendra advised me to read *The Discovery of India* he told me this would help me understand the 'true history' of India. Not long afterwards, Sayaji informed me that the epic poems of the Ramayana and Mahabharata were 'false history', penned by Brahmans to prop up the fraudulent edifice of Hinduism. Throughout the year Mahendra, Sayaji and their friends warned me about the dangers of false history, both ancient and modern, and urged me to familiarise myself with an 'alternative' or 'true' history put forward by Ambedkar. This history revealed how Buddhism had once been at the heart of an ancient India governed on principles of rationalism and egalitarianism and that, in order to transcend the social fragmentation of caste Hinduism, Buddhism is needed again to achieve an ideal, unified India.

Scientific rationalism and the future of India

These ideas, so at odds with the strident *Hindutva* choking public discourse, are in fact implicated within the fabric of India's nationhood. In his final speech to the Constituent Assembly in November 1949, Ambedkar invoked Buddhist *sanghas* (monastic communities) as an ancient example of the democracy to which India would be returning upon adoption of the Constitution (Ambedkar, 2014a, pp. 1214–15). Two years earlier, the newly independent India had adopted a state emblem based on the Lion Capital of Ashoka at Sarnath, a column head erected by the much-lauded Indian Buddhist Emperor Ashoka in the third century BCE. The emblem features four lions standing above an Ashoka Chakra, a symbol the emperor used on many of the edicts he inscribed on stone pillars across his territory, and which is now printed at the centre of the national flag.[6] It is something of a floating signifier, variously said to represent duty, the passage of time, the qualities of an ideal human and, according to Dalit scholar Gopal Guru, a principle of self-realisation whereby power is (re) distributed equally throughout society, and as such the basis on which Dalit nationalism is articulated (2016, pp. 239 and 248–9). The Ashoka Chakra is also used as a more general logo of the Ambedkarite community, including in the flags of political parties such as the RPI(A).

The claim to be Indians, firstly and lastly is therefore an explicit rejection of the hierarchies and superstitions of caste Hinduism in favour of Buddhism. Mahendra, possibly influenced by Nehru's insistence that India 'lessen her religiosity and turn to science' (2004, p. 579), once told me that Buddhism is 'scientifically proven'. Anish agreed, explaining that the Buddha was the first scientist. For Manish, Buddhism's uniqueness and superiority came from its flexibility as a religion of principles rather than a religion of rules, a distinction echoing the one Ambedkar made in his 1936 *Annihilation of Caste* (Ambedkar, 2013, pp. 68–72). All other religions are prescriptive, he argued – Christianity demands its followers go to church on Sunday, Islam demands *namaaz* five times a day, Hinduism dictates what you can and cannot eat – but to be Buddhist, it is only required that you think correctly and do not lie. Even then, said Manish with his customary quiet earnestness, should lying be necessary to achieve good, this is permissible too.

While they frequently expressed the opinion that in Buddhism lay the answer to India's problems, I was surprised by how rarely the Jay Bhim Katta crowd discussed Buddhism's potential for global reform. Teasing suggestions were sometimes made that I should spread Ambedkar's message back home, and, at the concert commemorating the mass conversion, one speaker proposed Buddhism as the solution to the 'war' between the US and North Korea. Otherwise the focus remained squarely on India and few appeared concerned with the situations unfolding in neighbouring countries Sri Lanka and Myanmar, where government policy and popular discourse has been profoundly influenced by Buddhist nationalist organisations, often to specifically anti-minority ends (Schonthal and Walton, 2016).

It was never clear to me whether this reflected a calculated reluctance to discuss the less savoury manifestations of Buddhism, or simply a lack of knowledge. When I asked Anish a question about the Bodu Bala Sena, an extremist Buddhist-nationalist organisation in Sri Lanka that has self-professedly 'wreak[ed] havoc' on the country's Muslim minority (Holt, 2016, p. 4), he seemed genuinely unaware of the group's existence. Instead, he showed me a WhatsApp forward about Japanese funding for the Mumbai–Ahmedabad high-speed rail corridor and made the point, later echoed by Mahendra, that India's technological progress is largely bankrolled by 'Buddhist countries'.

The particular strain of Buddhism I encountered in the BDD Chawls owes much to Ambedkar, who announced his intention to leave Hinduism in 1935 and considered alternatives including Christianity and Islam before settling on Buddhism, in part due to its 'secular ethics' (Tejani, 2013, p. 119).[7] Ambedkar's particular reading of Buddhism draws deeply from a nineteenth-century tradition often referred to as 'Protestant Buddhism'. This was a hybrid tradition born out of mixing, in Sri Lanka (then Ceylon), between British civil servants, American Buddhist converts and Ceylonese reformers (Omvedt, 2003, p. 234) and characterised by its use of 'Western sources and English translations of the scriptures' as well as emphasis on the rational, non-theistic nature of Buddhism (Beltz, 2005, p. 72) and the scientific explanation of miracles (Fiske and Emmrich, 2004, p. 11).

The extent to which these interventions represent an attempt to secularise Buddhism is open to debate. Ambedkar maintained that Buddhism was a scientific social philosophy and moral code (Beltz, 2004, p. 7), but he also insisted that the values of liberty, equality and fraternity that underpinned this philosophy are rooted in 'religion' and the teachings of the Buddha, rather than the 'political science' of the French Revolution (Keer, 1971, p. 459). My interlocutors themselves never appeared especially concerned by such metaphysical nuances and in our conversations the Buddha, like Ambedkar, slid between the status of *bhagwan* (god) and *bhagwan jaise* (like a god). Likewise, they appeared to inhabit a comfortable equilibrium in which prayer was a matter for the individual, while the quest for social justice it underpinned was a community affair.

Invading Aryans and Ambedkar's alternative history

Ambedkar was not only drawn to Buddhism for its secular ethics, but also because of its status as an ancient and indisputably Indian religion. Accordingly, many of my conversations at the Jay Bhim Katta about Buddhism and nationalism were imbued with a sense of proximity to an ancient and glorious past – the true history of India. Buddhism was a solution to India's contemporary problems, I was often told, precisely *because* it had been the religion of ancient India, a wealthy polity governed on casteless egalitarianism. The Mahars and other Dalits had been part of this ancient utopia, meaning that the 1956 conversion movement should more accurately be regarded as a reconversion movement. Today's caste inequalities were a direct consequence of Hinduism which, I was informed, had not arisen within India but rather had been imposed on the country by outside invaders.

Manish referred to these invaders as fair-skinned Persians, while Mahendra called them 'Eurasians', telling me they had come from Afghanistan to acquire more pastoral land, destroying India's indigenous Buddhist culture in the process. Anish labelled the invaders *arya* (Aryans), and explained that they were the first Brahmans who had come to India 3,000 years ago from Europe 'for business purposes', leading to political domination. Sayaji agreed, adding that Buddhism was originally practised well beyond the confines of today's India, perhaps even as far as Europe and America, and also that there is genetic evidence to prove that Brahmans were originally from Portugal.

Despite these minor disagreements over details, there was a general consensus that the invaders were something akin to settler colonials who had arrived thousands of years ago and had used the apparatus of Hinduism – fake gods, false history, the caste system – as a weapon with which to control the minds and bodies of indigenous (Buddhist) Indians. As a result, Hinduism today is a religion of blind, unquestioning adherence. After the Maharashtrian Hindu New Year (Gudi Padwa), Mahendra bridled at my asking him if he had taken part in the festivities. 'No!' he replied sternly in English. 'Hindus blindly follow, but Buddhists always ask "why?"'

Although at times I found elements of this alternative history outlandish, I recognised its pedigree immediately. Anish's use of *arya* explicitly referenced the so-called Aryan Invasion Theory that posited 'an ancient clash between a light-skinned [Aryan] race bringing Sanskrit and civilisation to an India inhabited by dark-skinned, savage speakers of Dravidian [south Indian] languages' (Trautmann, 2005, pp. xxxi–xxxii). This theory became a dominant paradigm among European Indologists in the nineteenth century following discoveries of the relationship between Sanskrit to Greek and Latin.[8] German philologist Max Müller conceptualised an Aryan race that encompassed dominant-caste Hindus and Europeans, binding them together in a 'mutual, emphatic connection' many decades before this idea found its most notorious expression in the political project of Nazi Germany (Birkvad, 2020, pp. 62–3 and 75–6). Accordingly, several British colonial historians invoked the Aryan invasion as a justificatory parallel to the British colonisation of India (Thapar, 2005, p. 115). Likewise, for some elite Hindu reformers and *Hindutva* ideologues the Aryan concept was a 'potent political currency' that allowed them to claim a connection to the British rulers (Birkvad, 2020, p. 76), and Bal Gangadhar Tilak, the famous Maharashtrian Brahman freedom fighter, even went so far as to posit the original home of Aryans as the North Pole (Doniger, 2009, p. 89).

But the theory was also used as a justification for several of the popular movements that sprang up in the late nineteenth and early twentieth centuries to challenge Brahmanic hegemony (Omvedt, 2006, p. 35). In Maharashtra, the social reformer Jyotirao Phule established the Satyashodhak Samaj (truth-seekers' society) in 1873 to campaign for equal rights for marginalised castes and untouchables, whom he considered the indigenous survivors of India's 'pre-Aryan Golden Age' (Hansen, 2001, p. 29). For Phule, the Aryans were the worst in a long line of subsequent invaders, since their power was consolidated through hierarchical religious structures premised on trickery and superstition (Omvedt, 2006, pp. 20–2).

Much of the alternative history I was taught at the Jay Bhim Katta draws on this heritage and can be traced at least indirectly to Phule, whose accessible Marathi-language tracts contrast strikingly with the denseness of Ambedkar's English prose (Rao, 2009, p. 39). Generally speaking, however, my friends attributed their knowledge of history to Ambedkar. Anish told me that Ambedkar had devised an alternative history of India after reading 50,000 books. At the time I dismissed this as a wild exaggeration and only much later discovered, with due embarrassment, about Ambedkar's 50,000 book collection at his house in Dadar, much of which is now in the library of Siddharth College in south Mumbai (Queen, 2004, p. 134).

Ambedkar in fact rejected the Aryan Invasion Theory in his 1946 *Who Were the Shudras* as an 'absurd' invention (1990a, pp. 78–80). In his unpublished *Revolution and Counter-Revolution in Ancient India,* on the other hand, he argues that 'If Hindu India was invaded by the Muslim invaders so was Buddhist India invaded by Brahmanic invaders ... [who] drove out Buddhism as a religion and occupied its place' (Ambedkar, 1987a, pp. 273–4). Although he is actually referring to the internal counter-revolution of Pushyamitra, a Brahman army general who persecuted Buddhists and established a Hindu Empire, the scope for misinterpretation is evident. In any case, there appears to be a degree of blurring in my interlocutors' accounts between the original Aryan invasion and the revival of Brahmanism that reached its height in the fourth and fifth centuries under the Gupta Empire. Like the eagerness among some to over-credit Ambedkar for his role in establishing reservations (see Chapter 2), there is a comparable eagerness to frame Ambedkar as the lone scholar who revolutionised the study of Indian history.

Nehru's account in *The Discovery of India* shares much with the histories I was taught at the Jay Bhim Katta. He refers to 'Aryan migrations' resulting in a 'synthesis and fusion' with pre-existing populations that gave rise to the 'basic Indian culture' (Nehru, 2004 p. 69), including the caste system (p. 81). Hinduism, Jainism and Buddhism all emerged from this synthesis (p. 70–1), and the latter is treated with an unashamed personal reverence (p. 132) while the 'astonishing' rule of Ashoka is recounted in hagiographic terms (p. 136). Nevertheless, Nehru's description of what follows differs starkly from Ambedkar's and those of the Jay Bhim Katta symposia when he assures his readers that there was 'no widespread or violent extermination of Buddhism in India' (2004, p. 187), and that the Hindu revival under the Guptas was 'not anti-Buddhist in any way' (p. 188). I never got a chance to discuss this with Mahendra, so I am unclear how familiar he was with Nehru's reading of the Hindu revival or how he would respond to it. However, his own claim that the 'Eurasians' first came to India to graze their cows accords with Nehru's description of Aryans as agriculturalists (2004, p. 82) and is consonant with a more general shift in academic understanding towards a 'slower, more gradual migration of Aryans into India' (Trautmann, 2005, p. xxxvii) that is supported by a considerable body of linguistic, textual and genetic evidence.[9]

In contrast to Tilak, some Hindu thinkers vociferously rejected the possibility that Hinduism came from outside India (for example Vivekananda, 1973, p. 293). The second leader of the RSS, M.S. Golwalkar, who openly expressed his admiration of the way Aryan racial purity was maintained in Nazi Germany,[10] domesticated Tilak's Arctic homeland claim by insisting that thousands of years ago, the North Pole would have been located in present-day Bihar, and thus (Aryan) Hindus were 'indigenouse [sic] children of the soil always, from time immemorial' (Golwalkar, 1939, p. 8). This 'Out of India Theory', placing India as the sole historical source of Hindu culture and the Sanskrit language, has become a mainstay of contemporary Hindu nationalist discourse albeit with limited traction in the wider academic world.

The topic remains hotly contested in India, not only in politics and academia but in the chawls and tea stalls.[11] Highlights from new genetics studies are excerpted in Indian-language newspapers, such as a Marathi article that Pradeep once flashed before me on his phone during a discussion, claiming with conviction that '*ye final proof hai*' (this is final proof). Final proof, he meant, that Dalits, not Brahmans were the original Indians. Since the residents of Chawl M are Marathas, not Brahmans, they are actually victims of this brainwashing invasion too, but since they only care about their caste status, they have themselves joined the ranks of the oppressors. Unlike the Mahars, they have not been liberated from the chains of false history into Buddhism rationalism, and they are therefore unable to see that they, too, are Indians, firstly and lastly.

Contested spaces and everyday chawlness

It would be satisfying at this point to shift the gaze to the Maratha community and listen to their views on Buddhism, the Aryan invasion and the origin of caste, but I am hampered by a lack of data. With a few exceptions, ancient history was apparently not a preoccupation for my Maratha interlocutors in the way that it was for many Dalit Buddhists. Mohan, a young man from Chawl B who I helped with English conversation practice, sometimes talked me through battle sequences from the Mahabharata but expended most of his historical enthusiasm on the life of his seventeenth-century hero Chhatrapati Shivaji. Shivaji was a popular subject of discussion among my Maratha friends (Tukaram included) and to a lesser extent among Dalit Buddhists, and these debates will form the basis of Chapter 6.

On a return visit to the BDD Chawls in late 2018, I found that almost everybody – Dalit and Maratha – was exercised by the subject of Ayodhya. In this small town in Uttar Pradesh, the sixteenth-century Babri Masjid ('Babur's mosque') had been demolished on 6 December 1992 after a sustained campaign by the Vishva Hindu Parishad (VHP)[12] in anticipation of the (re)-construction of a Hindu temple that they believed had historically stood on the site marking the birthplace of Lord Ram, incarnation of the deity Vishnu. The Ayodhya dispute, as it is known, is a prime example of Hindu majoritarian clout and Muslim 'feeling[s] of being an endangered minority' and as such is highly significant for religious identity formation in contemporary India (van der Veer, 1994, p. 10). In late 2018, the VHP organised a Dharma Sabha (religious meeting) in Ayodhya, drawing hundreds of supporters together to demand the construction of the as-yet-unbuilt Ram Mandir.

Commenting in the folly of such gatherings, Vinod (the journalist I met on my first visit to the Jay Bhim Katta) claimed that in fact Ayodhya had originally been a Buddhist town called Saket. He said that a Dalit activist, Chandrashekhar Azad, had marched to Ayodhya the previous month to present the Ayodhya District Magistrate with a copy of the Indian Constitution, reminding him of his constitutional duties to protect minorities, and simultaneously calling for the renaming of Ayodhya to Saket and the construction of a Buddha Vihar.[13] For Mahendra, cases like Ayodhya were illustrations of a broader historical phenomenon that he elaborated as follows:

> Har church ke niche, har masjid ke niche, har ghar ke niche, har hinduo ke mandir ke niche jitne bhi utkaran hote hai unne vaha pe archaeology department ko sirf Buddha ke murtiya, Buddha ke sculpture, Buddha ke sign ye milte hai.
>
> (Mahendra, interview, 3 December 2018)
>
> (Underneath every church, every mosque, every house, every Hindu temple, however much the Archaeology Department excavates, only Buddhist signs and sculptures are found).

Atreyee Sen points out that religious tension in India so often plays out as a battle for space, 'be it through the [Ayodhya] mosque/temple argument at the national level, for housing space at the slum level, or just a place to sit at the insignificant level of an outing by the sea' (2007, p. 102). For the Dalit Buddhists of the BDD Chawls, the Buddha Vihar is not only a sacred space but it is also a tangible symbol of belonging, to the neighbourhood and also to the nation. When the Marathas of Chawl M argue about paving stones, therefore, the Buddhists do not view it merely as a neighbourhood squabble about space. For them, every insult landed by the Marathas perpetuates a power structure imposed on both communities by an invading force and constantly replicated over thousands of years by means of a false ideology. Marathas can thus simultaneously be victims of Brahmanic brainwashing *and* caste oppressors, and as long as they remain in thrall to Hinduism, India will not truly be a nation.[14]

On a day-to-day level in the BDD Chawls these ideological tensions manifest in subtle rather than overt ways. Although in the aftermath of the Buddha Vihar incident Dinesh suggested that I should stay away from the BDD Chawls for some time as violence might break out, these fears fortunately proved unfounded and, in fact, I saw very little evidence of open hostility between the Dalit Buddhist and Maratha communities during my fieldwork. To my knowledge, there has been no recent history of communal rioting on the scale of the Hindu–Buddhist riots that engulfed the larger BDD Chawl site in Worli in early 1974.[15] Shashank More, a retired RPI(A) secretary and respected Chawl F resident, told me that in contrast to the 'dangerous' residents of the Worli BDD Chawls, those at Delisle Road were *sochnewale* (thinkers, or thoughtful) and so people generally get along.

Of course, fights sometimes broke out: friends in Maratha-dominated Chawls J and K recalled skirmishes with Dalit-dominated Chawl L in the 1990s, in which tube lights were hurled from the rooftops at adversaries on the road below. Nevertheless, in my own snapshot of

BDD Chawl life the prevailing mood was one of calm everyday chawlness. What caste conflict there was mostly played out either at the political level, such as the disputes over the chawl redevelopment plans I will discuss in Chapter 7, or at the level of snide remarks and microaggressions.

A Maratha lawyer from Shivaji Nagar, the newer building at the entrance to the BDD Chawl site, explained why rooms in certain chawl buildings commanded a lower rent than others. 'Where Dalits are there, speaking very frankly … the environment in those chawls, the cleanliness is very least. Everything are scattered, beds are outside.' Only '15 to 20 per cent' of the people living in the BDD Chawls are casteist, he claimed without a trace of irony; the remainder simply dislike the environment of those Dalit-dominated buildings. Satyajit, another highly-educated Maratha friend, told me that nobody wanted to live in the Worli BDD Chawls anymore because of its large Dalit community. Another time he talked in reverent tones about a cricketer friend from Chawl G who had recently died from jaundice. Not only was he a great cricketer, said Satyajit, but he was also 'very good in speaking', so that you would never guess he was a Dalit. 'He was like a Brahman!'

In fact, I encountered many friendships between members of the Maratha and Dalit Buddhist communities and both Sayaji and Mahendra introduced me at various points to Hindu 'best friends'. One Jay Bhim Katta stalwart, a young man called Vikrant who was always actively involved in any function or celebration, surprised me by telling me he was Maratha, and his family, now living in a nearby apartment block, had previously lived in Chawl M. After we had got to know each other better I asked him how he felt about the tensions between Chawl M and his Buddhist friends. He said that he had not heard about the Buddha Vihar incident and that as far as he knew, everything was calm between the communities. If it came to it, he claimed, he would support the Buddhists because – gesturing to his heart – he is like one of them.

Most surprising of all was the discovery that both Sayaji and Mahendra, arch-critics of Hinduism, are married to Hindus as are several other members of the community. Sayaji, at least, attended a number of Hindu celebrations during the year with his father-in-law. When I asked Mahendra if his wife still practised Hindu ritual, he gave a brittle laugh and said she did, but that there are no tensions between them as she is 'pure'. Dinesh, on the other hand, told me that his mother had officially converted to Buddhism on marriage but continued to practise Hinduism until he and Sayaji explained the error of her ways.

As far as I could establish, some of these Hindu wives were Marathas while others were from Chambhar families. Although the Chambhars are also a Dalit community, they are Hindu, not Buddhist, and the Mahar–Chambhar relationship comes with its own share of tension. Aside from Anish's Ambedkar Jayanti collection that targeted all Dalit communities in the BDD Chawls, I saw little other evidence of pan-Dalit solidarity, and Chambhars were often the object of mild ridicule among several of the Buddhists. Anish, for example, derided their ideological vacillation which results in a tendency to ally themselves with whichever community is in a position of local influence. One of his friends explicitly warned me against conducting research among the Chambhars due to their casteist mentality and insincerity. 'Ham log frankly speaking hai' (we speak frankly), he said.

Even in Ambedkar's time, apparently, 'Chambhars considered Mahars, Dhors and Matangs as inferior and fought for a better position in society' (Beltz, 2005, p. 98) and there was a 'striking' absence of Chambhars from Ambedkar's Indian Labour Party (Zelliot, 1996b, p. 106). A particular sore point among the BDD Chawls Buddhists is the lack of respect Chambhars accord to Ambedkar, who they regard as a purely Mahar leader, rather than a general social reformer (see also Beltz, 2005, p. 99; Zelliot, 1996b, p. 106). As with the Marathas, I heard stories of physical fights that had broken out between Dalit Buddhists and Chambhars, although in general, according to Gautam from Chawl H, the mood was that of a 'cold war', especially among members of the two communities living within Chawls F and G who simply avoided each other's festivals and weddings.[16]

At the level of the (imagi)nation

History lessons at the Buddha Vihar

I returned to the BDD Chawls for a few weeks in late 2018 still full of questions about 'Dalit Buddhist nationalism' – what kind of nationalism is it? What does it mean? What does it do? Is it really nationalism? I was immediately struck not only by the tiled new footpath leading to the Buddha Vihar but also by a totally revamped facade. In place of the old simple signboard with the words *samyak buddh vihar*[17] under a small sketch of the Buddha's head, was a long multicoloured banner comprising portraits and text (Figure 4.2). Ambedkar and Shivaji gaze out with steely resolve either side of an Ashoka Chakra, flanked by, among others: Ashoka himself; the Phules, Jyotirao next to Ambedkar, his wife Savitribai further towards the end; Shahuji, a Maharajah of Kolhapur renowned for his welfare activities and campaigns against Brahmanic hegemony; Ambedkar's first wife Ramabai; and various poet-saints including Rohidas (also known as Ravidas), Tukaram and Kabir, all of whom my interlocutors consider significant voices in the historical struggle against caste. In addition to the labels *samyak buddh vihar* and Republican Party of India are the words *bahujan hitaya bahujan sukhaya* (for the welfare of many, for the happiness of many), a dictum articulated by the Buddha that is also used, printed around an Ashoka Chakra, as a motto for the national public broadcaster All India Radio. Overlooking this panoply is a seated Buddha, and running underneath are the stripes of the international Buddhist flag.[18]

It is a confident (re)assertion of belonging in the neighbourhood and the prominent incorporation of Shivaji might been seen as a gracious acknowledgement of the feelings of the Marathas next door, although as we shall see in Chapter 6, Shivaji also plays a bona fide role in Dalit Buddhist cosmology. Above all, it is an eloquent articulation of Ambedkarite Buddhist thought and a visual history lesson in what it means to say: 'We are Indians, firstly and lastly'. What is excluded from the image is just as revealing as what is included. There are no Hindu gods, of course, in this place of Buddhist worship where Hinduism is seen as a foreign imposition stunting the country's development, and hence the antithesis of true Indian nationalism.

Figure 4.2 Renovated facade of the BDD Chawls Buddha Vihar. © Author.

Neither do the familiar figures of the mainstream Independence movement get a look in. This is hardly surprising in the case of Gandhi, who was generally referred to with little enthusiasm, and only slightly more so for Nehru, whose appreciation of India's Buddhist past commanded Mahendra's respect but was never otherwise discussed. The symbology here and at the Jay Bhim Katta suggests that British colonial rule looms far less large in the historical sense of the users of these spaces than does ancient Aryan 'colonialism'. In the face of my frequent anticolonial handwringing, Anish and friends would remind me that they actually regarded British rule as a liberation from the brutality of the Brahman Peshwa polity that preceded it, an uncomfortable conundrum that forms the basis of a fuller discussion in Chapter 6. This position nevertheless coexisted with a pride in India's independence and nationhood, most sharply in focus during the annual celebrations of Republic Day and Independence Day, both of which are readily celebrated through an Ambedkar-centric lens.

This is a far cry from the rhetoric in a 1972 article by Dalit Panther cofounder Raja Dhale who branded 15 August as Black Independence Day and compared the national flag, in its inability to protect the rights of Dalits, to a 'piece of cloth to be stuffed up the savarna's [caste Hindu's] ass' (quoted in Rao, 2009, p.189). My interlocutors' softer stance is partly explained by the Republican Party of India label at the bottom left of the banner. While many Buddhists of the BDD Chawls have historical Dalit Panther connections – relatives of another cofounder, J. V. Pawar, live in the neighbourhood – the radical activism of the 1970s has been somewhat submerged into the respectability of party politics under the auspices of the RPI(A). The fact that party leader Ramdas Athawale is a member of the Rajya Sabha (parliamentary upper house) further contributes to their sense of electoral investment in the nation.

On the other hand, the RPI(A) coalition with the BJP, which has been in force since 2011, is only reluctantly accepted as a necessary piece of strategy and does not prevent Anish and friends from openly deriding the BJP as representative of everything they detest about Hindu nationalism. This supple pragmatism recalls David Lloyd's (1997) concept of 'nationalisms against the state', which is based on studies of anticolonial nationalist movements within which internally competing ideologies are temporarily 'subordinated' only to re-emerge after independence (1997 p. 182). There is nothing illogical, Lloyd argues, in socialist feminists playing a leading part in the Irish struggle for independence in 1919–21 and opposing the Irish Free State that was subsequently established (Lloyd 1997, pp. 184–6).[19] However, he warns, nationalism against the state is a fundamentally dynamic position, constantly at risk of being co-opted in service of the state (Lloyd, 1997, p. 182).

If the Dalit Buddhist community is uniquely well-positioned to frame themselves as nationalists, given their connection to ancient India through Buddhism and to modern India through the Constitution and several of the symbols of state, their position is also vulnerable to co-option. Indeed, there have been 'constant efforts' by Hindu nationalists to 'integrate Ambedkar in their own ideology' (Beltz, 2005, p. 107), for example by incorporating commemorations of his death into the anniversary of the Ayodhya mosque demolition (Hansen, 1999, p. 226) and also by reclaiming Buddhism as a 'sect of Hinduism' (Teltumbde, 2017, p. 162), a claim made by Savarkar himself. Modi has shown himself to be fluent in this language when the occasion demands (PTI, 2021).

Beltz argues that these Hindu nationalist 'appropriations' of Ambedkar's legacy have 'compelled the Buddhists to take a stand, to defend themselves and to constantly reiterate their differences' (2005, p. 108). As we have seen, 'taking a stand', for my research participants at least, does not entail a quest for a separate Dalitstan akin to the demands articulated by liberation movements in the north-east of the country or in Kashmir. On the few occasions Kashmir cropped up in conversation at the Jay Bhim Katta, the general tenor seemed to be one of sympathy towards the plight of Kashmiris suffering under the weight of heavy-handed Indian government policy paired with a belief that, ultimately, greater integration with India, not independence, was the solution.[20]

Neither does taking a stand entail any obvious emulation of the majoritarian Buddhist nationalism currently ascendant in Sri Lanka. Granted, the two traditions draw extensively on a shared heritage of 'Protestant Buddhism', and Sri Lankan Buddhist nationalism is also undergirded by claims of scientific rationalism and a Buddhist golden age lost to colonial invasion (Schonthal, 2016, pp. 99–105).[21] Otherwise, there are far more commonalities between Sri Lankan Buddhist nationalism and (Indian) Hindu nationalism, and the label *sinhalatva* is sometimes applied to Sri Lankan Buddhist nationalism in a deliberate reference to *Hindutva* (Schalk, 2006). In both cases, majoritarian religious nationalism has formally taken root at the state level, while violent non-state actors appear to be unofficially tolerated and even supported by the government (Schonthal and Walton, 2016, p. 95).

Universal redistribution and recognition of difference

Neither Dalitstan nor *sinhalatva*-style Buddhist nationalism have a place in my interlocutors' worlds, so let us turn back to the Ashoka Chakra at the centre of the Buddha Vihar banner. Dalit scholar Gopal Guru argues that this emblem's inclusion in the Indian flag 'provides an opportunity for nationalism to save itself from falling into [the] paradox' of being unable to fulfil the promise symbolised by the *chakra* and enshrined in the Constitution (2016, p. 248). This promise he refers to as the 'rotation principle' whereby vertical social mobility is achievable and power is (re-) distributed equally throughout society (2016, p. 248). Aloysius, as we saw earlier, understands this 'homogenization of power within culture' as a necessary condition for any nationalist movement to succeed (1997, p. 54). In a South Indian context, anthropologist Hugo Gorringe argues that the 'radical potential of Dalit mobilisation' is 'a politics of redistribution that would grant everybody … a stake in the nation' (Gorringe, 2008, p. 145).

But the Dalit struggle is also a struggle for '*recognition* which acknowledges otherness … a society in which different communities coexist as equals, not in hierarchical relationships' (Fuchs, 2004, p. 292). These possibly contradictory urges evoke the language of Charles Taylor who elucidates, in his well-known essay 'The Politics of Recognition', the coexistence of a *politics of universalism* that seeks equal rights and equal dignity, and a *politics of difference* in which the distinctness of individuals and groups must be recognised and not 'ignored, glossed over, assimilated to a dominant or majority identity' (1994, pp. 37–8). Recognition, according to Taylor, is a human need that if not fulfilled can lead to 'real damage' and low self-esteem that can hold individuals or groups back, even after the 'objective obstacles to their advancement' are removed through a politics of redistribution (1994, pp. 25–6).

In the Dalit Buddhist struggle of the BDD Chawls, these two politics manifest in multiple ways. Being Indians, firstly and lastly, suggests an equality accorded to every Indian citizen (universalism; call for redistribution), and yet my research participants insist that they are *more* nationalist than other communities, including their Maratha neighbours (difference; call for recognition). Specifically, Buddhists are truer nationalists than non-Buddhists, but by viewing non-Buddhists as descendants of Buddhists who were brainwashed into Hinduism by outsiders and who could in theory reclaim their ancestral Buddhism, the possibility of equality is maintained. In practice, however, Dalits were Ambedkar's core audience, and Buddhism has remained a 'religion for

Dalits only' (Fuchs, 2004, p. 292). The RPI, likewise, was theoretically a party of the 'dispossessed' of India but in reality has remained a party (or group of parties) composed overwhelmingly of Dalit Buddhists (Zelliot, 1996b, p. 114).

Similarly, the Constitution is *both* a blueprint for Indian society as a whole, *and* an instrument that specifically safeguards the rights of Dalits, a tension reflected in ongoing debates about who should be entitled to reservations and whether and when these should be discontinued. Taylor conceptualises such debates in terms of the 'difference-blindness' that proponents of a politics of universalism can fall prey to, whereby the outcomes of a politics of difference, especially those involving affirmative action, are regarded as a 'betrayal' of universalist principles (1994, pp. 39–40). It is revealing that Mahendra, clearly advocating for a politics of difference, frames the need in terms of a politics of universalism when he asks how a country can walk on legs of unequal length.

The universalism-difference dialectic also cuts in at the larger scale of national versus global. In an era where 'progressive' politics is often associated with transnational movements and alliances (for example Black Lives Matter, global LGBTQ+ movements, climate activism) while nationalism towards established states is looked on by some as regressive, I initially found my Dalit Buddhist friends' sincere identification as nationalists profoundly disconcerting. Since many of them believe that Buddhism was an ancient global religion and a present-day solution to world problems, I sometimes wondered why they called themselves nationalists, rather than *inter*nationalists, notwithstanding their apparent lack of interest in the political affairs of their Buddhist-majority neighbours.

After all, in *The Discovery of India* Nehru called for a 'fusion' between the ideals of nationalism, internationalism and proletarianism in order to maintain a 'world equilibrium and a lessening of conflict' (2004, p. 45), and dreamed of a time when his compatriots, proud 'of their Indian heritage' would open their hearts and minds to 'become citizens of this wide and fascinating world' (2004, p. 583). But it is perhaps unrealistic to expect social movements so focused on their own struggles to make the necessary adjustments in perspective to accommodate struggles from other parts of the world. Even with the best intentions, such attempts may in any case founder. Ambedkar was largely unsuccessful at forging international coalitions with other civil rights movements, and despite showy rhetoric in their manifesto, the Dalit Panthers, hampered by state oppression, were unable to 'utilize their offices to build active partnerships with social movements around the world' (Yengde, 2018, p.104).

Perhaps, despite many academics (myself included) fondly imagining themselves as participants in a progressive global struggle, large sections of the world's population are still more comfortable 'thinking and waging struggles at the national level' (Bourdieu, 2003, p. 43). Intuitive as it is to conceptualise a response to the rising populist-nationalist tide at an international or subnational level, we owe it to those opposing their majoritarian governments to acknowledge that for some of them, it is the level of the established nation that exerts the strongest hold on their imaginations.

Who is Indian, firstly and lastly?

Dalit Buddhists, victims of caste Hinduism and viewed with suspicion by the *Hindutva*-aligned state, are not the most obvious nationalists. However, my interlocutors proudly use this label and describe themselves as Indians, firstly and lastly. In doing so, they are eschewing separatism and sidelining globalism in favour of claiming a space in the discursive imagination of the nation, while remaining openly critical of the majoritarian state and making their own prescriptions for the future of India based on a very particular understanding of its history.

Ultimately, they are appealing for a redistribution of power and opportunity while also demanding recognition. Owing to their unique relationship with the Constitution through Ambedkar, and their understanding of their place in an ancient Buddhist India they are readily able to frame these appeals as *rashtrawadi,* or nationalism, while critiquing the Hinduism that has denied them both redistribution and recognition. And given their conception of a 'true' history of India that is, as yet, only known by a handful of enlightened individuals, they can logically reconcile universalist and differentiating impulses. They are in essence arguing that, since much of the rest of India is brainwashed by Hindu superstition and caste hierarchy, they *alone* are Indians, firstly and lastly, but that if their fellow Indians would only lift the veil of false history, those compatriots, too, would understand the deeper reality that 'We are *all* Indians, firstly and lastly'.

Notes

1 See 'About this book' in the Introduction.
2 Savarkar profoundly influenced K.B. Hedgewar, who founded the Rashtriya Swayamsevak Sangh (RSS), a vast paramilitary network of volunteers operating in *shakhas* (cells) across India with the aim of spreading *Hindutva* through social service, physical discipline and education. The BJP,

founded in 1980 but with roots in the earlier Bharatiya Jana Sangh, is one of the most prominent organisations affiliated to the RSS under the Sangh Parivar ('RSS family').

3   V. T. Rajshekar, former editor of polemic anti-caste periodical 'Dalit Voice', argued for an independent Dalitstan (1987, p. 69), as did some of the Tamil Christian Dalits interviewed by sociologist Hugo Gorringe (2008, p. 140). Since Dalit communities are found across India, there is no single obvious location for this imagined nation.

4   A particular focus of these protests has been the Citizenship (Amendment) Act (CAA) passed in December 2019, which offers a sped-up path to citizenship for migrants who fled religious persecution in Afghanistan, Pakistan or Bangladesh prior to December 2014. Muslims are excluded from this path, a policy described by critics as 'inconsistent with the basic structure of the Constitution' (PTI, 2019).

5   Gellner states that 'nationalism is not the awakening and assertion of these mythical, supposedly natural and given units', but rather a 'crystallization of new units ... using as their raw material the cultural, historical and other inheritances from the pre-nationalist world' (1983, p. 49).

6   It was in fact Nehru who insisted on including the Ashoka Chakra, which he saw as a universally appealing symbol of India's past as an international centre, in the place of the more culturally-specific *charkha* (spinning wheel) favoured by Gandhi (Roy, 2007, p. 511).

7   Ambedkar saw Christianity and Islam as having comparable advantages in terms of broad geographic distribution, political entitlements and financial resources. He rejected Christianity on the basis that it 'will help to strengthen the hold of the British on this country', and Islam because a large number of new converts would heighten the 'danger of Muslim domination' (quoted in Jaffrelot, 2005, p. 122). Conversion to either religion would 'denationalise' Dalits, unlike conversion to Sikhism which he also considered quite seriously in 1936–7 but ultimately rejected due to a variety of factors including concern over the status of existing Sikh Dalits (Jaffrelot, 2005, p. 130).

8   This linguistic discovery is usually attributed to British judge Sir William Jones who was tasked by the colonial judiciary with mastering Sanskrit, and wrote in 1786 that he found the language bore 'a stronger affinity' to Greek and Latin 'than could possibly have been produced by accident' (quoted in Anthony, 2007, p. 7).

9   For a nontechnical summary of this evidence, see Doniger (2009, pp. 86–102).

10 See Golwalkar (1939, pp. 77–8).

11 References to Aryan invaders conquering an indigenous Dalit population have been encountered by numerous anthropologists including Johannes Beltz, among Dalit Buddhist communities in Pune (Beltz, 2005, pp. 141–4) and Nicolas Jaoul witnessing an Ambedkarite Dalit procession in Kanpur, Uttar Pradesh (Jaoul, 2012, p. 110). Even Dalit Christians in South India have used these ideas to construct a theology that aims to recover an 'autochthonous, pre-Aryan, non-Sanskritic culture and identity', which rejects both *Hindutva* and a 'Hinduiz[ed]' Christianity that allowed caste to thrive (Mosse, 2012, p. 209).

12 Translating literally as 'World Council of Hindus', the VHP is another member of the Sangh Parivar, the 'family' of organisations spawned by the RSS.

13 Azad also pointed to the date of the Babri Masjid demolition (December 6th), claiming that this date, Ambedkar's death anniversary, was chosen 'deliberately to make people forget Babasaheb' (The Wire, 2018). As Hansen shows, Ambedkar's legacy was in fact instrumentalised by RSS and VHP leaders who, on the first anniversary celebrations of the mosque demolition, 'shower[ed] praise on Dr Ambedkar and condemn[ed] the practices of untouchability' while 'significantly downplay[ing]' the theme of *Hindutva* (Hansen, 1999, p. 226). Meanwhile, the importance of Ayodhya/Saket as a Buddhist site of historical significance has been championed by historian Hans Bakker who has argued that, for perhaps a thousand years, 'it was mainly Buddhism ... that determined the religious significance of the town on a supra-regional level' while 'the all-India importance of Ayodhya within Hinduism arose only during the second millennium' (1986, p. 36).

14 In a village context, Bahujan intellectual Kancha Ilaiah points out that it is through the daily interaction between Dalits and 'neo-Kshatriyas' (a category that Marathas might loosely be said to belong to) 'that unequal power relations are perpetuated' (1996, p. 38). Likewise, in everyday rural Maharashtra, Marathas rather than Brahmans have 'often appeared as direct exploiters, the main perpetrators of atrocities on the Dalits' (Omvedt, 1994, p. 198).

15 These riots reportedly started as a response to obscene comments about Hindu deities made at a Dalit Panther meeting convened to uphold an electoral boycott in protest against an RPI alliance

with Congress and the Shiv Sena (Rao, 2009, pp. 199–200). Stones, bottles and fluorescent light tubes were hurled between Hindu-dominated and Buddhist-dominated chawls, and 'symbols of Dalit pride, such as Ambedkar photos, were targeted' in a manner that Rao suggests 'were systematic attempts by Hindus to overthrow the neo-Buddhists' (2009, pp. 200–1).

16 Interestingly, several of my Dalit Buddhist friends from Chawls F and G told me they had no problem with the Chambhars of other buildings, and during my fieldwork year they attended a Chambhar wedding in Chawl N.

17 *Samyak* is an almost untranslatable word used in various Indic religious traditions including Buddhism with connotations of goodness, rightness and completeness.

18 This flag was initially designed in 1885 by the Colombo Committee in Sri Lanka (then Ceylon), and adopted by the World Fellowship of Buddhists in 1950.

19 Rahul Rao has also used the analytical frame of 'nationalism against the state' with respect to the prominence that the anti-CAA protests have accorded to the Constitution and the flag (Rao, 2020a).

20 There are some parallels between Dalit Buddhist nationalism and the 'visceral nationalism' that anthropologist Veronique Bénéï (2008, p. 195) encountered in a Muslim-run school in Kolhapur, west Maharashtra. Muslims, even more than Dalits, are presumed to be anti-national in majoritarian Hindu discourse and the school's medium of instruction was Urdu, which is the official language of Pakistan as well being closely associated with India's Muslim community. Bénéï describes the eagerness with which the teachers and students demonstrated their loyalty to the nation in daily performances of the national anthem and pledge of allegiance, and more elaborate parades on national holidays (2008, p. 197). These are not simply 'ostentatious' displays for self-preservation, Bénéï argues, but reflect a 'deep-seated sense of belonging' embedded in an understanding of Indian history that elevates the 'glorious contribution' of past Islamic rulers, thus forging a connection to the wider Muslim world without relinquishing India's claim to Kashmir or claiming any special relationship to Pakistan (Bénéï, 2008, pp. 191–200).

More generally, a consistent pan-India Dalit–Muslim political unity in the face of Hindu nationalism has thus far proved elusive (see Kumar and Ansari, 2022), perhaps unsurprisingly given the lack of any pan-Dalit unity. Of the myriad protests that erupted across India in response to the Citizenship (Amendment) Act (see endnotes 4 and 19, this chapter), many featured symbolic displays of Dalit–Muslim unity, often including public readings of the Constitution, for example in Delhi at the Jama Masjid and Shaheen Bagh (Rao, 2020b). Hyderabad MP Asaduddin Owaisi, who also led such readings of the Constitution (Rao, 2020b) entered his All India Majlis-e-Ittehadul Muslimeen party in coalition with Prakash Ambedkar's Vanchit Bahujin Aghadi in the 2019 Maharashtra State Elections, but this alliance was short-lived. My Dalit Buddhist interlocutors never spoke to me about the potential of such alliances and in general seemed to maintain a sympathetic distance from debates about the plight of India's Muslims.

21 There is a striking resemblance between Anish's description of Buddha as the first scientist and Sri Lankan diplomat Dr G.P. Malalasekera's much earlier claim that 'The Buddha was the first great scientist to appear among men … [and] discovered what scientists have only now discovered' (quoted in Gombrich, 1988, p. 196), as well as political activist Dilanthe Withanage's view of Buddhism as 'the most scientific, most logical philosophy we can think of' (interviewed in Schonthal, 2016, p. 105).

5
Village histories, urban futures

With their corner shrines and framed images of deities, the first Gramastha Mandals I encountered were visibly Hindu places. Curious, I asked Vaibhav from Borgaon Gramastha Mandal whether Borgaonkars of different religions came to live in his room. Yes, he said, there are people of many religions living together. On my pressing him for specifics, he clarified that technically he was referring to 'sub-religions' which he listed as 'Maratha, OBC, General Caste and SC'. When he referred to 'SC' (Scheduled Castes), I asked, did he mean Dalit Buddhists or Dalit Hindus? Actually, he explained, there are no Buddhists in Borgaon, hence there are no Buddhists in the Borgaon Gramastha Mandal. Likewise, there are no Muslims in the village and only a few Catholics, none of whom are currently in Mumbai.

In search of corroboration, on my next visit to a Borgaon Gramastha Mandal room I asked one of the boys whether there were any Buddhists living in the room. 'In another room', he replied, to my surprise.

'Why not in this room?'

'Because of casteism,' one of his roommates chipped in.

'Gaon mei aisa rehte,' (it's like that in the village) said a third.

I asked where the room was, and after some discussion they told me it was in Chawl F or G, the buildings in which many of my Jay Bhim Katta friends lived. By this time Vaibhav had come in and I said I would like to meet the Borgaon Buddhists.

'Any particular reason?' he asked, smiling, but – it seemed to me – a little suspicious.

'Just for my research,' I said, pulling out my usual trump card.

'OK, I will definitely give you a phone number by tonight.'

'What if I just visit and say that I'm friends with you and the others?'

'Yes, yes, but we don't know their schedule.'

No phone number materialised that night, or in the days and weeks that followed, but a few afternoons later, Anish beckoned to me from the Jay Bhim Katta and pointed out an upstairs window in Chawl N, Mahendra's building. Did I know, he asked me, that that room was also a Gramastha Mandal, and that only Buddhists lived there. Intrigued, I slipped off as soon as I politely could and headed directly to the room Anish had pointed to. I knocked on the door, which was labelled Jay Bhim. A few men were sitting inside and I explained that I was a researcher and a friend of Anish, whereupon they immediately invited me in.

None of the men recognised the name Vaibhav, and it transpired that this room was not linked to Borgaon village as I had supposed but was open to residents of four different villages. One of these was Amrutwadi, the same village that gives Vikas' Amrutwadi Gramastha Mandal its name. The others were all in the Ajara *taluka* of Kolhapur, and included a village adjoining Katkarwadi, and another called Dorli. When I asked them whether the room had a name, they simply said they call it *sarvajanik* (public), but I started thinking of it as the 'Buddhist Gramastha Mandal'. They told me that Hindus were welcome to come and chat with them in the room, but only Buddhists were allowed to live there. At the time, 18 men of widely varying ages lived in this room, mostly working in the same kind of low-paid occupations as many of their Hindu counterparts – drivers, security guards and office clerks.

In many respects, the room was similar to all the other Gramastha Mandals I had visited, with trunks stacked on shelves midway up a partly-tiled wall, and a mezzanine *potmala* above the *mori* which had the usual complement of pots and water butts. A cluster of tiffin containers aroused my suspicion, later confirmed, that the room residents got their meals from a mess. However, the corner shrine, a focal point of any Hindu Gramastha Mandal, was absent, and in place of the usual images of Hindu deities were framed pictures of Ambedkar, the Buddha, Phule, and Shahuji Maharaj of Kolhapur. A gap in the gallery was explained, by Pravin from Amrutwadi, as the space where a picture of Shivaji had hung until someone accidentally knocked it on the floor. The welcome I received in this room was certainly as generous as in any other Gramastha Mandal, and I took to visiting on a regular basis.

Meanwhile, Vaibhav kindly took me himself to visit the room for Borgaon Buddhists (in Chawl F) a few weeks after the initial conversation we had had on the topic. He seemed a little reluctant, reminding me en route that his fellow villagers there would give me exactly the same information that he already had. I decided not to call him out on his earlier misstatement that there were no Buddhists in the village; perhaps he had misunderstood my question, I speculated, or maybe I had misunderstood his answer. Once inside, we met one of the room's four residents, who Vaibhav introduced as an old school friend. They seemed on friendly terms and there was no discernible awkwardness between them. When I made a return visit to the room a week later, the friend asked me how Vaibhav was and reiterated that he and Vaibhav were old friends but they do not see much of each other now since they work in different jobs.

Borgaon Gramastha Mandal is not alone in its restrictive eligibility criteria. As far as I could ascertain, 11 out of the 18 Gramastha Mandals I interacted with were restricted to Hindus, and some of these explicitly limited their entry to Marathas. Aside from the Chawl N 'Buddhist Gramastha Mandal' room, and the room in Chawl F for Borgaon Buddhists, I did not encounter any other Buddhist-only Gramastha Mandals, although four Hindu-majority Gramastha Mandals had a few Buddhist members living alongside the Hindus in their rooms. There is also a Buddhist-run cooperative bank (*patpedhi*) in Chawl Q, providing a small dormitory for Buddhist migrants from Ajara *taluka*.

By and large, the Buddhist Gramastha Mandal residents seemed to be a little more involved in the wider BDD Chawls Buddhist community than were many of the Hindu Gramastha Mandal residents with the Hindu community. While Tukaram and his friends laughed at my interest in the Bandya Maruti Seva Mandal, Pravin and others were members of the Yuvak Kranti Seva Mandal, linked to Chawls F and G. They joined in the candlelit march on Ambedkar's death anniversary, and several of them took part in an expedition on 31 December to commemorate a Mahar military victory at Bhima Koregaon village (see Chapter 6). This may be the result of a more conscious attempt by the Jay Bhim Katta circle to include rather than exclude. Even so, there was no mistaking the amusement with which Anish and his friends viewed the attention I paid to my Gramastha Mandal friends, none of whom were regulars at the Jay Bhim Katta.

Kunduri (2018) argues that while 'the process of migration is strongly represented as a means of breaking away from traditional hierarchies', caste identities 'often provide context and meaning(s) to how the migration process is envisaged'. In this chapter I probe this context and meaning, questioning the common narrative that urban migration can break down community divisions in favour of a deeper village solidarity (see Rowe, 1973, p. 229). By analysing the Gramastha Mandals as sites in which exclusionary village history is reproduced and reconfigured, I show that the process by which village migrants become city dwellers has had a profound role in solidifying broader patterns of division in the BDD Chawls. Whether the current trend towards settling permanently in Mumbai's outer suburbs and satellite cities will disrupt these patterns or not remains unclear. I further consider the different impacts of the mill closures and ensuing economic liberalisation on community relations in the Gramastha Mandals, demonstrating how divisions have been softened in some cases and potentially exacerbated in others. Overall, I conclude that, on migrating to Mumbai, Hindus and Buddhists construct their village-based identity too differently to bring them together as *gaon bhai* (village brothers) in any meaningful sense, but I nevertheless end the chapter on a faint note of hope.

'We are all Marathas': importing rural divisions

Next to remittances, I found the question of eligibility and exclusion in Gramastha Mandals one of the most challenging to research. Asking questions about caste felt awkward and also intrusive, since it drew attention to my researcher status in an unambiguous way that a question about types of mess food available or the timings of water-pipe flow did not. When I brought the topic up, it was often in a deliberately nonchalant manner that suggested it was something that had occurred to me on the spur of the moment and did not really matter to any great extent. Unsurprisingly, the information I came by was often confusing and sometimes downright contradictory. For example, I asked Sameer on two occasions who could live in his Gaowadi Gramastha Mandal room, and both times he told me that anybody from Gaowadi was welcome. In addition to Hindus there are Dalit Buddhists, Christians and Muslims in the village, and there are no restrictions on any of them joining the room, although he noted that those communities do not tend to come to Mumbai for work.

On a visit to Sameer's room, however, a different story emerged as his fellow Gaowadikars informed me pointedly that '*Ham log sab Maratha hain*' (we are all Marathas). Eventually I asked them whether they would allow other communities, like Dalit Buddhists, to live in their room. '*Nahin!*' (No) they roared in response, and Sameer made a punching motion with his fist. There was a lot of noisy discussion, during which one resident said that '*Ve log a sakte hain, lekin ve nahin ate hain*' (those people *can* come, but they don't come), while others said that Dalits could stay in the room for a few days but wouldn't be allowed to live there permanently. I asked whether there was any rule to this effect, but while this prompted further discussion it did not result in any agreement.

In general, I found it very difficult to gauge the exact status or cause of these community-based restrictions, since Gramastha Mandals do not tend to have written constitutions. In Bhandewadi Gramastha Mandal, and a few parallel cases, I was told that room places were only open to descendants of the original residents, all of whom had been Hindu. In two other cases, Katkarwadi included, the caste profile of the room was simply explained as a reflection of village demographics: since only Hindus lived in the village, the only people who could join the Gramastha Mandal were Hindu. In some of the other Gramastha Mandals with restrictive eligibility criteria the reasoning was less clear. Some residents simply shrugged, saying *'niyam hai'* (it's the rule) or openly attributing it to casteism, as Vaibhav's friends in Borgaon Gramastha Mandal had. 'It's a mentality, not a rule,' explained Yogesh, from Amrutwadi Gramastha Mandal, while one of the Buddhists from the Chawl N Gramastha Mandal said of the Hindus in his village that:

> Unke sochne ka tarika alag rehte, hamare sochne ka tarika alag rehte, to … unko inconvenient rahega, yahan rehne.
> (Ananda, interview, 7 January 2018)

> (Their way of thinking is different from ours, so … it would be inconvenient for them to live here).

The bluntest example of this mentality came out during my (JG) interview with Mahadev, a resident of Chincholi Gramastha Mandal in Chawl E:

JG: *Gaon mein sab Maratha jati se hain ya alag-alag jati se bhi …?* (In the village is everyone from the Maratha caste, or do other castes also live there?)

Mahadev: *Hai na. Hindu hain, Muslim hain. Ye kaun sa? Bal katnewala kaun hain?... Barber* (Yes others too. Hindus, Muslims and what do you call them? Barbers.)

JG: *Nhavi? Hindu hai na?* (Nhavi [a barber caste]? They're Hindus, right?)

Mahadev: *Hindu Nhavi. Hindu Chambhar. Hindu Mhang. Sab jat ka rehte.* (Hindu barbers, Hindu Chamars, Hindu Mang. All castes live there.)

JG: *Jay Bhim?* (Dalit Buddhists?)

Mahadev: *Jay Bhim* (Yes, Dalit Buddhists.)

JG: *Aur sab jati se room mein a sakta hain?* (And can all these castes come to the room?)

Mahadev: *Nahin, nahin, nahin, nahin* [echoed vigorously by the room]. *Khali Hindu. Maratha.* (No, no, no, no! Only Hindus. Marathas.)

JG: *Kyon? Kya niyam hai?* (Why? Is that a rule?)

Mahadev: *Niyam kya malum hai? Vo log barobar achcha rehte nahin. Ghanda rehte… Is ke liye… Aur khud bhi ghanda rehte aur jagah bhi ghanda karege. Is ke liye un ko allowed nahin.* (What do I know about rules? Them lot don't live properly. They're dirty … So … And if you're dirty yourself, the place you live is also going to be dirty. So for this reason they're not allowed.)

(Mahadev, interview, 3 December 2017)

Abhinav, from Jhambe Gramastha Mandal, told me that there are a few Christians and Muslims in Jhambe, but 'We are more concerned to Hindus' due to their majority. Nevertheless, he added, other communities are welcome to apply to stay in the room and their application will be considered by the Gramastha Mandal committee, although in practice this has not happened. After several minutes of dancing round the elephant in the room, he leaned towards me:

Errr … To tell you very frankly, for Buddhists the entry is not allowed … Because you know, during the foundation of these rooms … Everyone was supposed to do [a] fund which, you know, will be a helping hand to us to buy a room … but [the Dalit Buddhists] they strictly refused. At that time they said: "No we are not interested in this concept, and we will not give you anything, and we will not come with you in future as well." … [So] the restrictions are being made, and due to that they are not allowed … It has been strictly decided.

(Abhinav, interview in English, 11 December 2017)

A similar situation was described to me by Sunil and others from Kingaon Gramastha Mandal who explained that when the rooms were purchased 30–40 years ago, only certain village members paid shares towards them. Since no Buddhist paid for shares, they are still excluded from the room.

Of course, these accounts simply shift the cause back to the villages themselves. Sunil told me bluntly that Dalit Buddhists live in a separate part of Kingaon. 'I don't know them so I have no information … They cannot come to our room. They cannot come into our area [in Kingaon]. I can talk to them but I don't make friends with them. I don't like. Not only me. All Hindus.'

Spatial divisions between castes and religious communities in Indian villages have been described extensively by social scientists, anthropologists and of course the resident chroniclers of the villages themselves. Kancha Ilaiah, for example, sets out with painful clarity the way Dalits and dominant castes lived almost entirely separate lives in his natal village in Telangana, their houses in different parts of the village and their lifestyles, languages, religions and occupations dividing them culturally and psychologically as well as physically (1996, pp. 1–19). In Maharashtra, as Rao describes, the separate 'residential area for Dalits, called the Maharwada or Baudhwada, is usually located at the southern end of the village, and is almost always outside the village boundary' (2009, p. 230).[1] Dalit literature in Marathi abounds with references to the Maharwada: Shankarrao Kharat (2009) recounts searching round the Maharwada for bones to sell to an itinerant bone merchant, while for Sharankumar Limbale (2009) it was the site of an illicit affair. Most poignantly, in his autobiography *Baluta*, Daya Pawar tells readers that the image of the Maharwada of his childhood 'lingers with me forever' (Pawar, 2009, p. 98).

In addition to Sunil, other interlocutors made occasional references to such spatial divisions in their villages, some suggesting that the boundaries were slowly being eroded. However, Sayaji's city-born son Dinesh, who had moved to his grandfather's village in Ratnagiri for work, implied divisions remain strong:

> In Konkan side the people, they are not mixed up. All Muslims stays in mohalla ... where the Buddhists live that is called Buddhawadi. Where all the ... Chambhakars live ... so it's called Chamarwada. Where the Marathas live, it's called Marathawad.
> (Dinesh, interview in English, 20 December 2017)

Gaon bhai in the city? Reconfiguring rural divisions

Should we be surprised that divisions encoded through centuries of village life are reproduced in cities? Or, if not exactly reproduced, then – to a certain extent at least – *reconfigured* in the social structures and built environment of the city? Dandekar, reflecting on her dominant-caste research assistant's friendship with a Dalit in Bombay, hints at the opposite with her observation that 'friendships and alliances are established' in the city 'that could never flower in the jealous village' (Dandekar, 1986, p. 254).

This is hardly a novel proposition, and the idea of the city as a place where people are 'set loose from the structures of kin and clan, free to mix, mingle and run amok' is a common enough trope in fiction and news media, and a 'familiar refrain for anthropologists' (Ring, 2006, p. 19).[2]

In a Chennai slum, Nathaniel Roberts records his Dalit interlocutors' insistence that caste exists in the village of the past and not in the present-day city, although he interprets this claim as a response to painful memories and a determination to look forward (2016, pp. 54–8). Many of my research participants told a similar story of Mumbai as a place where everybody mixed together, in contrast to the village, where conservative dominant-caste grandparents were still rumoured to prohibit Dalits entering their houses and to offer them water in special glasses they kept separately to avoid contamination.

This is a common narrative of Mumbai, or perhaps more accurately Bombay, which has been fabled as a place of 'intensity, heterogeneity and … radical mixing' (Hansen and Verkaaik, 2009, p. 10). Prior to the 1992–3 riots, Hansen argues, the city was 'marked by a relatively high degree of ethnically mixed neighbourhoods' (2001, p. 160). Relatively high, perhaps, but evidence suggests that social fragmentation along community lines has always been a feature of Bombay's neighbourhoods (Kosambi, 1995, p. 8; Masselos, 2019, p. 311; Wacha, 1920, pp. 425–8). While 'most of the settlements in Mumbai are fairly mixed', Govind Narayan reflected in 1863, residents usually 'prefer to stay close to members of their own caste' (Ranganathan, 2008, p. 130).

In a 1960s study of a Maharashtrian village, Valunjkar noted that most of the Mahars who migrate to Mumbai stay in the same chawl, since 'persons migrated to the places where their kinsmen and castemen were situated' (Valunjkar, 1966, p. 72). However, other studies of village migration and specifically Gramastha Mandals tend either to be silent on issues of caste or to celebrate the *'esprit de corps'* found in the city, in contrast to the village (Dandekar, 1986, p. 255). In his 1973 study of migration to Mumbai from Senapur village in Uttar Pradesh, Rowe argues that among migrants in the city the 'ideal of all men of a village being *gaon bhai*, or village brothers, has greater meaning' and that 'relationships among men of different castes but of the same village may be much warmer and closer than in the village' (1973, p. 229).

To what extent do Hindu Vaibhav and the Borgaon Buddhists embody the ideal of being *gaon bhai*? The general impression I could gather from stray remarks and observations was of a cordial, if somewhat distant relationship between Hindu and Buddhist Gramastha Mandal residents from the same villages. Pravin, from the Chawl N Buddhist

Gramastha Mandal, explained that *'British samay mein'* (during the British time) there were over 10 rooms in the building for Mahar migrants from different villages, and there had been frequent brawls between Mahar and Maratha migrants. Even Ambedkar had once paid a visit to this very room, Pravin told me, in a bid to restore peace.

Today, Pravin and his friends insisted, no such tensions existed between Buddhists and Marathas. Since they were all from Amrutwadi, I asked them if they had attended the Independence Day celebrations held in the (Hindu) Amrutwadi Gramastha Mandal room. Pravin said he had, although his roommate had instead celebrated Independence Day with the Jay Bhim Katta crowd outside Chawl F and G. Likewise Ananda, a Buddhist from a village called Dorli, told me he knew and mixed with the residents of Dorli's Hindu-only Gramastha Mandal in a building near the BDD Chawls, meeting them for tea and snacks when they had time. They also invited him and fellow Dorli Buddhists to their annual *puja*.

Overall, Hindus and Buddhists alike seemed at pains to point out that they had no problem mixing socially with each other, but that living together is a different matter. Amid the confusion in the Gaowadi room, the one thing that all the residents agreed on was that, as Hindus, they do not eat beef, and hence they cannot eat at Dalit homes. Several of them attempted to soften their earlier bigotry by pointing out that they had Dalit friends. What really struck me in my interview with Mahadev, moreover, was not so much the casual casteism but the fact that, minutes beforehand, he had been telling me with every appearance of sincerity how he still kept in touch with and sometimes visited his Muslim ex-neighbours who had gradually left Chawl E for the suburb of Mumbra after the 1992–3 riots.

Even if there is no active animosity between Hindu and Buddhist individuals from the same village, however, the structure of Gramastha Mandal living makes in-group socialising much easier than between-group socialising. In-group socialising can occur simply by being in the Gramastha Mandal room and is hence woven into the fabric of everyday life, while Hindu–Buddhist mixing requires a conscious effort to bridge the gap between separate living spaces and uncertain schedules.

This structure runs deeper than the spatial separation of Gramastha Mandals, of course, since whole buildings are organised – some loosely, some more strictly – along community lines. This does not seem to have been the result of any official allocation policy. A 1923 *Labour Gazette* article reports that the Bombay Development Department made large-scale allocations of chawl rooms to the 'working class' (Punekar et al., 1988, p. 338). Although couched in class terms, in practice this probably referred to caste. As Vanessa Caru explains, due to difficulties faced by untouchable communities in finding housing, 'various associations argued for government aid through the provision of rooms in ... [the] BDD Chawls', and hence requests were made for the allotment of rooms for the 'Depressed Classes' (2011, pp. 33–4). Pendse et al. imply that these, and other, room allocations were made evenly across all buildings, rather than in specific buildings, in an attempt to 'homogenize' the chawls 'along linguistic and caste lines' (2011, p. 3).

If official policy was to promote community integration, how did today's segregation come about? Piecing together the evidence I presented in Chapter 3, I suggest that male-only dormitories, including but perhaps not limited to Gramastha Mandals, were one of the most common forms of habitation in the BDD Chawls until the second half of the twentieth century, and that many of the chawls' social institutions, such as Mitra Mandals, were established by Gramastha Mandal migrants themselves. Only gradually did this bachelor-dominated community give way to the families that now predominate in the neighbourhood, and a common mechanism by which this occurred was when migrants brought their families to live with them, in some cases in the same building.

It has similarly been argued that 'the initial single migrant and later the families imported the village or subdivision (tahsil/taluka) specificities to their neighbourhood' and it was precisely the 'concentration of population brought about by the chawl' that allowed this level of cultural specificity to be maintained in the city (Pendse et al., 2011, p. 3). So it is that in Chawl K I met families with links to Borgaon and Katkarwadi, villages that own multiple Gramastha Mandal rooms in the same building, and in Chawl M I knew a family with roots in the same village as that of the Gramastha Mandal directly across the corridor. And a few young men who I encountered as Gramastha Mandal residents had actually grown up in the same chawl, only shifting to the Gramastha Mandal when their parents retired to the village.

Importantly, it is for this reason that Chawls C, D, J, K and M, where so many of the Maratha-only or Maratha-dominated Gramastha Mandals have rooms, house families that are not only from the same part of southern Kolhapur District as the bachelor migrants, but are also almost all Marathas themselves. While chawl living enabled a degree of 'amalgamation between different castes – often through romances and marriages' (and, I would add, through structures like the Mitra Mandals) Dalits were often 'assiduously excluded from the buildings ... and not allowed to mix freely with others' in defiance of government regulations (Pendse et al., 2011, p. 3). There is clearly nothing incidental about the fact that the two Buddhist-only Gramastha Mandals I encountered are in Chawl F and Chawl N, and the Buddhist-run cooperative bank is in Chawl Q. All these buildings, according to their older residents, were once almost entirely occupied by Dalits and remain predominantly Dalit even today.

As far as living arrangements are concerned, then, there is no obvious reason why migration to Mumbai will necessarily bring Hindus and Buddhists any closer together than they are in the village. Community divisions are perpetuated by the Gramastha Mandal migration mechanism and, as a consequence, are still embedded to a certain extent into the demographic layout of the BDD Chawls.

What about the role of work, and in particular the impact of the mill closures on this social reality? Sumeet Mhaskar disputes the claims of 'modernisation theorists' that India's economic liberalisation of the 1990s should replace caste-, religion- and gender-based discrimination with egalitarian conceptions of 'efficiency and skill', demonstrating that Muslim ex-millworkers face discriminatory hiring practices in contemporary Mumbai and are underrepresented in service sectors while overrepresented in 'ghettoised' repair and processing industries (2013, p. 149). Elsewhere he concludes that neoliberal restructuring has simply 'reworked' existing factors that disadvantage Muslims, such as the *karahiyat* (abhorrence, disgust) with which caste Hindus perceive Muslims as beef-eaters living in unclean neighbourhoods (Mhaskar, 2018, pp. 31–6). His observation that these perceptions also apply to Dalits in Mumbai (Mhaskar, 2018; 2013) is borne out by my own: beef-eating and uncleanliness were precisely the terms in which the Gaowadikars and Mahadev justified their inability to share a living space with Dalits.

Since I only met a handful of Buddhist Gramastha Mandal migrants, my conclusions regarding occupational patterns in the post-mill era are cautious. Today's Buddhist migrants are typically drivers, security guards and office clerks. While these roles overlap with those of many of the Hindu migrants, the white-collar professions (like those of civil engineer Rohan or IT manager Abhinav) appear to be missing among the Buddhists. Likewise, none of the Buddhist migrants I encountered were pursuing further education in Mumbai, although Ananda (and quite possibly others) had completed a Bachelor of Arts in Ajara, the nearest small town to his village. In light of this patchy evidence, I can only suggest that these better-paid corporate professions remain a rarity among Gramastha Mandal migrants, for whom low-paying precarious positions are the norm, and exceptional cases appear to be the preserve of a handful of Marathas.

That the type of job a person does will impact on the extent to which they interact with their colleagues is well-documented. For example, in a study of community relations in a Mumbai manufacturing plant, Panjwani (1984) found that, in general, workers from different backgrounds 'may spend their entire occupational lives working [together] ... without visiting each other's homes' or socialising together (1984, p. 281). Only in the small, stable and highly-skilled team working in the foundry section was camaraderie found to extend beyond working hours (Panjwani, 1984, p. 283). A somewhat similar study by M.S. Gore (1970) also suggests a positive correlation between education or skill level and a propensity to form connections with people of a different community background. These findings do not, in the short term at least, bode well for an increased level of intercommunity mixing among the precarious workers that constitute the majority of Gramastha Mandal migrants in the post-mill era.

Becoming urban

There is much, it seems, in city life, that militates against the ideal of being first and foremost *gaon bhai*. In particular, it is the process by which village migrants become city dwellers that has itself had a profound role in cementing the building-wise segregation of communities in the BDD Chawls. In earlier decades, however, numbers opting to settle permanently in Mumbai were low, and for most, the Gramastha Mandal room represented an interlude in the lives of most of its circular migrant residents. In the 1980s, Dandekar observed that 'most migrants cannot save enough to buy an apartment or live in the city after retirement, [so] they must retire to Sugao'. The handful of 'educated middle-class' migrants who managed to buy property in the city were 'exceptions rather than the rule' (Dandekar, 1986, p. 244). Over a decade earlier, Gore found that over half the Marathi-speaking migrants he interviewed wished to retire to their villages, many having already made definite arrangements to do so, while less than 10 per cent wished to stay in Mumbai (1970, p. 146).

Today, numerous ex-residents of Gramastha Mandals now own rooms in the BDD Chawls and live there with their families, such as the husband of Tukaram's *khanavalwali* Kanchan as well as some of those involved in the running of the Mitra Mandals. The demographic shift from bachelor-dominated to family-dominated, and the accompanying accretion of an urban identity based on belonging and rights, is succinctly conveyed in Prasad Shetty's fictional history of a chawl he calls Ganga Building:

> Once primarily male labour-dormitories, the chawls began changing into housing colonies for [the migrants'] families. The tenement occupancy changed from a set of friends to an extended family. This new sense of property created a new city; a city where people had claims, where people not only came to earn money to send to their village, but more often came to settle and join in with the city's destiny.
>
> (Shetty, 2011, p. 61)

One who joined in with the city's destiny was Datta, whose job history as a compounder, waiter, millworker and currently Conscious Foods packer I outlined in Chapter 3. He was not educated beyond his early teens and can hardly be said to belong to Dandekar's 'educated middle class'. Due to his father's early death, it was Datta's responsibility to look after his brother Nutan's education from a young age, hence his shift to Mumbai aged 12. Thirteen years later, in 1985, Nutan joined him in the same Katkarwadi Gramastha Mandal room and, some time after this, the extended family arranged Datta's marriage to a girl from a nearby village. After marriage, he continued to live in Mumbai while his wife, and later son and daughter, lived in Katkarwadi and he might only see them once a year.

In 1994, more than 20 years after leaving the village, Datta teamed up with his brother to buy a room in BDD Chawl U. Nutan lived there with his wife for a few years before moving to the satellite suburb of Vashi for work, whereupon the brothers rented out the room for another 20 years. During this time, Datta's son Ajay came to study in Vashi, living with Nutan and his family, before going to Kolhapur city for a further engineering course. Meanwhile his wife and daughter remained in Katkarwadi until the daughter got selected for the Maharashtra police and also came to live in Vashi. Throughout this time, Datta stayed in the Katkarwadi Gramastha Mandal, and it was only in 2014, when Ajay's studies were complete and he started working, that father, mother, son and daughter moved together into the family-owned room in Chawl U. The family still own property in Katkarwadi but the house remains empty except when they visit, and they have allowed others to make use of their land without paying any rent. Ajay previously had a girlfriend, but they split up some time back and he is now preparing for an arranged marriage in the next two years. Once his son's life 'barobar chalte hai' (is running smoothly), Datta and his wife, who are bored of living in Mumbai, plan to move back to their house in Katkarwadi and live out their retirement there.

Datta's story is not unusual, although it is probable that even in 1994 he belonged to a substantial minority, rather than a majority, who bought property and continued to live in Mumbai. Tukaram's father, for example, is one of six cousins who came to work in Mumbai, and, out of these six, two have bought property in the city while the other four have returned to Katkarwadi. Today, however, the experiences of my interlocutors would suggest that it is becoming increasingly common to buy property in Mumbai with a view to settling more permanently.

Furthermore, new ways of settling in the city are becoming popular. Rather than buying chawl rooms in Lower Parel, as Datta did, most opt to buy flats in one of Mumbai's satellite cities such as Kalyan, Virar or Nallasopara where property prices are considerably cheaper. I was surprised by the number of migrants who already owned a flat but chose to rent it out while remaining in the Gramastha Mandal rooms, as Datta had done until 2014. In many cases they planned to move after getting married but a number of others, like Datta, were still living in the Gramastha Mandal room several years after their marriage and the birth of one or more children back in the village. Of those who did not own their own flat, several were saving money for a future purchase and for this reason had been excused from remitting money home. Some were even anticipating financial support from their parents in buying a flat. Tukaram told me that this was the case, although typically his plans were fluid and hard to pin down, sometimes featuring a flat in nearby Dadar or far-off Panvel, to be purchased jointly with his brother, and sometimes a featuring a flat of his own in Pune or Bangalore. A few years after my fieldwork was complete, he moved into a flat in the suburb of Dombivli where he is now living with his brother and sister-in-law as well as his parents who have moved from Katkarwadi. The family continues to divide its time between Mumbai and the village.

Tukaram's dreams aside, moving from Mumbai to other cities does not appear to be a particularly popular option. A number of Katkarwadi Gramastha Mandal residents shifted to live in shared accommodation with other Katkarwadikars in Pune during my fieldwork period, and Vipin moved to Kolhapur although this was intended as a temporary move followed by a return to Mumbai. I only heard of a few cases of moving outside Maharashtra, including Nutan, Datta's younger brother, who now lives in Hyderabad, and another former Katkarwadi Gramastha Mandal resident who had worked in Qatar and Nigeria, although had since settled in Dombivli.

Moving itself can be a phased process. Saurabh from Katkarwadi owns a flat in Kalyan and stays there at weekends with his wife, brother and sister-in-law. During the week he still lives in the Katkarwadi Gramastha Mandal room as this is more convenient for his work as a security guard during the day and bouncer at night. I met others who usually lived full time in their own homes but had returned for six months or so to their previous Gramastha Mandal accommodation while their wives had returned to their villages to give birth. They made no secret of the fact that they were relishing the shorter commute to work in the city centre and enjoying the camaraderie of bachelor life.

Even among those who have moved out more completely, many maintain a close relationship with their Gramastha Mandal, irrespective of whether they live in local chawls or distant suburbs. Several Gramastha Mandal committees are run by former residents, like the president of Kingaon Gramastha Mandal who lives in Virar and comes back for committee meetings. Former room members also return in force for the Gramastha Mandal-based functions that replicate annual village festivals or national celebrations. They sometimes bring their wives and children and generally make themselves at home in their old rooms. At a *puja* in honour of folk-deity Mhasoba in Katkarwadi Gramastha Mandal, for example, Tukaram snidely referred to the crush of middle-aged men taking up space in his room as show-offs who only come back to flaunt their success. At Borgaon Gramastha Mandal's Mahalaxmi festival, celebrated in January in the space between Chawl J and K, a former resident told me he found coming to the BDD Chawls from his Kalyan flat an easy alternative to travelling back for the full-scale festival, which is celebrated in Borgaon on the same day. In effect, the Gramastha Mandal has become another point of return alongside the village.

Given the frequently-articulated claims about the uniqueness of open-door chawl culture, any new identity that emerges among these new suburban homeowners is likely to be rather different from that of the Mitra Mandal stalwarts whose sense of belonging is rooted in chawlness. The impact this might have on intercommunity mixing is also unclear, although global literature on relocation to high-rise blocks suggests that a radical decline in mixing of any kind, in favour of a more insular domestic life, is a likely outcome (Coleman, 1985; Ghannam, 2002; Tamburo, 2020). In Mumbai specifically, the preponderance of housing blocks that restrict eligibility to vegetarians and hence, by implication, dominant-caste Hindus and Jains (cf. Holwitt, 2017), might signal an even further decline in the 'radical mixing' that Bombay-nostalgists already lament so enthusiastically. In short, there is no compelling reason to assume that the trend of buying property in Mumbai's far-flung suburbs will do anything more to reunite sundered village brothers than settling permanently in the BDD Chawls did in previous generations. (Hansen and Verkaaik, 2009, p. 10)

Gaon bhai in the future: disrupting rural divisions?

One result of the mill closures that might actually have the effect of softening rural divides is the marked decrease in occupant numbers of each room. Some Gramastha Mandals are taking in occupants from other villages, while others are renting out whole rooms to families and yet others have sold off one or more of their rooms altogether. In a few cases, however, formerly Hindu-only Gramastha Mandals have opened their doors to Dalit Buddhists. Shiravali Gramastha Mandal, for example, although still dominated by Marathas, now has a small group of OBC and Dalit Buddhist residents. When Namdeo, an older Maratha resident, arrived in 1997 the Gramastha Mandal had a rule restricting residency to dominant-caste Hindus. Once the men of his father's generation retired and left for the village, the remaining residents relaxed the eligibility criteria to include any (male) resident of Shiravali. Namdeo did not specify whether this was principally a result of the younger generation's more relaxed approach to caste purity, or whether it was part of a strategy to broaden the pool of potential rent payers.

One of the Buddhist residents works as a security guard, like the majority of the room members, although unlike his Hindu roommates he does not belong to the Security Guards Board. It was not clear to me whether this was the result of deliberate exclusion, but in the limited interactions I observed, he seemed well-integrated into the social life of the room although I never not got the chance to talk to him individually. However, Namdeo and his fellow Hindu roommates laughed at my suggestion that they put up a picture of Ambedkar alongside the images of Hindu deities, telling me that their Buddhist roommates are not 'proud' of being Buddhist and instead worship alongside them at the room's Hindu shrine. While this sounds like peer pressure of the most egregious kind, it must be remembered that not all Dalit Buddhists are as principled in their rejection of Hindu worship as are my interlocutors at the Jay Bhim Katta (cf. Beltz, 2005, pp. 188–9). Indeed, a resident of Chawl Q once joked that he and his friends were Buddhists that had 'not fully converted'.

Three other Gramastha Mandals had similar eligibility rules, while a fourth, although currently restricted to Marathas from the village, had relaxed an even more stringent earlier policy restricting entry to Maratha *millworkers* and their descendants. One of the younger room members confided in me that the Maratha-only policy restriction was an old one, and he personally thought the room should be opened up to others, including Buddhists.

Furthermore, in contrast to the general picture I have drawn of increasing fragmentation, I heard a number of encouraging stories of cross-community mixing, such as that of the Buddhist Gramastha Mandal migrants who took part in wedding celebrations hosted by the Hindu family that lived opposite them. On one of my visits to their room, in fact, I accompanied Pravin and a few of his friends to their Hindu *khanavalwali's* room down the corridor, where we were given tea and biscuits. Pravin said that this kind of social mixing was completely normal now, although acknowledged that it had only become the case in the last two or three decades. But people are educated now, he said, and have left caste behind, both in Mumbai and the village. A middle-aged Hindu man from one of the four villages linked to the Buddhist Gramastha Mandal painted a rosy picture of village progress during a chance conversation. In his grandparents' time, he explained, Mahars and Marathas never mixed and would not even shake hands, but today community members visit each other's houses and celebrate each other's festivals without a second thought.

This view finds some academic support. In an otherwise pessimistic musing on the contemporary Indian village, Dipankar Gupta offers a somewhat hopeful view on rural caste relations, maintaining that following a 'gradual diminution of status of the dominant castes ... the assertion of [marginalised] caste identities is becoming much more strident and out in the open' (2005, p. 753). Save a few 'pockets of upper caste intransigence' he contends, '[u]ntouchability is not practiced widely' (Gupta, 2005, p. 757). Not everybody agrees: in Chapter 2 we heard Anand Teltumbde opining that the Khairlanji massacre shatters any illusion that 'economic development does away with casteism' (2007, p. 1019). Neither do all Pravin's roommates share his optimism. Ananda told me that the divisions in his village, Dorli, are less stark than they used to be, but casteism persists and he does not envisage it disappearing in the near future. His words echoed those of one of the Hindus from Amrutwadi, who described casteism as a 'mentality' that would never change.

In some ways, the Gramastha Mandal experience might actually help to reinforce, rather than undermine, division back in the village. Just as the Hindu-only Gramastha Mandals maintain institutional links to their villages to help fund new infrastructure and new temples, there are numerous similar Buddhist organisations linked to specific villages, such as the Panchashil Tarun Mandal originally set up in Dorli but now with a Mumbai chapter established by its Gramastha Mandal migrants. The main function of this society is to encourage Dorlikars in Mumbai to contribute funds and organisational assistance to Buddhist festivals in the village. A Buddhist cultural centre and temple were recently established in Dorli with assistance from the Panchashil Tarun Mandal alongside government funding. Likewise, a Buddha Vihar is also under construction in Borgaon, partly funded by the Borgaon Buddhist Gramastha Mandal, and I was aware of other Buddhist-only committees in Mumbai that were associated with a particular village and were primarily concerned with issues relating to the village's Buddhist community.

Dandekar suggested back in the 1980s that migrants tend to 'adopt more progressive attitudes ... than those who stay behind' and hence 'if caste and class relationships are to be jolted into the countryside, the impetus will probably have to come from the city' (1986, pp. 254–6). When I think of these community-based organisations that channel city wealth back to the village, often with equally community-specific ends, I wonder if this view was in fact wildly optimistic. Inclusive eligibility rules might have sprung up in a few Gramastha Mandals, but in most cases village spatial practices from the middle of the last century have ossified through this migration mechanism, despite – or perhaps because of – the socio-economic transformation of Girangaon.

Uncertain futures

Ultimately, can we determine whether Gramastha Mandal migration reinforces or diminishes the social and spatial community divides of the village? A survey of the somewhat limited literature on the topic would suggest that in the city these sharp divisions collapse into a shared sense of belonging to the same village, that transcends community differences (Adarkar and Menon, 2004, p. 100; Dandekar, 1986, p. 255; Rowe, 1973, p. 229). However, this narrative overlooks the ways in which village-belonging is constituted differently by the different communities, meaning its potential to unify these communities is consequently rather weak. A Dalit Buddhist and a Maratha from the same village will, traditionally at least, come from distinct parts of the village and may have quite different personal histories and understandings of village life, rooted, for example, in different temples, different festivals and different social networks circumscribed by casteism.

Meanwhile, their city experiences, although likely to have many similarities, will be in large part defined by the Gramastha Mandals they belong to, meaning that their day-to-day lives and social activity will overwhelmingly take place among members of the same community. This community specificity of the Gramastha Mandals is likely to have been a strong contributing factor towards the building-level community segregation still found in the BDD Chawls and elsewhere in Mumbai. Migrants are to a large extent surrounded by members of their community, or at least co-religionists, even though social interaction between migrants and longer-term family residents is often extremely limited (as discussed in Chapter 3). Meanwhile, it is unclear what impact the increasing trend towards buying property in the outer suburbs will have on these community relationships.

Today, at any rate, Mahadev can glibly write off whole swathes of society as dirty, and Sameer can punch the air in anger at the thought of having to live with a Dalit. On the other hand, Mahadev apparently has a genuine affection for his Muslim ex-neighbours with whom he still keeps in touch. Pravin's best friend is a Hindu, and I have lost count of the number of other close friendships between Hindus and Buddhists that I encountered, both among Gramastha Mandal migrants and longstanding chawl residents. As eligibility rules are relaxed in response to dwindling levels of demand, Hindus and Buddhists *are* living in the same rooms together and, if my admittedly superficial impressions from Shiravali Gramastha Mandal are any indicator, navigating this challenge successfully. Amid the pessimism prompted by my study, in other words, there is perhaps some room for hope.

Notes

1 In the 1970s Sugao, for example, the 'Mahars are segregated in a distinct area outside the main village', while the houses of the prominent Maratha families 'are in two clearly separated wards to the north and south of the village's main axis lane' (Dandekar, 1986, pp. 63 and 54).
2 In *The Triumph of the City,* urban enthusiast Edward Glaeser celebrates the city as a place where people can 'connect with a broader range of friends whose interests are well matched with their own' (2011, p. 128).

6
Shivaji contested: on being Maharashtrian

As the fieldwork year wore on, the spectre of redevelopment loomed ever larger and protest banners appeared around the neighbourhood. These were authored by my Dalit Buddhist friends from the Jay Bhim Katta who were largely opposed to the proposal, in contrast to the Marathas who, by and large, supported it. The substance of the protest will be discussed in Chapter 7, but a sentence from the bottom of one banner in particular caught my attention: *Shivaji Maharaj shejarchya nahi, amchya sarvachya gharat janmava ahe tari amhala chalel*.

Although Vikas characteristically professed a complete lack of involvement in the redevelopment debates, I enlisted his help in translating this, and the English approximation we arrived at was: 'It's OK for us if Shivaji Maharaj wasn't born in a neighbour's house but in all our houses.' This made little sense to us. Vikas said it was probably intended to be sarcastic, as he could not imagine the Dalit Buddhists writing about Shivaji in any positive light. He gently pointed out that, in his view, Dalit Buddhists always emphasise their separateness from other groups.

It was only later that I discovered *Shivaji janmava pan shejarchya gharat* (Shivaji should be born, but in the neighbour's house) is a well-known Marathi phrase, lampooning the passivity of those who are happy to ride on the coat-tails of heroes so long as they do not have to put up with the inconvenience of actually having a hero living in their house. Seen in this new light, the banner clearly subverted this sentiment through an appeal to home-grown heroism in opposing the redevelopment, an interpretation that Manish later confirmed was correct. Rather than sarcastically emphasising community division, as Vikas had assumed, it was an attempt for the largely Dalit Buddhist-led protest movement to reach out to other communities through their common reverence for Shivaji.

Vikas' assumption that any Dalit Buddhist reference to Shivaji was probably sarcastic did not surprise me. I had initially been puzzled myself at Shivaji's inclusion on the back screen of the Jay Bhim Katta, in a triptych with Ambedkar and the Buddha, given that he is not popularly associated with the Ambedkarite movement in the way that Jyotirao Phule, for example, is. Those coming to Mumbai for the first time are likely to encounter Shivaji as a mainstream Hindu icon whose name is attached to the city's airport and major rail terminus and, of course, to the Marathi-regionalist, Hindu right-wing 'Army of Shiva[ji]': the Shiv Sena.

But Shivaji's appeal extends well beyond the Shiv Sena voter base, while pride in being Maharashtrian is by no means the sole preserve of the Marathas. The following section describes a commemoration of a historic battle that, in and of itself, seems to underscore the antagonism between Dalit Buddhists and Marathas, not least due to the celebration's violent aftermath. However, a closer inspection of the context of these events forces us to grapple with the different meanings that 'Maharashtra' and 'Shivaji' have had for different communities over time and complicates any simple Maratha-Buddhist binary. It also brings us back to the issue of (anti-)nationalism and reveals Dalit memories of British colonialism that are (to me, at least) unexpected and uncomfortable, reminding us once again that people's ideas and beliefs do not always match up to our preconceptions.

I ask what Shivaji signifies today, both in the BDD Chawls and in wider popular culture, and how different conceptions of Shivaji are embedded in different historical narratives of both Maharashtra and India. I draw on the work of Govind Pansare (among others) to reveal how Shivaji has been the victim of 'false history' and the fakery of deification (2015, p. 96). This leads to an extended discussion on Maratha identity, presented through a diachronic series of snapshots. The first deals with the non-Brahman movement that arose in the late nineteenth century and the Maratha quest for Kshatriya (princely/warrior caste) status. The second concerns the rise of the Shiv Sena and its implications for the Maratha community, and the third looks at the contemporary demand for recognition as a Socially and Educationally Backward Class (SEBC) entitled to reservations (quotas) in educational institutions and public-sector employment.

Finally, I return to the Dalit Buddhist community and consider the extent to which it is able to claim belonging to Maharashtra and participate in a Maharashtrian identity. I show that my Dalit Buddhist interlocutors are not immune to the rhetoric of a Maharashtrian Mumbai being undermined by outsiders, and I explore the community's own tangled relationship with the Shiv Sena and Maharashtrian politics in general. I conclude that just as there is no single way of being Indian, 'Maharashtrian' is also too elusive a category and Shivaji's legacy correspondingly too contested, for these to bring the BDD Chawls' diverse Marathi-speaking communities together in any common sense of purpose.

The Battle of Koregaon: blue, saffron and colonial complications

In January 2018, a new name entered India's political vocabulary: Bhima Koregaon. A small town by the Bhima river outside Pune, Koregaon was the site of an 1818 battle that was little known, except among certain groups of Dalits and historians, until events occurred on its bicentenary that shook the nation. Skirmishes between Dalit Buddhists and Hindus near the site of the battle spilled over into protests in Mumbai and fed into a bitter conversation in the national media about caste and exclusion and the state of Indian society.

I was lucky enough to have been aware of the battle months beforehand. Since March, Anish and others had regularly reminded me to keep the night of 31 December free to accompany them to the anniversary celebrations of a military victory in which a 500-strong battalion of Mahar soldiers defeated the much larger army of the Peshwa. The Peshwa were a Brahman dynasty who had been effective rulers of the Maratha Empire from the early eighteenth century, gradually assuming the mantle of power from Shivaji's descendants. Given this victory, Anish's cousin Kunal told me: 'We are proud to be Buddhist but we are proud to be Mahar too.' A party from the BDD Chawls make a commemorative visit to Koregaon every year, both as a tribute to their forebears' bravery and as a protest against casteism, a tradition apparently popularised by Ambedkar (Kumbhojkar, 2012, p. 105). The 1 January 2018 celebrations were to be of particular significance, however, as they marked the battle's two-hundredth anniversary.

No explanation of the wider context was given in these initial conversations, and it was only through independent online research that I found out that the Mahar battalion had actually been fighting on behalf of the British East India Company. Part of the Third Anglo–Maratha war, the Battle of Koregaon was in fact a critical step in the British conquest of western India (Bakshi and Sharma, 2000 p. 43; Kulkarni, 1996, p. 176). Appalled, I asked Nitesh, one of the regulars at the Jay Bhim Katta, why he celebrated a British victory that helped to consolidate colonial rule in India.

He seemed genuinely puzzled by the question, pointing out that the battle was a Dalit victory over Peshwa oppression. He went further, however, telling me that for the Mahars, life under the British was an improvement on the humiliation and oppression endured under Peshwa rule.[1]

This made me uncomfortable. I had grown up with a general sense that the British Empire was an immoral enterprise, but one that had undoubtedly left some beneficial legacies – the railways! democracy! – and it was only in the years preceding fieldwork that I had come to appreciate the depths of colonial brutality and rapaciousness. While living in Mumbai I read Shashi Tharoor's (2016) *An Era of Darkness,* a meticulous chronicle of the ways in which the British had damaged India through an enormous programme of wealth extraction, resource mismanagement, divide-and-rule policies, violence in the name of law and order, and the destruction of existing education systems. Its author is a dominant-caste MP and a notable, if increasingly controversial, presence on the international stage, but Anish was unimpressed when I showed him my copy of the book, brushing it off as ill-informed Hindu hysteria. 'Dalits and British, we are friends', he said, interlocking his hands in a vigorous gesture of comradeship, 'since 1818.'

My discomfort was in a similar vein to the discomfort I felt towards Dalit Buddhist nationalism and gender relations – a set of expectations of what 'progressive' politics (Shaikh, 2016 p. 126) would look like (gender-egalitarian, non-nationalist and, surely, anti-colonial) that was continually thwarted. In this case, the discomfort was compounded by my sense, as a British researcher, of being forced to reckon with my own history rather than simply watch others reckon with theirs. I tried to explain to Anish and his friends why I believed that India's railways cannot be regarded as an uncomplicatedly benevolent British bequest, since they were built to facilitate resource extraction and functioned initially as a get-rich-quick scheme for British investors while Indian passengers were crammed into overcrowded third-class compartments (Tharoor, 2016, pp. 205–7).[2] These conversations were never satisfactory, and we often seemed to end up talking at cross-purposes. Since then, in fact, there has been a growing trend of Hindu nationalist politicians co-opting the concept of 'decolonisation' in service of *Hindutva* and the demonisation of minorities, especially Muslims (see, for example, Shivasundar, 2023; Truschke, 2022).

At the time, a deeper familiarity with Ambedkar's work might have better prepared me for this shock. While Arun Shourie's accusations that there is 'not one instance' in which Ambedkar contributed to the independence struggle (1997, p. 3) are grossly unfair, Ambedkar, as we saw in Chapter 4, remained profoundly sceptical of the Congress-led independence movement. Moreover, while he made it clear that the British were 'quite incompetent to tackle our problems' (Ambedkar, 1982c, p. 504), his account in *Annihilation of Caste* of the humiliations endured by the Mahars under Peshwa rule is considerably more damning (Ambedkar, 2013, p. 18). Perhaps unsurprisingly, therefore, he responded to accusations that the Mahar battalion's role in the Battle of Koregaon was 'an act of gross treason' by arguing that it was just one of many historical examples of 'one section of people in a country [showing] sympathy with an invader, in the hope that the new comer will release them from the oppressions of their countrymen' (Ambedkar, 1993, p. 86).

Braced to protest the continuing oppressions of their countrymen, more than a hundred bikers, all male, set off from the Jay Bhim Katta at midday on 31 December (Figure 6.1), while the more cautious among us travelled alongside in a chartered bus. A predeparture ceremony outside Chawl G had featured a round of speeches, a short play and the usual chants of *'Dr Babasaheb Ambedkarancha – Vijay Aso!'* (triumph be to Dr Babasaheb Ambedkar) followed by similar homages to Shivaji and other historic figures. The journey to Koregaon itself was excruciatingly slow, but momentum was kept up by chanting Ambedkar slogans at every tollgate and we stopped at several Buddhist temples for speeches and

Figure 6.1 Dalit Buddhist bikers from the BDD Chawls en route to celebrate the Battle of Koregaon, 31 December 2017. © Author.

prayers. We finally reached Koregaon after midnight and, even then, it was a few more hours before we could approach the Vijay Stambh, the British-built obelisk commemorating the Mahar Regiment's victory. After a short speech from the organiser of the rally, a few final chants and some group selfies, it was already time to get back on the bus. By 9 a.m. on 1 January I was back in my Mumbai flat, feeling so exhausted that I shut the door on the outside world until the middle of the following day.

By the afternoon, unbeknownst to me, stories of violence were surfacing in the press. The *Indian Express* reported 'incidents of stone pelting and vandalism' (PTI, 2018a) and *India Today* later revealed that 50 cars had been damaged and one person killed (PTI, 2018b). Left-leaning online magazine *Scroll* relayed rumours that the attackers were waving saffron flags, heavily implying the involvement of the Hindu-nationalist right (Chari, 2018a). Through videos circulated over social media, a narrative emerged of an angry dominant-caste Hindu mob sabotaging a Dalit celebration they considered 'anti-national' for its commemoration of a British victory (Bhattacharya, 2018). One death was reported, a young Maratha man called Rahul Phatangale, although who killed him was not immediately clear and remains the subject of controversy.

On 2 January, in a retaliatory move, Dalit groups blocked roads across Mumbai and on the following day Ambedkar's grandson, a politician himself, called for a statewide *bandh* (shutdown) which was vigorously enforced by a broad coalition of Dalit activists (Express Web Desk, 2018). National newspapers fixated on this disruption with sensationalist headlines like 'Cops look on as mobs hold city to ransom' (TNN, 2018), often paying scant attention to the original violence. Inevitably, perhaps, this was followed by a backlash in the liberal-left sections of the media with some writers pillorying the predictability of a public response that prioritised traffic disruption over centuries of caste oppression (Venkataramakrishnan, 2018) and others lamenting the exclusion of Dalit voices in a mainstream media 'soaked in caste privilege' (Rajmani, 2018).

The atmosphere at the BDD Chawls was tense on the day of the *bandh*. Many of my Dalit Buddhist friends were circling the neighbourhood on motorbikes to ensure that shops remained shut, while Sayaji, magisterial as ever, kept an eye on things from the Delisle Road pavement. An enduring memory for me is that of a group of Dalit Buddhist women, including Sunita, haranguing the pavement fish vendors to shut down their operations. There was a stronger police presence in the area than I had seen outside election time, with several vans next to the Jay Bhim Katta. Buddhist friends warned me to be careful: 'Things are different now', said Anish. Many of my Maratha friends, on the other hand, seemed relaxed about the whole affair and more excited to have the day off work than annoyed about the strike. Several expressed the opinion that Hindu–Buddhist tension was less worrying than Hindu–Muslim tension.

Away from the streets, the tension also played out on WhatsApp. When schools stayed closed on 3 January, which is the birthday of Bahujan (marginalised caste) educationalist Savitribai Phule, a popular circular among Maratha-dominated WhatsApp groups expressed outrage that education was being withheld from Maharashtra's children on this day of all days. 'But when have you ever cared about the Phules and their caste fellows,' I only just restrained myself from shouting, 'except when it gives you ammunition to complain about Dalit politics?'

Meanwhile, several of my Buddhist contacts changed their profile pictures to an image of a white Ashoka Chakra on dark blue background, an all-purpose Ambedkarite signifier,[3] while large numbers of Maratha faces were replaced with the *bhagwa jhanda,* the forked saffron flag variously associated with Hinduism, Hindu nationalism and the Maratha Empire and sometimes printed with an image of Shivaji. I quizzed a number of Maratha friends about this, and they invariably framed it as a response to the Dalit Buddhists. '*Unhone unka colour dala',* explained one, tilting his head in the direction of Chawls F and G. *'Isliye* … [pointing at his WhatsApp profile] *hamara bhagwa'* (They've put their colour on, so we're showing our saffron).

The clear-cut blue versus saffron narrative is a reassuringly simple way to look at the Bhima Koregaon violence and the wider political economy of Maharashtra: on the one hand, an oppressed minority of Dalit Buddhists protesting with blue flags, on the other, a Maratha Hindu majority, emboldened by centuries of saffron-coloured privilege. Shivaji is held up as a saffron icon by many Hindu nationalists in Maharashtra, including the Shiv Sena whose rhetoric is steeped in 'the glories of Shivaji's heyday and his resistance against the Mughal Empire' (Chandavarkar, 2004, p. 51). This draws on a well-established tradition, strongly associated with Bal Gangadhar Tilak, the orthodox Chitpavan Brahman scholar and independence activist who popularised a vision of Shivaji as both 'a national and anti-Muslim hero' (Hansen, 2001, p. 30).

But if Shivaji was firstly and lastly a hero of Hindu resistance, why did the Dalit Buddhist bikers invoke his name alongside that of Ambedkar in the short ceremony that preceded our departure for Bhima Koregaon? And why is his image often found next to that of Ambedkar in the BDD Chawls, not least on the triptych at the back of the Jay Bhim Katta? In short, who was Shivaji?

Shivaji kon hota? (Who was Shivaji?)

Mahendra once told me that Dalit Buddhists never took issue with books about Ambedkar, whereas anybody attempting a biography of Shivaji risked angering Hindu readers and being murdered as a result. He may have specifically had Govind Pansare's *Shivaji kon hota?* (Who Was Shivaji?) in mind. In this popular 1988 biography, Pansare, a communist politician, argued that Shivaji's legacy has been 'cynically used to serve selfish interests' both by the British colonial rulers and by organisations like the Shiv Sena who 'propound a false history', distorting Shivaji into an upper-caste Hindu fundamentalist and anti-Islamic *go-brahman pratipalak,* or 'Protector of Cows and Brahmans' (Pansare, 2015, p. 96). He accredits the popularisation of this epithet to Marathi historian B. M. Purandare and disputes the evidence on which Purandare claims Shivaji himself employed it, suggesting conversely that 'Brahmans do not seem to have [had] any privileges in Shivaji's kingdom' (Pansare, 2015, pp. 75–6).

Parts of Pansare's book read like hagiography – 'Shivaji's personal morality was impeccable' (2015, p. 49) for example – while the references throughout to Shivaji's protection of the rights of peasant cultivators perhaps reveal more about Pansare's own politics than they do about Shivaji's. Overall, however, the book is a clearsighted corrective to the hysteria surrounding its subject, and Pansare emphasises Shivaji's religious tolerance, citing the large number of Muslims who 'held very important positions in [Shivaji's] army and administration' (2015, p. 59), while at the same time dismissing claims that Shivaji was secular or a socialist as 'ridiculous' (2015, p. 80). On 13 February 2015, Pansare was shot by unidentified gunmen while on his morning walk, and died four days later (LeftWord, 2015, p. 7). Arrests have since been made, and the suspects linked to the Sanatan Sanstha which has been described as a 'Hindu extremist group' whose members have also been accused in the murder of journalist and anti-*Hindutva* activist Gauri Lankesh (The Hindu Bureau, 2022).[4]

The Tilakite, *go-brahman pratipalak* version of Shivaji that Pansare so vigorously contested is somewhat similar to the one I often encountered in the Maratha-dominated sections of the BDD Chawls, although nobody used this expression in my hearing. His image is a common sight in public and private spaces and, as Ambedkar does for the Dalit Buddhist community, Shivaji appears to encapsulate the identity and pride of the Marathas, many of whom are supporters of the Shiv Sena or its ideologically similar breakaway, the Maharashtra Navnirman Sena

(MNS). Stories of Shivaji's bravery often surfaced quite casually in conversation, and several young Maratha men I knew styled their beards to emulate him.

One of these was Mohan, from Chawl B, who I sometimes helped with English conversation practice. In his frequent panegyrics, he described Shivaji's famous campaigns, against Afzal Khan, a general of the Adil Shahi Sultanate of Bijapur, and Shaista Khan, an emissary dispatched by the Mughals (see Laine, 2003, p. 25). For Mohan, what appeared to matter was that these adversaries were Muslims, a community for which he openly expressed his disdain, legitimated by the inevitable assurances that '*mere kuch Musulman dost hain*' (I have Muslim friends). If Shivaji hadn't been born, he said, there would be no Maharashtra: Shivaji gave us our independence. 'From whom?' I asked. 'From the Muslims. The Mughals.'

In practising for a job interview, he shoehorned the Chhatrapati into answers with ease. He met 'What are your hobbies?' with 'I like reading books about Shivaji Maharaj', and 'What motivates you to do a good job?' with a homage to the inspiration set by Shivaji who he described as his 'ideal person'. Some weeks into the new job, he told me with indignant approval about a bust-up that had occurred over lunch when one of his fellow Maharashtrian colleagues had slapped a co-worker from Uttar Pradesh for referring to Shivaji as a *pahadi chuha* (mountain rat).[5] 'We never call him this,' he fumed. 'For us he is *bhagwan*. He is like a god.'

Govind Pansare writes that there are in fact 'a large number of people who sincerely believe Shivaji was genuinely an incarnation of God' (2015, p. 88). I never heard any Dalit Buddhists describe Shivaji in such terms, but his companions on the Jay Bhim Katta back screen, Ambedkar and especially the Buddha, occupy that indeterminate status that oscillates between *bhagwan* (god) and *bhagwan jaise* (like a god). Shivaji is portrayed on a golden throne embossed with lions, surrounded by members of his court (see Figure 2.1). Since I knew Anish had helped to source internet images for the banner, I asked him why Shivaji was included in the main triptych, while Jyotirao Phule is only represented by a portrait on the smaller front banner.

The first part of the answer was disappointingly prosaic – they wanted to show a 'scene', not just a portrait, and there were no such images for Phule online. But, he went on, there is also a direct line between the three figures: Buddha was a king who worked on behalf of all his subjects and Shivaji was likewise a king who worked for everybody. Although not a king, Ambedkar shared this trait of egalitarianism. Shivaji rejected the *Manu Smriti* (Laws of Manu), while Ambedkar burnt a copy of the text at Mahad in 1927 on his campaign to gain access for untouchables to a public water tank. Anish explained that Shivaji's thought was actually the root of Ambedkar's thought, and that although he did not go as far as trying to dismantle caste, Shivaji treated all religions and castes well, including untouchables.

A Dalit Buddhist academic with connections to the neighbourhood once suggested to me that the Shivaji image in the Jay Bhim Katta is primarily a showpiece aimed at keeping the peace with the Maratha neighbours. In private Dalit homes, he said, you will find more images of Phule than Shivaji next to the ubiquitous portrait of Ambedkar. I found this deflating at first: an 'outsider' anthropologist lapping up everything his interlocutors told him, only to find out he had been duped. In time, however, I began to question this. Shivaji's image *was* in fact displayed in many of the Dalit Buddhist homes I visited, and in the corridors of the Dalit-majority buildings most of them lived in, as well as above the entrance to the Buddha Vihar. At Dalit Buddhist functions, including both the ceremony at the BDD Chawls prior to departure to Bhima Koregaon and also the protests against the ensuing violence, Shivaji was almost invariably invoked in second or third place after Ambedkar and alongside Phule. While this *could* all have been an elaborate performance for the sake of communal harmony, surely this would be counterproductive in the context of publicly protesting Hindu-led violence?

Either way, there was some disagreement among the Jay Bhim Katta regulars about the details of Shivaji's life. Sayaji once asked me why, if Shivaji was a Hindu, there were Muslims in his army. Mahendra went further and informed me that there is strong evidence to suggest that Shivaji was not a Hindu but actually followed the traditions of the Shakya, the Buddha's own clan. When I relayed this to Anish, he grimaced and said that '*Vo galat information bolte hai*' (he's telling you false information) but he seemed less concerned with these discrepancies than he was with the Brahmanical 'false history' of which Shivaji is a victim. For example, he claimed, Shivaji's first campaign was not actually against a Muslim, but a Brahman, although this has been edited out of mainstream history.

When I asked Anish where he got his information from, he explained that Phule had written a *pavada* (ballad) on Shivaji's life, in which he described the Maharaj not as a *go-brahman pratipalak*, but as a *kulwadi bhushan* ('pride of peasants'). Published in 1869, Phule's ballad represented Shivaji as a low-caste leader and 'strongly denied Brahman agency in the creation of the Maratha state', thus presenting a claim for non-Brahmans (including Marathas) as 'the rightful leaders of Maharashtrian society and the representatives of its traditions' (O'Hanlon, 1983, p. 3).[6]

Struck as I was by the differences between Anish's Shivaji and Mohan's Shivaji, I also began to perceive certain similarities. Dalit Buddhists and Marathas alike seemed to frame Shivaji as part of their *national* (as opposed to purely regional) mythology, perhaps not surprising given that the Maratha empire at its height covered much of today's India. Both communities also stressed Shivaji's religious tolerance. Just as Sayaji highlighted the role of Muslims in Shivaji's army, so did Yogesh, one of Vikas' (Maratha) roommates in the Amrutwadi Gramastha Mandal. Yogesh also held up Shivaji's Mahar bodyguard as evidence of his belief in human equality, as did Anish who told me that if Shivaji believed in *unch–nich* ('high–low') where caste was concerned, he would not have had a Mahar *killedar* (fort custodian) at his capital, Raigad.

A possible source for these overlaps is the Maharashtra State Board school history textbook for Class 4. Entirely devoted to the life and achievements of Shivaji, the text emphasises his quest for justice, tolerance and religious freedom albeit couched in terms of Hindu self-rule:

> He established swaraj. He did this so that *everyone would live in peace and follow his religion without any outside interference*, so that Marathi language and Hindu religion would acquire their due place of honour. He toiled all his life for the prosperity of his language, his religion, and his country ….
>
> (quoted in Laine, 2003, pp. 84–5, my emphasis)

In turn, the textbook itself has been heavily influenced by M. G. Ranade's famous 1901 *Rise of the Maratha Power*, in which Shivaji's Maratha Empire is framed as a model for postcolonial India, a socially and spiritually reformed 'one nation' built on an inclusive idea of Maharashtrian identity that 'could even absorb Muslims' (Laine, 2003, pp. 74–6).

Nevertheless, according to Anish:

> School book mein kuch jankari sab jhooti jankari thi, kyonki unhone school book mein aise banaya … ki Shivaji Maharaj sirf larai karte dikhay diya … lekin Shivaji Maharaj ka jo actual kam hai, vo nahin dikhaya unhone … Kyonki is desh ki jo education system thi, vo sab brahmano ke pas thi.
>
> (Anish, interview, 30 November 2018)

> (There is false information in the school textbook, because [the authors] only show that Shivaji Maharaj fought wars … but they

don't show the actual work of Shivaji Maharaj ... Because the whole education system in this country was in the hands of Brahmans).

Veronique Bénéï, in her ethnography of schooling in Kolhapur, points out that the supposedly secular textbook focuses heavily on 'warfare and acts of aggression' and is framed 'in Hindu terms' such that Shivaji's legendary religious tolerance is presented as a contrast to the Islamic rule that preceded it (2008, pp. 146–9). This rupture from the supposed dark days of Mughal intolerance is of course the hallmark of Mohan's vision of Shivaji's rule. It is also behind Tukaram's description of Shivaji as a contrast to Mughal Emperor Aurangzeb, who was an '*ek number madarchod*' (first-class motherfucker), worse even than Donald Trump.

Despite this apparent common ground, therefore, Shivaji's tolerance can mean something very different depending on whose vision of Maharashtrian history it is embedded in. For many Marathas it is framed, in opposition to Islamic fundamentalism, as a model for a contemporary India with Hinduism at its heart. For the Dalit Buddhists, on the other hand, Shivaji's thought was a blueprint that reached its most radical and mature form under Ambedkar, whose rational Buddhism, as we discovered in Chapter 4, is the foundation on which an egalitarian India can be built.

Contested gurus and tangled (hi)stories: a tale of three Sambhajis

Manish also mentioned the Class 4 textbook when, on a trip to a local library, he told me he had become part of an *andolan* (movement) that aimed to pressure the State Education Board to correct 'wrong information' in history textbooks. This included the question of Shivaji's guru. Anish had previously explained that, contrary to popular belief, Shivaji did not turn to the Brahman saint Ramdas for spiritual advice, but to a non-Brahman saint called Tukaram. Manish agreed that Ramdas played no part in Shivaji's spiritual life but insisted that neither had Tukaram, and Shivaji's only guru had been his mother, Jijabai. These debates follow a well-trodden path. Historian S. H. Mohite argued in a 1936 treatise that Jijabai would have provided sufficient guidance to the future Chhatrapati (Deshpande, 2007, p. 187 n. 25), while James Laine also maintains there is little evidence that Shivaji had significant contact with either saints Ramdas or Tukaram (2003, pp. 52–4).[7]

I was not familiar with Laine's work when, on our first ever encounter at the Jay Bhim Katta, Mahendra asked me if I had heard of

'James Klein'. At the time I struggled to follow his point, but I understood I was being warned about the trouble I could get into as a researcher. This was nerve-wracking enough in itself but became more so when I found out that James Laine's (2003) historiographical study *Shivaji: Hindu King in Islamic India* had been banned in India after a Maratha-activist organisation called the Sambhaji Brigade attacked the Pune-based Bhandarkar Oriental Research Institute (BORI) that had provided some assistance to Laine in his research.

In Laine's own account, it was not primarily his questioning Shivaji's 'connections to Tukaram or Ramdas', which he dismisses as 'old stuff', nor his portrayal of Shivaji's various alliances with Muslims that chiefly irked the Sambhaji Brigade and earned the writer two death threats (2011, pp. 153 and 158–9). Rather, it was a single paragraph, in which Laine (2003, p. 93) recounts jokes told by Maharashtrians about Jijabai, that caused the outrage.

Manish, however, was emphatic that the most problematic part of the book was the way (he believed) it presented Ramdas as Shivaji's guru, a consequence, he said, of Laine's failure to 'cross-check' his sources. When I pressed him, he confirmed that he had never actually read the book, and most of what he knows about it comes from WhatsApp circulars. In any case, he argued, the real target of the Sambhaji Brigade's anger was not Laine himself but BORI, which he described as a Brahman organisation. As James Laine recalls, the leader of the Sambhaji Brigade's parent organisation, the Maratha Seva Sangh, derided him as 'merely an instrument of Brahman conspirators [i.e. BORI] who long disparaged Shivaji for reasons of caste prejudice' (2011, p. 164). Manish said he did not support the vandalisation of the institute, but he understood the anger behind it.

This Dalit Buddhist sympathy for a Maratha-led campaign against Brahmanical agents of false history is a far cry from the clear-cut blue–saffron clash I read in my WhatsApp feed in January 2018. Several days after the Bhima Koregaon trip, in fact, I was skim-reading a news article about the criminal cases being filed against the figures suspected of inciting the violence and thought I noticed a reference to the Sambhaji Brigade. Homing in on the passage in question I realised it actually concerned a man called Sambhaji Bhide.

Both these Sambhajis in fact owe their names to Chhatrapati Sambhaji, the son and heir of Shivaji whose burial site near Pune is at the centre of another strand of the dispute over the contested history of Bhima Koregaon.[8] This aside, there is little else in common between Sambhaji Bhide and the Sambhaji Brigade. Bhide is a Brahman physicist turned *Hindutva* activist and popular guru known for the simplicity of his lifestyle and the admiration he commands from powerful figures including Narendra Modi. He has been described by one journalist as 'deliberately profess[ing] Maratha history in a Brahminical perspective' (Sutar, 2018), comparing the rule of Shivaji with the utopian Hindu rule of Lord Ram, and over the past few decades he has attracted a string of allegations of inciting religious violence. He has repeatedly been implicated in the Bhima Koregaon skirmishes, although he was cleared of all charges in 2022 (Haygunde, 2022).

The Sambhaji Brigade, on the other hand, describes itself in terms that resonate surprisingly with the professed intentions of the activists at the Jay Bhim Katta, as an organisation dedicated to spreading the 'thoughts' of Shivaji, Phule and Ambedkar among other 'Bahujan mahapurush' (great men of low caste) and bringing 'the hidden history to people' (Sambhaji Brigade, n.d.). Shashank told me that the Sambhaji Brigade had actually supported the Bhima Koregaon celebrations, and a few months later the organisation gave its support to rallies demanding the arrest of Sambhaji Bhide (Chari, 2018b). That this position does not enjoy the support of all Marathas was made clear by a number of my Maratha friends in the BDD Chawls who claimed that if Sambhaji Bhide were arrested, the Marathas would organise their own *bandh* to which the Buddhist-led protests would pale in comparison. Would you join these protests, I asked Amrut from Katkarwadi Gramastha Mandal. 'Yes', he replied. '*Ham bhi Maratha hain*' (We are also Marathas).

Who are the Marathas?

How can we reconcile the Maratha-led and sometimes violently anti-Brahman Sambhaji Brigade, devoted to uplifting the marginalised, with the young Maratha men in the BDD Chawls ready to march in defence of Brahman ideologue Sambhaji Bhide? One narrative that emerged from the post-Bhima Koregaon analysis merits closer inspection, for the way it challenges easy 'blue versus saffron' interpretations. 'Real tussle between right-wingers & Marathas' a *Times of India* headline declared on 4 January (Radhyesham, 2018), while Smruti Koppikar writes in *Scroll.in* that the 'age-old power struggle between the Brahmins and the Marathas' lies 'at the heart of the Bhima Koregaon story' (Koppikar, 2018). This is not a new claim, and Hansen argues that the mediaeval history of this part of India was dominated by 'tensions between Maratha elites and Brahman communities' (2001, p. 24).

I received a salutary lesson on this tension while waiting to approach the obelisk at Bhima Koregaon. I asked Vinit, one of the expedition organisers, why we had chanted 'triumph be to Chhatrapati Shivaji' that morning, given that we were celebrating a decisive military blow against the empire Shivaji had established. Vinit shook his head vigorously, but his response threw me: the Battle of Koregaon was a battle against the Peshwa, not the Marathas. 'But the Peshwa ruled the Maratha Empire!' I replied. He shook his head again and told me I was confusing 'Maratha' and 'Marathi' – the Peshwa were Marath-*i* but they were not Marath-*a*. I understood this to mean that as Brahmans, albeit Marathi-speaking ones, the Peshwa did not belong to the Maratha caste cluster. By this time Pradeep had joined us and he reiterated the now familiar story that Shivaji was a fair leader who ruled for the benefit of all his subjects and it was only after the Peshwa came to power that the Bahujan castes were oppressed.

Asking 'Who was Shivaji?' therefore leads inevitably to the broader question of who the Marathas are, both in the BDD Chawls today and more generally across Maharashtra and across recent history. Several of my research participants recounted the story of Shivaji's coronation, where he assumed the title of Chhatrapati, 'one who is entitled to have a *c[h]hatra:* a large parasol or canopy ... and a sign of dignity or grandeur' (O'Hanlon, 1985, p. 19). Custom dictated that Shivaji needed to be declared of Kshatriya (princely/warrior caste) status, but Brahmans from across present day Maharashtra refused to take part in this coronation ceremony. Eventually a Brahman from Varanasi called Gaga Bhatt was persuaded to declare that Shivaji was actually a descendant of the Sisodia Rajput clan 'whose standing as Kshatriyas could not be questioned' (O'Hanlon, 1985, p. 20).

Maratha Yogesh told me that Shivaji truly was a Kshatriya, but his clan had been scattered by the Mughals, meaning that most Brahmans refused to believe his true status until it was proved by Gaga Bhatt. For Anish, in contrast, the story was proof of Shivaji's low-caste status and he instructed me to ask my Maratha friends why, if Shivaji was a Kshatriya, so many Brahmans refused to crown him. He derided the continuing pretensions of Marathas to a Kshatriya status and defined 'Kshatriya' simply as one who does not question Brahmanical hegemony, as opposed to Shudras (labouring castes), who, like Buddhists, ask questions.[9]

Marathas and the non-Brahman movement

Vinit's forceful distinction between the Maratha Shivaji and the Marathi-speaking Peshwa recalls Phule's reading of the Peshwa takeover of the Maratha Empire as 'a symbol of treason and oppression' (Hansen, 2001, p. 27). It was on this basis that a cluster of non-Brahman movements emerged in late nineteenth-century Maharashtra which sought to counter the effects of 'rigid, hierarchical, and overly ritualized Brahman dominance' (Hansen, 2001, p. 29).

The most prominent such movement was the Satyashodhak Samaj ('Truth-Seeking Society'), founded by Phule and others in 1873, which set up educational institutions, charitable trusts and print media. In its early days, the Satyashodhak Samaj was dominated by Phule's own Mali caste, but it also included Mahars and other untouchables as well as Marathas and a few Muslims (Hansen, 2001, p. 32; O'Hanlon, 1985, p. 249). Five years after Phule's death in 1890 however, the society decided to ban untouchables from its meetings, and its inclusive ethos gradually began to give way to a more 'exclusive [Maratha] identity tied to a ritual Kshatriya status' (Rao, 2009, p. 47).

A key patron of the movement in the early twentieth century was Shahuji Maharaj of Kolhapur, a descendent of Shivaji. Like his ancestor, Shahuji campaigned to be recognised as a Kshatriya, but his response to Brahman non-recognition was to establish a school for non-Brahman priests and to steer a middle course between the conservative 'Kshatriya ideology' and the 'more radical Satyashodhak ideology' (Omvedt, 1976, p. 136). He is well-regarded by many Dalits in Maharashtra for his pioneering social-welfare policies (Teltumbde, 2017, pp. 46–7); his portrait is displayed next to Phule on the front banner of the Jay Bhim Katta, and on the revamped banner of the Buddha Vihar.

The non-Brahman movements staked an emphatic claim to Shivaji's legacy, incorporating 'Chhatrapati Melas' that celebrated their hero's life into the annual Ganeshotsav festival. Unlike celebrations of a 'violent and aggressive' Shivaji led by Tilak in the late 1890s, the Chhatrapati Melas 'ridiculed' the power-hungry Brahmans and 'praised the Marathas as the true people of the Deccan and of the nation' (Hansen, 2001, pp. 30–1). After independence, this assertive anti-Brahman identity continued to thrive among Maratha communities, who dominated Maharashtra's sugarcane-based rural economy and the regional branch of the Congress Party (Hansen, 2001, p. 34). Following Gandhi's assassination by Chitpavan Brahman Nathuram Godse, a wave of anti-Brahman violence spread across Maharashtra, overwhelmingly led by Marathas (Pawar,

2017, p. 16). Hansen suggests this violence was 'subtly encouraged by non-Brahman Congress leaders' thus 'further entrench[ing] the link between the Congress and the Maratha identity' in post-independence Maharashtra (2001, p. 34).

Marathas and the Shiv Sena

The non-Brahman legacy is hard to detect among the Marathas I met in the BDD Chawls. While I heard snide remarks about Muslims and Dalits on a depressingly regular basis, anti-Brahmanic sentiment was almost entirely absent. How has this Brahman-adjacency come about? To better understand these shifts in Maratha identity, it is useful to unpick the community's entanglements with the Shiv Sena which has been a dominant force in Maharashtrian politics since its election to state government in coalition with the BJP in 1995.

The context in which the Shiv Sena emerged in 1966 was the recently-formed state of Maharashtra, born from the campaigning of the Samyukta Maharashtra movement which united right- and left-wing intellectuals in the name of Marathi speakers, exploited by 'alien (predominantly Gujarati) capital' (Heuzé, 1995, p. 187). From the outset, founder Bal Thackeray claimed to be acting in defence of this generalised *Marathi manoos* (ordinary Marathi speaker), a category that has political power because it is imprecise and is defined against a shifting roster of 'others' whose spectre Thackeray raised to galvanise the anxieties of his supporters. Prominently, he targeted South Indians and communists, and indeed shared opposition to communism was a critical factor in the various opportunistic alliances the Sena made with other political parties, notably the Congress (Hansen, 2001, pp. 64–7). Thackeray himself was hardly a marginalised figure, belonging as he did to the Chandraseniya Kayastha Prabhu, a dominant-caste community typically considered 'socially proximate' to the Chitpavan Brahmans (Béteille, 1992, p. 48).

Although Hindu nationalism was a 'possibilit[y] always folded into' the operational milieu of the Shiv Sena, Hansen argues, it was after communal riots in Bhiwandi in 1984 that the organisation pursued a 'radical anti-Muslim strategy' (2001, pp. 9 and 76)[10] and, in 1989, an alliance with the BJP. In the notorious communal riots that engulfed Mumbai in 1992–3, it was the Shiv Sena who positioned themselves as the 'ultimate defender of the Hindus … against the Muslim menace' and mobilised a systematic campaign of looting and burning Muslim-run businesses in retaliation for the burning to death of a Hindu family in January 1993 (Hansen, 2001, p. 122–5).

Notwithstanding the Shiv Sena's popularity among the BDD Chawls Marathas today, in general terms it has never primarily been linked to the Maratha community. Before the 1995 Shiv Sena-BJP Maharashtra Assembly victory, state politics was dominated by a series of Maratha chief ministers, most belonging to the Congress Party. More recently, it is the breakaway Nationalist Congress Party (NCP), a party founded in 1999 on principles of Gandhian secularism by Maratha political stalwart and three times Chief Minister Sharad Pawar, that has popularly been regarded as the 'party of the Marathas' (Deshpande and Palshikar, 2017, p. 80).

Nevertheless, in Mumbai's lower-income neighbourhoods, formerly bastions of communism and the trade-union movement, the Shiv Sena has embedded itself through a network of *shakhas*, or cells, such as the Delisle Road *shakha*, which has an office attached to Chawl Q. These *shakhas* are often closely linked to the Mitra Mandals (cf. Hansen, 2001, p. 73). In the BDD Chawls, for example, the Bandya Maruti Seva Mandal receives financial support from the Delisle Road *shakha*, as does the Satyam Krida Mandal and various others, many dominated by Marathas. During Ganesh Chaturthi in 2017, the most impressive *pandal* in the BDD Chawls was the one, situated between Chawls J and K, hosted by the N. M. Joshi Sarvajanik Utsav Mandal which is controlled by the Delisle Road *shakha*.[11]

The Shiv Sena strategy of appealing to Marathi-speaking Hindus has enabled them to forge a strong and diverse base of support among Brahmans and Kayasthas as well as marginalised-caste groups. Crucially, this militant brand of Hinduism has proved appealing to elite Marathas whose 'declining hegemony' led them to seek an 'alternative ideology to help re-entrench their dominance' and to 'infiltrate' the Shiv Sena, using it 'to their own advantage' (Lele, 1995, p. 202). The high-handed treatment of the Maratha leadership by Congress Prime Minister Indira Gandhi, not least 'her decision to prop up a Muslim' Chief Minister (A.R. Antulay) in the early 1980s, was another factor that arguably pushed Marathas away from Congress and towards the Shiv Sena (Kumar, 2009, p. 11). By the turn of the twentieth century, the Maratha vote in state elections was split between the Congress-NCP and the BJP-Shiv Sena but it shifted 'decisively' in favour of the BJP-Shiv Sena alliance in 2014, most notably in Mumbai (Deshpande and Palshikar, 2017, p. 81). Municipal election results in the BDD Chawls appear to bear this out, as the Shiv Sena captured 52.4 per cent of the total vote, compared to the Congress Party's 6.2 per cent (BMC Elections, 2017).

Ek Maratha Lakh Maratha

The effect of the Shiv Sena's rise to prominence under a *Hindutva* banner has been a further erosion of any unified non-Brahman identity, eclipsed in political salience by the umbrella term *Marathi manoos* that more often includes Brahmans than Dalit Buddhists. But nesting within this category is that of Maratha, whose continuing relevance I saw vividly demonstrated in a rally outside the outside the Brihanmumbai Municipal Corporation building on 9 August 2017. Huge crowds were gathered, many waving forked saffron flags and almost all wearing at least one saffron item of clothing such as a shawl, cap or custom-made shirt emblazoned with the words *Ek Maratha Lakh Maratha* (One Maratha, One Hundred Thousand Marathas).

Tukaram and Ramesh and many of their friends had been present and the next day they showed me photographs of themselves decked out in saffron scarves and waving flags. They told me the demonstration was a silent march called a *Maratha Kranti Morcha* (Maratha Revolution Rally), and that these had been occurring in various locations across Maharashtra since August 2016. While framed as protests for justice in a case of gang-rape and murder of a Maratha schoolgirl in Ahmednagar (by Dalits), these marches, that profess no political alignment, included a range of demands. Most prominent was the demand for Marathas to be included in the OBC category to take advantage of reservations (quotas) in state-run educational institutions and government jobs (Firstpost, 2018).

My friends were adamant that reservations for Marathas were essential, given their marginalised economic status in contemporary Maharashtra. Tukaram asked me how I would feel if a large number of Indians came to the UK and had 75 per cent of jobs specifically reserved for them. I laughed, which upset him, and, apologising, I explained that his analogy baffled me. No community in Maharashtra had anywhere close to a 75 per cent quota for job positions (the total for all communities at the time of this conversation was 52 per cent), and trying to frame the beneficiaries (Schedule Castes, Scheduled Tribes and OBCs) as immigrant outsiders was at best ill-informed, if not actively disingenuous. In any case, the signifier *Ek Maratha Lakh Maratha* papers over deep ideological cracks within a caste cluster that includes impoverished cultivators and urban elites, right-wing Hindu nationalists and left-leaning social activists.

This aspiration for downward mobility, apparently at odds with a centuries-long struggle for recognition as Kshatriyas, is not unique to the Marathas. Other communities of a similarly indeterminate status but with a strong historic tradition of dominant-caste identification, such as the Patidars (Patels) of Gujarat and the Jats of Haryana, have made equivalent demands in recent years. The Maratha demand, in particular, is premised on the claim that the community, suffering from declining agricultural returns, faces challenges when participating in the service sector and knowledge economy due to heavy existing reservations for OBCs (Kumar, 2009).[12]

Superficially redolent of the original Satyashodhak Samaj and its radical anti-Brahman stance, the Maratha campaign might more realistically be viewed as a symptom of further fragmentation among the non-Brahman castes. It is precisely *because* Dalits and OBCs have made gains through reservations and protective government acts that Marathas have adopted a disadvantaged status of their own. Although broad international comparisons should be made with care, it is hard to resist thinking of other instances of traditionally powerful majorities reimagining themselves as victims of marginalisation, such as the popular white-American claim of reverse discrimination.[13]

Albeit couched in Maratha-specific terms, Tukaram's claim to victimhood is clearly inflected with Bal Thackeray's 'sons of the soil' rhetoric in which the *Marathi manoos* is the true inheritor of Mumbai, perpetually beleaguered by competition from immigrant labour. One of the demands made in *Shiv Sena Speaks,* the organisation's early English-language publication, is that '80 per cent [of] jobs, skilled or otherwise, must be reserved in Governmental, semi-governmental, private and public undertakings' for 'Maharashtrians' (Kapilacharya, 1967, pp. 3 and 47). Since then, the Shiv Sena's stance on job quotas has fluctuated, and in 1990 Bal Thackeray strongly opposed Prime Minister V.P. Singh's decision to implement the Mandal Commission's recommendation of reserving 27 per cent of central government and public sector jobs for OBCs. In recent years, however, the Shiv Sena appears to have thrown its weight behind the Maratha demand for reservations (see Firstpost, 2018).

Ironically, it was a Brahman BJP member, Maharashtra's Chief Minister Devendra Fadnavis, who championed a Bill in November 2018 designating the Marathas as a Socially and Educationally Backward Class (SEBC) entitled to 16 per cent of seats in educational institutions and positions in the public sector (Bare Acts Live, 2018). This effort to woo the electorate made its mark, since a months-long delay in passing the Bill did not deter approximately 59 per cent of Marathas in Maharashtra from voting for the BJP-Shiv Sena alliance in the May 2019 Lok Sabha elections (Sutar, 2019). In June 2019 the Bombay High Court found the Bill constitutionally valid (Srivastava, 2019), but two years later it was struck down as unconstitutional by the Supreme Court in May 2021 (Saigal, 2021). At the time of writing the issue remains unresolved, and with it the question of what it means to be Maratha.

The Gujaratis are coming! Dalits and Maharashtrian pride

As the status anxieties of a hundred thousand Marathas are given voice in confusing polyphony, it is easy to understand Vikas's misreading of the Dalit Buddhists' protest banner. But what he saw as sarcasm at the Marathas' expense was actually, in its call for a Shivaji to be born in every house, an attempted appeal to a common Maharashtrian identity shared across communities.

Standing on the Chawl G roof back in March 2017, Anish pointed at One Avighna Park, a block of luxurious apartments, and complained about the Gujarati families, many of them Jain, that would move in and enforce their strict vegetarian dietary rules on the building, empowered to do so by their wealth. 'Marathi people live in small houses,' he said bitterly and warned me that if I return to the area in 20 years I will not see any Maharashtrians as they will have been forced out by wealthy Gujaratis. Soon enough, he was explicitly framing the BDD Chawls redevelopment project as a policy-driven attempt to squeeze the Maharashtrians out of the area in favour of more moneyed communities. Likewise, in a wide-ranging conversation about the neighbourhood's future, Dinesh predicted an influx of rich Gujarati families that would prompt a neighbourhood-wide 'partition' and an overall loss of Maharashtrian identity and culture.

The boundaries of the population that can lay claim to this Maharashtrian identity are as imprecise as those of Thackeray's *Marathi manoos*. My research participants used the expressions '*Marathi log*' (Marathi people) and sometimes '*Maharashtrian log*' (Maharashtrian people) indexing an importance attached to both language and territory. Taking this to refer, approximately, to Marathi-speakers born in Maharashtra, it can include Dalit Buddhists, Hindus, Marathas and Brahmans as well as other dominant castes, OBCs and possibly some Christians and Muslims – in short, the vast majority of BDD Chawls residents.

Among the regulars at the Jay Bhim Katta, there never seemed to be any doubt over their entitlement to claim a place in this category. When I first met Shashank More's son Prabhu, a talented singer of *bhim geet*[14] he had just returned from a television interview and was fulminating against the inability of somebody at the studio to speak Marathi despite being in

Mumbai. Other Dalit Buddhists made similarly disparaging remarks about those who came to Mumbai without learning Marathi, a trope more commonly associated with supporters of the Shiv Sena. Many also maintained strong links with their ancestral villages and expressed a pride in the locally-specific culture and cuisine of their districts, mostly within the Konkan and Ghat subregions. Historically, indeed, sections of the Mahar community have claimed to be the *dharniche put,* or 'sons of the soil' of Maharashtra, such as Kisan Fagoji Bansode, a community leader prior to Ambedkar who 'spoke of pre-Aryan land ownership to try to build the pride and spirit of the Mahars' (Zelliot, 1996b, p. 87).

Just as the extent and intensity of a common Maharashtrian identity has fluctuated over time, so has the Mahars' ability to participate in it. Despite the 1895 ban on untouchables in the Satyashodhak Samaj, Ambedkar 'unequivocally identif[ied]' with the movement (Omvedt, 1994, p. 148). However, he was highly critical of the absorption of non-Brahman movement politicians into the Congress Party and, as we saw in Chapter 4, had deep concerns over the Congress-led independence movement which he feared would simply lead to an 'aggressive' new imperialism of elite Hindus (Ambedkar, 1990b, p. 9). After the formation of Maharashtra, the politically dominant Maratha elite tended to exclude Dalits from the state's 'common regional identity', even though the Scheduled Castes Federation (precursor to the RPI) had participated in the Samyukta Maharashtra movement (Rao, 2009, p. 183).

Dalit Buddhists were also excluded from Maharashtrian identity by the Shiv Sena, who instead embraced Dalit Hindus by nominating candidates from the Chambhar community (among others) to contest elections (Lele, 1995, p. 206). The long-term success of this strategy is evident in the support the party continues to enjoy among the Chambhars of the BDD Chawls. Even so, Ramdas Athawale, eponymous leader of the RPI(A), has landed numerous times 'at the feet of Thackerays' in political coalitions with the Shiv Sena (Teltumbde, 2012), and poet Namdeo Dhasal, founder of the Dalit Panthers and vociferous critic of such alliances, later joined the Shiv Sena himself, supposedly following a row with Ambedkar's grandson Prakash (Namishray, 2018).[15]

Meanwhile, the insidious incursion of well-to-do Gujaratis and other communities into the formerly Maharashtrian strongholds of south-central Mumbai is a popular trope among left-leaning writers with sympathies for the plight of the ex-millworkers, despite the same writers' vehement opposition to the Marathi chauvinism of the Shiv Sena. In his compelling epitaph for the bygone mill era, Naresh Fernandes quotes an ex-millworker who points to the disappearance of chicken butchers in his neighbourhood as a sign that Maharashtrians and Muslims 'were being eased out of Girangaon and that vegetarian Gujarati and Jain traders were taking their place' (Fernandes, 2013, p. 117). Further south in Girgaon, meanwhile, Pablo Holwitt reports that, following redevelopment projects, 'many Maharashtrian chawl-residents blame Gujaratis and Marwaris of driving them out of "their" neighbourhood and denying them basic rights' (2017, p. 339).[16]

Some of my interlocutors blame this de-Maharashtrification on the Shiv Sena, who they claim have sold off the city to the highest bidders even while trumpeting their role as the defenders of Maharashtrian interests. Vinod, the journalist from Chawl F, told me that while Bal Thackeray himself had supported Maharashtrians, his successor Uddhav Thackeray is only interested in money, as is his nephew, the MNS leader Raj Thackeray. Anish, with his usual frankness, once described the Shiv Sena as a *madarchod* (motherfucker) party for claiming to care about Maharashtrians while doing nothing to actually benefit Maharashtrian communities.

These perceptions appear to have some empirical basis. The city's mercantile classes have long been dominated by various Gujarati and Marwari communities and this broad segment of society was a key beneficiary of economic liberalisation and the associated housing development policies of the early 1990s. As housing activist P.K. Das argues, these policies 'have never reflected the needs and aspirations of the slum dwellers and the working class', instead favouring 'business interests in land and housing' (Das, 1995, p. 170). Since these changes occurred under the watch of a Congress-led state government, the Shiv Sena was able to gain political capital from framing them as disadvantageous to the *Marathi manoos* (D'Monte, 2002, p. 151) and campaigning in 1995 on a 'platform of opposing the sale of lands and closure of the textile mills' (Krishnan, 2000, p. 12). However, nothing changed during the party's tenure in power, and 'workers of Girangaon continued to be crushed by an alliance of politicians, builders and land sharks, mill-owners and underworld interests' (Krishnan, 2000, pp. 12 and 15).

In general, moreover, the Gujarati-dominated capitalist class had never been one of the more significant targets for the Shiv Sena. The 1967 publication *Shiv Sena Speaks* even makes the claim that, far from being considered 'outsiders', the Gujaratis are the Maharashtrians' 'partners in every noble cause … hav[ing] closely identified themselves with this soil for over two hundred years' (Kapilacharya, 1967, p. 7). Lele suggests that the Shiv Sena's highly publicised fixation with the supposed threat of South Indian migration 'deflected attention' from the protection it provided to 'unchecked capitalist development' (1995, p. 190). Indeed, the Sena functioned as 'a valuable tool for industrialists', with strike-breaking gangs that often divided the workforce on 'the lines of language and region' (Krishnan, 2000, p. 12).

Perhaps this discourse has seeped into the general population, since other than a handful of generic comments, such as those from Anish and Dinesh, I heard very little anti-Gujarati rhetoric from any Maharashtrians, Dalit Buddhist or otherwise. Neither did I hear of any tension with the small number of Gujarati families living in the BDD Chawls. Both Sayaji and Mahendra told me that a demographic change had already occurred in their buildings, which predominantly housed Dalits in the 1960s but now had a more mixed population including Marathas and Gujaratis. Neither spun this change in an especially negative light: Mahendra described his building, with seeming approval, as 'cosmopolitan', while for Sayaji the shifting demographic evidenced an increased standard of living and another sign of the neighbourhood's arrival into the ranks of the middle classes.

Being Maharashtrian

Contestations over revered historical figures often take 'for' or 'against' positions. During my year of fieldwork, for example, the *Guardian* back in the UK printed an article in which Afua Hirsch lays bare the 'white supremacist' politics of Admiral Horatio Nelson (Hirsch, 2017), a framing vigorously rebutted a few years later by The Nelson Society (2020). The legacy of Nelson's adversary Napoleon has likewise been wrangled over in France, including on questions of racism (Daut, 2021). Shivaji's legacy divides Marathas and Dalit Buddhists in a different way. For members of both communities he is a much-loved figure, but he is embedded in very different visions for India and their respective places in it.

Many Marathas premise their ideal version of India on *shiv rajya*, the tolerant, just rule of Hindu Shivaji over a predominantly Hindu nation, a marked contrast to the perceived Islamic imperialism that preceded Shivaji and the British imperialism that followed. Yogesh, Tukaram and Mohan all, in their various ways, stressed what they understood as the inequality and oppression of Islamic rule, and framed Shivaji as a liberator and the ideal Indian ruler.

Many Dalit Buddhists also view Shivaji as a revolutionary figure, but they regard Brahmanic caste hegemony, more than Islamic or British rule, as the oppressive structure against which he can be compared. This category (Brahmanic caste hegemony) is expansive and can include anything from the original 'Aryan invasion' (see Chapter 4) to contemporary *Hindutva*, taking in en route the Maharashtrian Brahmans who refused to crown Shivaji and the Peshwa who later assumed power over his empire. Through this lens, the British on whose behalf the Mahar battalion had fought the Peshwa at Bhima Koregaon, can be remembered as liberators, or at least the lesser of two evils.

Some Dalit Buddhists, like Mahendra and Sayaji, even go so far as to question Shivaji's Hindu identity that the Marathas (and other Maharashtrian Hindus) hold so dear. Unlike for the Marathas, moreover, for them Shivaji's rule does not represent a transcendent ideal so much as a stepping stone towards the rational Buddhism of Ambedkar. As explained in the song at Dhammachakra Pravartan Din, Shivrao wielded a sword but it was Bhimrao who had the superhuman intellect to be able to change India with a pen.

Underlying both narratives, is a keen sense of belonging to Maharashtra as part of a broader Indian identity. Pride in the Marathi language and its literature appears to be almost universal among the Marathi-speaking communities in the BDD Chawls. Similarly, my friends at the Jay Bhim Katta exhibit as sincere an attachment to their natal villages as do second- and third-generation Mumbai Marathas like Satyajit and Sushil. The Dalit Buddhists, by calling for Shivajis in 'all our houses', were therefore attempting to appeal to this shared belonging in the face of a threat from a capitalist state housing agency (which, it should be noted, sat at the time within the umbrella of a state government presided over by a Brahman Chief Minister) that does not have Maharashtrians' interests at heart.

But there is too little common ground here for this appeal to be successful. The Marathas, by and large, subscribe to a rather conservative 'Kshatriya ideology' (Omvedt, 1976, p. 136), which places them as the dominant caste of Maharashtra, infused with the Hindu nationalist sentiment of the Shiv Sena. Despite the centuries-long struggle for Brahman recognition of their caste status, I never heard Brahmanism invoked by the Marathas of the BDD Chawls as a significant threat to their identity today. Instead, Brahman ideologues such as Sambhaji Bhide enjoy considerable popularity, and some of my Maratha interlocutors even claim that an insult to Sambhaji Bhide is an insult to them as Marathas.

Meanwhile, the threat of displacement by a vegetarian middle class, facilitated by the state government's corporate greed, is apparently not compelling enough for most Marathas to join the Dalit Buddhists in protesting against the redevelopment proposal. Instead, the biggest threats are those that are seen to undermine their status, either specifically as Marathas or as the more generic *Marathi manoos*: migrants from elsewhere in India, Muslims, and the beneficiaries of reservations such as OBCs and Scheduled Castes, their Dalit Buddhist neighbours among them.

Just as the history of India is conceived in very different ways by these different communities, their modes of being Maharashtrian are articulated in fundamentally different allegiances and histories – Maratha, Kshatriya and Hindu on the one hand, Mahar, Dalit and Buddhist on the other. As was made painfully obvious during and after the clashes at Bhima Koregaon, where the role of the British Empire was also contested in a way that hit uncomfortably close to home for me, any shared idea of Maharashtra that exists is too superficial and weak to transcend the divisions between communities. Few Maharashtrians, I imagine, would claim in public that they did not want a Shivaji born in their own houses, but those expecting a Protector of Cows and Brahmans, or a Hindu-nationalist Maratha waving away 'Islamic intolerance' with a saffron flag, might baulk at the arrival of an Ambedkarite anti-caste peasant revolutionary.

Notes

1. See Beltz (2005, pp. 173–4) and Thapar (2005, p. 111) for examples of similar claims.
2. In fairness to Anish and his companions, it should be acknowledged that members of the Mahar community did benefit from British military recruitment and employment opportunities (cf. Zelliot, 1996b, pp. 88–93). Such benefits of colonialism must, of course, be viewed in the context of its many and extreme deleterious effects on Indian society as a whole.
3. For details on the significance of Ashoka Chakra, see Chapter 4, subsection 'Scientific rationalism and the future of India'.
4. The Sanatan Sanstha itself purports to be an organisation that 'impart[s] spiritual knowledge' (Sanatan Sanstha, 2022).
5. This epithet was allegedly used by Mughal emperor Aurangzeb in reference to Shivaji.
6. In *Gulamgiri*, four years later, Phule rails against the Brahmans who claim Shivaji 'sought to protect cows and Brahmans' and imbue him with 'false religious patriotism' (quoted in O'Hanlon, 1985, p. 169).
7. The Ramdas legend appears to derive from eighteenth-century texts of Mahipati, a poet heavily involved in the cult of Vithoba at Pandharpur, and Laine suggests that Mahipati's 'portrayal of [Shivaji] lavishing worship on his saintly guru is clearly an invitation to the worldly powers of [Mahipati's] day to continue patronage of religious personages of the Pandharpur cult' (2003, p. 54). Where the saint Tukaram is concerned, Laine cites Phule, who argued that Shivaji was 'truly devoted to the nonbrahmin Tukaram' and hence 'all these stories of devotion to Ramdas [were] a brahmin plot to make the king a servant of brahmins' (Laine, 2003, p. 52).
8. See Chari and Satheesh (2018) for a detailed account.
9. Ambedkar himself discussed Shivaji's coronation in *Who Were the Shudras*, where he argues that the Shudras were a clan of Aryan kings who, following a conflict, were socially degraded through the Brahmans' refusal to initiate them with Vedic rites, thus becoming a fourth varna (caste grouping). He presents Shivaji's protracted struggle to gain recognition as a Kshatriya and the continued struggles of his descendants to retain this status as evidence of the Brahmans' ongoing power to confer or deny caste status (Ambedkar, 1990a, pp. 175–85).

10 In 1973, in fact, the Shiv Sena had even entered into a short-lived alliance with the Muslim league, thereby taking the mayoralty of the then Bombay Municipal Corporation (Rodrigues and Gavaskar, 2003, p. 146).
11 Raminder Kaur (2003) has estimated that the Shiv Sena controls around two thirds of Mumbai's Ganeshotsav Mandals (neighbourhood associations specifically established to coordinate local Ganesh Chaturthi celebrations) and describes in compelling detail the tableaux in the pandals (temporary shrines) erected by two of these organisations for Ganesh Chaturthi in 1995. Both proclaimed the new Shiv Sena-BJP coalition in the legislative assembly as *shiv shahi* (rule of Shivaji), and presented Thackeray and Shivaji as part of a line of nationalist heroes who struggled against misrule by Muslim 'tyrant[s]', British colonisers and corrupt Indian governments (Kaur, 2003, pp. 169–75).
12 The validity of these claims has been disputed by several official commissions on backward classes (Kumar, 2009, p. 12) and by a recent study that analysed data from the 2011–12 India Human Development Survey to conclude that the 'claim to backwardness is empirically unjustified' since the Marathas, Jats and Patels are 'closer to dominant than disadvantaged groups' across multiple socio-economic indicators (Deshpande and Ramachandran, 2017 p. 81; see also Mhaskar and Sapkal, 2022). An independent survey of rural Maharashtra found that, while Marathas are on average better off than OBCs in terms of landholdings, their education levels are actually a little lower (Anderson et al., 2016).
13 According to the 2016 PRRI/Brookings Immigration Survey: 'Approximately six in ten (57 per cent) white Americans and roughly two-thirds (66 per cent) of white working-class Americans agree that discrimination against whites is as big a problem today as discrimination against blacks and other minorities.' (Jones et al., 2016, p. 2).
14 Songs associated with the Ambedkarite movement and struggle.
15 In her visceral and moving autobiography, Dhasal's widow Malika Amar Shaikh implies he was a 'sell-out' since 'he tied up with the Shiv Sena and I did not approve at all' (Shaikh, 2016, p. 158–9).
16 Like Fernandes' informant, Holwitt examines this phenomenon through the lens of eating practices, suggesting that the purchasing power of Marwari and Gujarati Jains, who 'would not tolerate the smell of non-vegetarian food' ensures that builders typically exclude non-vegetarians from their buildings (2017, p. 339).

7
'Smiles or fraud?': when chawlness falls apart

Partway through the year, a bright-blue corrugated-metal enclosure appeared at the corner of the *kabaddi maidan*. I would often walk past to inspect the transformation taking place inside: a hole in the ground, an ever-more complex scaffolding structure, concrete blocks piled on top of each other, and eventually a small, two-bedroom flat with a Divali lamp and a doormat reading 'Welcome' at the entrance. This structure was a sample flat, designed to show current residents what their new homes would look like once the appointed builder, Shapoorji Pallonji, had demolished the existing buildings and replaced them with high-rise residential towers.

In many stories of urban redevelopment, hardworking, honest residents are pitted against the capitalist greed of the property developer or the interfering hand of the state. Protests against the redevelopment of the docklands in east London in the 1980s used the language of 'big money' pushing out 'local people' (Leeson, 2019, p. 9) while more recent anti-gentrification marchers in Berlin proclaimed that 'the streets are ours' and expressed their opposition to a capitalism that meant only the wealthiest can afford to purchase property (Reuters, 2019).

In some 'developers versus the people' cases, indeed, the external threat unites disparate elements, such as protests against the Dakota Access Pipeline in the US which brought together environmentalists and indigenous activist groups (Steinman, 2019). Likewise, in the 2003 Hindi film *Praan Jaaye Par Shaan Na Jaaye* where, facing a decision from their landlord to demolish his chawl and develop a shopping mall, tenants belonging to various castes and religions sing together in protest with 'multi-cultural gusto' (Gangar, 2011, p. 92).

No such songs were sung in the BDD Chawls, where any 'developers versus the people' narrative was complicated by the fact that, in theory at least, the 'people' were to be rehoused in the new development in spacious flats, for free. But ideas of falseness and fakery circulated here too. A protest movement, predominantly spearheaded by members of the Dalit Buddhist community, arose due to scepticism over the government's promises to rehouse existing chawl residents and fear that stringent eligibility criteria could be used to exclude the majority of them. The protestors were also concerned about the burden of future maintenance costs that would be imposed on them and frustrated by the lack of clarity on all these issues from local government representatives. The title of a well-known Marathi play (*Hasva Fasvi,* or 'smiling deceit') was adapted in one of the protest banners to *Hasvi ki Fasvi?* (smiles or fraud?) which asked whether the state government's promises could be trusted. It was on another such banner that Vikas and I found the puzzling expression of welcome for a Shivaji to be born in every house.

Conversely, many members of the various Hindu communities (including Marathas and Chambhars) enthusiastically supported the proposals, in no small part due to the endorsement the redevelopment received from the local branch of the Shiv Sena. My Dalit friends ascribed this enthusiasm, and the corresponding lack of interest in their objections, to casteism and (according to Anish) also to the ease with which Hindus were 'hypnotised' by false promises. Just as shared village nostalgia and a shared sense of belonging to India have limited potential to bridge community differences, the neighbourhood redevelopment proposal served to widen, not narrow, the cracks that already existed within the 'chawlness' narrative of shared neighbourhood belonging and local history.

'Hasvi ki fasvi?' (smiles or fraud?): Buddhist opposition

As March turned into April, the redevelopment proposal started gathering momentum. '5,904 families of BDD chawls to get free houses!' a news headline declared on 22 April 2017, the body of the article explaining how BDD Chawls families were set to receive a 'bonanza of spacious flats, free of cost and free of maintenance charges', with work expected to start by June (Vernekar, 2017). The trigger for this, and a host of similarly enthusiastic reports, was the redevelopment *bhoomipujan* (groundbreaking ceremony) that day, presided over by the Chief Minister Devendra Fadnavis at a big open space in the Worli BDD Chawls site called the Jambori Maidan.

I received a very different account of events through a series of WhatsApp messages from Anish in the afternoon:

2:37 p.m.: Do you know Jhon
2:37 p.m.: Worli police arrested mr.sayaji mama [uncle] for the [protest] against the development
2:38 p.m.: We are going to agripada police station

A news report that day confirmed that *'BDD Chawl Ke Redevelopment Project ka Virodh karnewale ko Police ne kiya Giraftar'* (Police have arrested protesters against the BDD Chawls Redevelopment) (Gallinews, 2017). Less than two hours later, however, Dinesh reported that everything was alright, and by the evening Sayaji was back in Chawl G, playing the genial host for his niece's wedding party that took place the same night. He later told me that he had not been taken to jail, only the police station, where he was given food and drink and 'full respect'. I asked him whether the tensions were now over and everything was *shanti* (calm). *'Nahin! Shanti nahin! Tension chalu hai'* (No! Not calm! The tension carries on) he said, but he was smiling.

At the time I regarded this incident as an interruption to my fieldwork, and I did not make any particular effort to find out anything more about who had organised the protest and who else had participated in it. It also reinforced my instinct that, as a foreign researcher in Mumbai by the grace of the Indian government, it would be unwise to get too involved in public events connected to the redevelopment. Although a combination of curiosity and weak will caused me to ignore my own advice at times, much of what I learnt about the redevelopment came from discreet observation and private conversations and through following news reports. More than in almost any area I felt my outsider-ness as an obstacle to my research, and the account that follows is undoubtedly quite different from the account that a resident of any of the BDD Chawls might produce, or indeed that of a Marathi-speaking investigative journalist for whom the redevelopment represented their primary, or only interest.

While strong undercurrents of opposition were already in place prior to the *bhoomipujan* (see Dhupkar, 2017), from my perspective it was in the weeks that followed that a more cohesive protest movement became evident among my interlocutors. Spearheading this Dalit Buddhist-led movement were Sayaji and Mahendra, with support from Anish, Manish and others at the Jay Bhim Katta. But the movement drew others from across the BDD Chawls into its ambit, including some Marathas like Sushil from Chawl B and an edible lime manufacturer from

Shivaji Nagar. Outside Delisle Road, a prominent Congress Party member, himself a Dalit Buddhist, galvanised a similar movement in the Naigaon BDD Chawls. By and large, the manifestations of the movement that I was able to observe were overwhelmingly dominated by men, although I understand from discussions with Tejaswini and Sunita that Dalit Buddhist women were also involved.

Questions of nostalgia aside, it was a struggle at times to appreciate the depth of opposition to a project that, after all, was offering residents a spacious modern flat with two bedrooms and a bathroom, entirely free of charge. The first detailed articulation of the group's objections to MHADA's[1] proposal came in the form of a large poster that was displayed in four locations around the (Delisle Road) BDD Chawls in early May 2017. It was the headline of this poster that asked *BDD Punarbandhani Yojna – Hasvi ki Fasvi*? (loosely translated as 'BDD Chawls Redevelopment Plan – Smiles or Fraud?') in a play on a well-known Marathi drama *Hasva Fasvi* ('Smiling deceit'). The subheading exhorted 'BDD Chawls residents, brothers and sisters' to 'ask these questions to MHADA', elucidating said questions in a wall of small-font text. Through the conversations that this poster prompted, and the follow-up posters and leaflets that were produced, I gathered that the opposition crystallised around a few key objections and uncertainties.

First was the lack of clarity over whether the promised 500 sq. ft. referred to 'built-up area' or 'carpet area' (standard Indian real-estate terminology distinguishing between the total building floor area, wall thickness and balcony area included, and the internal, liveable area that could theoretically be covered with a carpet). A second area of concern was the Rs 1 lakh (c. £1,000) 'corpus fund' that MHADA was proposing to offer each resident to meet maintenance costs for the first 10 years of the development. According to Anish this was grossly insufficient, as maintenance fees for the new buildings, covering lift maintenance, security and cleaning, among other services, would likely to come to Rs 2,000/month, or Rs 3 lakh (c. £3,000) over the 10 years. A more general source of tension was the unclear timescale of the project and associated provisions for temporary 'transit camp' accommodation while building work was taking place.

Underpinning these objections were a few broader concerns. One was the issue of consent. The proposed redevelopment of the BDD Chawls is classified as an Urban Renewal Scheme under the Development Control Regulations for Greater Mumbai, 1991, which in the ordinary scheme of things would mean it is subject to a requirement for 'irrevocable written consent by not less than 70 per cent of the eligible tenants/occupiers'

(Maharashtra Housing and Building Laws, 2014, Appendix III.2 – 3(a)). However, on 27 December 2016 a new Regulation 33 (9) B, with specific reference to the BDD Chawls redevelopment, was introduced through a Sanctioned Modification to the earlier regulation (Government of Maharashtra, 2016) that 'waived [the] crucial condition of seeking consent of 70 per cent of the tenants for the project' (PTI, 2017). This understandably incensed many BDD Chawl residents, and at a demonstration in June, one of the placards produced by my friends at the Jay Bhim Katta simply read (in Marathi): 'Cancel! Cancel!! Cancel!!! / Regulation 33 (9) B III. / Cancel!!!'

Another major concern can be gleaned from the initial protest poster, which asks '*500 sqft carpet ki built up likhit karar ka nahi?*' (Why is there no written agreement on whether [residents will receive] 500 sq. ft. carpet area or built-up area?) and '*Corpus fund (maintenancesathi) 1 lakh jahir kelyanusar likhit karar ka nahi?*' (Why isn't the 1 lakh corpus fund, for maintenance, declared in a written agreement?). Indeed, the lack of any *likhit karar* (written agreement) from MHADA that the redevelopment project would be carried out as outlined in oral presentations and word-of-mouth assurances remained a significant bone of contention.

This links to a third, and equally contentious issue that exercised the opponents of MHADA's redevelopment plan, which was that of eligibility. The original Urban Renewal Schemes policy states that 'No new tenancy created after 13/6/96 shall be considered' (Maharashtra Housing and Building Laws, 2014, Appendix III.2 – 2(a)). This cut-off date is reiterated in the 2016 modification meaning that only those who had had possession of their tenancy since before June 1996 would be eligible for a new flat. The relevant clause also states that a 'Competent Authority' will be appointed to establish eligibility, and that 'if necessary [the government] may issue comprehensive guidelines for determination of eligibility and tenants therein' (Government of Maharashtra, 2016). The means by which MHADA decided to determine eligibility, a biometric survey, prompted further outrage given that residents were expected to undertake the survey in the absence of any written agreement.

On 17 May 2017 MHADA sent teams round to conduct biometric tests in those buildings earmarked for the initial phase of demolition (Chawls C, D, O2, R1, R2, W and X). In response, a large group, including many of my Dalit Buddhist friends, staged a demonstration outside one of the chawls, encouraging residents to refuse to undertake the test. Alongside the placard urging cancellation of Regulation 33 (9) B III, another read: 'First agreement with us / then do your paperwork!!' I was not in the BDD Chawls that day but saw a news report which was uploaded to YouTube the following day and shared widely on Facebook. It begins with the anchor in the newsroom:

> Government's ambitious plan of redeveloping 100-year-old buildings also known as BDD Chawls in Lower Parel and Naigaon has run into severe opposition from residents. While there were residents who wanted the much-needed facelift, several others refused to take part in the biometric survey. Many alleged that the government has not shared any proposal with them and that they will refuse to co-operate until that happens.
> (Mirror Now, 2017 0:01 – 0:24)

The scene then cuts to the entrance of one of the chawl buildings where a reporter, after a brief introduction in English, turns to a young man and asks in Hindi *'Sir aap pehle bataye kyon aap nahin chahiye biometric survey?'* (Sir, first tell me why don't you want a biometric survey?). His reply, inaudible in places, is as follows:

> Kyonki … ham logo ko plan bhi nahin bataye, kya honewale, plan banewale … kuch nahin bataye. Ham logo ko patr bhi nahin diya. MHADA ka patr nahin diya. Sarkar ka … Government ka letter nahin aya, kuch bhi nahin aya.
> (Mirror Now, 2017 1:15–1:35).

> (Because … nobody has told us the plan, what's going to happen, what plan will be made … we've been told nothing. No letter has been given to us, no letter from MHADA, from the government … We've received nothing).

Later in the month, Sayaji, Mahendra, Anish and others organised a big public meeting in the Lalit Kala Bhavan, the hall adjacent to the *kabaddi* ground, to discuss their opposition to the redevelopment proposals with an audience from across the BDD Chawls. I erred on the side of caution and kept away, but I met Shashank More the following day at the Jay Bhim Katta and heard his summary version of events. The key point under discussion among the 300–400 attendees, he told me, was that the residents should refuse to take part in the biometric survey until MHADA provides them with a written agreement, with a government stamp, about the future ownership and size of the new flats. In addition, it was argued that the 1996 tenancy cut-off date should be extended to 2016. These demands will be made to MHADA initially, Shashank explained, but if that is unsuccessful, then the matter will be escalated to the High Court.

I asked him if everyone at the meeting agreed to these proposals. 'Listen', he said in Hindi, 'In every state there are political crosses,' – he said this last word in English and I took it to mean clashes – 'in America, there is Trump versus the Democrats. Here in the BDD Chawls, all the RPI supporters understand the importance of our points.' What about the others, I asked. '*Filhal, jo Shiv Sena ke log hai vo soch rahe hai. Meeting mein, chup chap*' (Currently those in the Shiv Sena are thinking about it. In the meeting they were quiet).

'*Hypnotise ho gaye*' (they were hypnotised): Hindu support

As Shashank explained it, the vanguard of the protest movement was the Dalit Buddhist community, composed largely of RPI(A) supporters but also including NCP-member Mahendra and the Congress politician from Naigaon, alongside a smaller number of members of other communities and political parties. In those first few months after the *bhoomipujan*, there was a palpable optimism among my Jay Bhim Katta friends that they would be able to bring others round to their way of thinking. After all, in Shashank's terms, the residents of the Delisle Road chawls are *sochnewale* (thinkers), unlike the rash-tempered crowd living in the larger BDD Chawls site over at Worli.

But as Anish would reflect several months later, the lure of a free new 500 sq. ft. flat was hard for many to resist. Just before reiterating the familiar story of the waived requirement for occupant consent and the lack of written agreement from MHADA, he described what he perceived as the government's strategy:

> Ye hamare nabbe sal purane buildings hai. Hame bhi naye building chahiye, hame bhi naye ghar chahiye … BJP government ka ek formula hai. Un logo ko sammohit kar de, hypnotise kar de. Jaise, is project mei bhi kiya. Inhone directly declare kiya … 500 sq. ft. carpet ka ghar denge. Directly declare kiya. Uske vajah se kya hua? Log hypnotise ho gaye! 500 sq. ft. ka ghar mil rahe hai. Ekdam mast! Lekin vo ghar dete samay, government ne ek law bhi banaya … 33 (9) B 3(a).
>
> (Anish, interview, 29 October 2017)

(Our buildings are 90 years old. Of course we want new buildings, new homes ... [But] the BJP have a formula. They hypnotise the people. They've done it in this project too. They directly declared that they will give people a 500 sq. ft. carpet area home, and what happened? People were hypnotised! We're getting a 500 sq. ft. home – great! But at the same time the government made a new law ... 33 (9) B 3(a)).

In early August 2017, MHADA again sent officials to conduct biometric tests in Chawls C, D, O2, R1, R2, W and X (those initially slated for redevelopment) and, as before, the opposition movement organised a demonstration, this time outside Chawl X. It was at this demonstration that I was first introduced to Satyajit, my Maratha friend from Chawl D, by Sagar, a Dalit Buddhist from Chawl G. Although I felt a jolt of pleasure in encountering a friendship that crossed community lines, this turned out to be the only time I saw the two together. Sagar had been showing Satyajit a copy of one of the contentious government regulations and beckoned me over to join them. Satyajit spoke good English and said he had spent time working in the UK, after which the two of us drifted off for a cup of chai at one of the nearby stalls.

Once out of Sagar's hearing, Satyajit confided that there had been disputes in the past between Maratha-dominated Chawls C and D on the one side, and Buddhist-dominated Chawls F and G on the other, so that he and his neighbours are not inclined to join the protesters from the Buddhist buildings. In fact, he said, his neighbours had faith in the BJP state government and hence had no problem with the biometric testing, but rather were concerned that opposing the project might risk delaying it until after the next state elections. If Congress were to come to power, he speculated, perhaps the BDD Chawl residents will be given a worse deal later.

A year later he told me that, having completed the biometric testing, the residents of Chawl D now had a written agreement from MHADA detailing the flats they would receive following redevelopment. It was only when he and I pored over the agreement his father had received that he realised this was actually an agreement for transit accommodation, and that the elusive *likhit karar* guaranteeing a free 500 sq. ft. flat had still not materialised. While I sympathised with his zeal to get things moving, and his fear that delays might lead to a worse deal for the residents, it was hard not to view the way that his faith in the 'good work' of the BJP trumped his attention to detail as an example of what Anish would consider hypnotism.

One point of common ground between Anish and Satyajit was their repeated references to the BJP, understandable since the party controlled the Maharashtra Legislative Assembly and hence MHADA. However, an influential manifestation of state power came in the form of the MLA for the local Worli Constituency who belonged to the Shiv Sena and publicly endorsed the redevelopment project. While Sayaji and Mahendra were going from chawl to chawl trying to persuade residents not to undergo biometric testing prior to a detailed written commitment from MHADA, Ram Patil, a Shiv Sena member from Chawl D who Anish described as a stooge for the MLA was doing precisely the opposite.

There was some confusion among my Dalit Buddhist interlocutors after the August 2017 demonstration over exactly who had or had not agreed to take part in the biometric tests. Tellingly, though, no residents in the Buddhist-majority Chawl O2 underwent the tests, while most or all in Ram Patil's Maratha-dominated Chawl D and its demographically similar neighbour Chawl C submitted to them. Satyajit described the Satyam Krida Mandal (jointly operated by Chawls C and D) as 'leading from the front' on the redevelopment, and another resident of Chawl D told me that Ram Patil was 'in charge' of the redevelopment, although in reality his role seemed to be that of liaison with MHADA and with the MLA.

My one meeting with Ram Patil, helpfully brokered by Satyajit, was of little success as it quickly became apparent he was suspicious of my motives and he passed me onto his friend from the same building. This man declared himself 'fully satisfied' with MHADA's proposal based on the meetings he had attended. The only problem he foresaw was that the redevelopment project would be derailed due to divisions between different groups of residents within the BDD Chawls, exploited by Congress and NCP politicians (he did not mention the RPI[A]) for their own gain. This was a speculation I heard on several occasions. Satyajit, despite claiming to be on good terms with Mahendra's brother, informed me that 'Mahendra is not known for good reasons in BDD' and surmised that his public opposition to the redevelopment might simply be a tactic to garner political support should he stand for the BMC elections in future.

For Anish, the prevailing tendency of the Maratha chawl residents to listen only to the MLA and ignore the voices of the predominantly Dalit Buddhist protest movement was yet another manifestation of casteism. He listed Chawls C, D, R1 and R2 as those that had for the most part acquiesced to the biometric test, describing them as 'Maratha buildings', and explained the situation to me as follows:

Yahan pe bhi casteism hai. Un char building mein, chay building mein, logo ko malum hai ki ham log sahi bol raha hain, ham log genuine bol rahe hain. "Bolnewala kaun hai? To Buddhist log hai. Vo sahi bhi batata lekin vo kaun hai? Vo untouchable hai. Previous … pehle untouchable hai … Nokar the. Abhi ye bada ho gaya aur ham ko sikhane lage." Isliye vo hamare sunte nahin. Lekin unke building ke jo achche admi hai, unko samaj mein a raha hai ke kya chalu hai.

(Anish, interview, 29 October 2017)

(Here there's casteism too. In those four or six [Maratha] buildings people know that we're telling the truth, that we're being genuine. 'But who's talking?' [the Marathas ask]. 'Buddhists. They're correct but who are they? Untouchables. Previously untouchable. Servants. Now they've got bigger [in stature] and they're starting to teach us.' So therefore they don't listen to us. But in those buildings, the good guys understand what's going on).

Tejaswini, likewise, complained bitterly that she and others had warned the people in the Maratha-dominated buildings not to agree to the biometric test until they had a written agreement from MHADA, but they had not listened. While none of my Maratha interlocutors framed their disagreement with the protest movement in caste or religious terms, a couple of further incidents lent weight to Anish's perception.

For example, on the one occasion I met the MLA – a typically chance introduction on the street followed by an invitation to a meeting at the local Shiv Sena *shakha* just next to Chawl Q – I mentioned that I knew many of the local supporters of Ramdas Athawale, specifically naming Sayaji and Shashank. 'Ramdas Athawale is in charge of a very small party,' he said, half his attention already elsewhere. Shashank, he added turning back to me, is a mature person, but the others – he mentioned Sayaji, Mahendra and a few other names I did not recognise – are not mature. I tried to explain that all they want is a written agreement with MHADA, to which he crisply replied that MHADA is following the process of the law. He said that he was a big supporter of the redevelopment project and that it was a great project for Mumbai, before turning his attention to the main business of the meeting.

Meanwhile, there was a persistent rumour in the BDD Chawls that flats in the new towers would be allocated on a lottery basis, potentially rehousing members of different communities in close proximity to each other. Nobody complained directly to me about this prospect, but there was a perception among some at the Jay Bhim Katta that the Maratha families were uncomfortable about the possibility of living next door to a

Dalit family. There was even a rumour that residents of some of the Maratha-dominated chawls had written a letter to MHADA specifically asking that they be rehoused with residents of their building or corridor, in effect requesting to live with members of the same community without directly referring to caste or religion.

If this rumour were true, it would hardly be unusual, at least in South Asia. Emma Tarlo has described a slum resettlement in Delhi in which, despite a policy 'designed to cut across social and religious divisions by mixing people up', different phases of the development have largely segregated into Hindu-only and Muslim-only buildings (2000, pp. 68–9). In a Karachi apartment block Laura Ring recounts how new residents, daunted by the building's 'extreme heterogeneity', attempted 'often desperately, to buy or rent flats adjacent to [members of their own families]' (2006, p. 15).

Most potently, Edward Simpson (2013) has argued in terms of a fundamental difference in the attitudes towards space held by residents of Bhuj, in Kutch, and by the urban planners who had come from all over India to help construct the town after the famous 2001 earthquake. While for the planners, thinking about urban space 'in terms of caste' was 'unconstitutional and retrograde', for the residents, space was, or at least should be, 'a manifestation of the caste order in the town' (Simpson, 2013, p. 142). The history of the BDD Chawls pieced together in Chapter 5 can be understood as a stubborn manifestation of caste order on the part of its migrant residents and their offspring, in the face of government planners' attempts to break down this order (cf. Pendse et al., 2011, p. 3). In the BDD Chawls today, conversely, it is the Dalit Buddhist residents who effectively argue that a spatial manifestation of caste is 'unconstitutional and retrograde' and believe that their Hindu neighbours are colluding with the planning authority in an attempt to maintain it.

The limits to chawlness

Not every anthropologist has an exit narrative, but, wanting one for myself, I approached my last visit to the BDD Chawls in 2017 with a sense of occasion. I had already hosted a large group of Dalit Buddhists for a valedictory mutton biryani in my flat, but Mahendra was adamant that I should visit the Jay Bhim Katta on my final evening in Mumbai for an additional send-off. If I questioned Mahendra's judgement in insisting, in the speech he gave, on the uniquely open-minded welcome I had received from the Buddhist community compared to the other communities in the BDD Chawls, I was nonetheless touched by the framed picture of

Ambedkar and copy of the Constitution of India my friends presented me with. I fought back tears as I made some goodbye remarks in Marathi and Hindi, and re-enacted my first encounter with Bharat and Anish on the benches of the *katta* before heading off for a farewell tour of the Gramastha Mandals. I spent the final half-hour of fieldwork with Tukaram eating tandoori chicken gizzards at a street stall.

I was profoundly grateful for these last acts of hospitality, which felt like a culmination of a year's chawlness, the term I introduced in Chapter 1 to convey a sense of shared history and belonging to the BDD Chawls based *inter alia* on ideas of an open-door culture, a neighbourhood origin-myth that cast the buildings as former jails and, today, a common aspiration towards middle-class status. On the surface, chawlness appears to be a powerful force with the potential to transcend the differences between the communities that participate in it. Even in light of the many layers of difference explored in subsequent chapters, it might be expected that when the very foundations of chawlness – the buildings themselves – are threatened, chawlness would act as a unifying force, in the manner celebrated in *Praan Jaaye Par Shaan Na Jaaye* (Gangar, 2011, p. 92).

Indeed, it is hardly surprising that the Gramastha Mandal residents, as the group who participate least in chawlness, given their strong ties of belonging elsewhere, are also the group least preoccupied with the redevelopment debate. It was never a topic that arose spontaneously in my visits to their rooms, and my attempts to start a conversation about it were usually met with shrugs of boredom. Since the rooms were registered in the name of one village member, as far as anyone could tell me the same village member would be entitled to a free flat in the new development. Nobody appeared remotely concerned that the official owner might decide to profit from the room in the new flat at the expense of the Gramastha Mandal, given the social ostracism that this would occasion back in the village.

Tukaram once acknowledged that he thought the proposal was good for him and his roommates since they would end up with a larger living space, but he was hazy on details about timescales and transit accommodation, and told me that in India nothing like this happens quickly. In late November 2017, an acquaintance from Jhambe Gramastha Mandal informed me that the biometric test had been completed for his room by a former resident who now lived in Virar, and as a result he and his roommates would be shifting to transit accommodation in a couple of months' time while they waited for their new flat. I asked him how he felt about this. '*Bura laga!*' (it feels bad!) he replied, but clarified that he was excited at the prospect of a 500 sq. ft. flat, and it was simply the upheaval of having to move out that was a nuisance. The residents of Manewadi

Gramastha Mandal, meanwhile, explained that only seven people would be allowed to live in each room in the redevelopment, so additional rooms will need to be bought elsewhere to house the remaining residents.

Among the permanent family residents, chawlness actually seems to count for very little in the context of a neighbourhood already rife with social tensions. Despite its spectacular power to respond to emergencies, on an everyday level chawlness is characterised less by a 'multi-cultural gusto' (Gangar, 2011, p. 92) and more by an 'edgy, intricate peace' (Ring, 2006, p. 28) marred by microaggressions and the Buddhist–Chambhar 'cold war' we encountered in Chapter 4. As explained in Chapter 1, indeed, everyday chawlness is experienced more at the scale of the *kattas* and corridors than that of the neighbourhood as a whole, and any unifying chawl identity exists more in the homogenising gaze of outsiders than it does in the daily experiences of the chawls' residents themselves. The Gramastha Mandal to Mitra Mandal pipeline, as we discovered in Chapters 3 and 5, has been integral to the emergence of chawlness but is also fundamentally tied up with a building-wise segregation of communities. Hence, as illustrated by 'The ideas of Ambedkar' in Chapter 2, chawlness actually does more to reinforce intra-community bonds than bring Dalit Buddhists and Marathas (or Chambhars) together.

For many, quite simply, the promise of a free flat and the shiny middle-class existence it would bring eclipsed the threat to the old way of life. This sense of anticipation was sharpened by a fear that the current favourable conditions under a BJP-led state government might not last and that the redevelopment was an opportunity that needed to be grasped immediately. These fears were played on by local politicians, notably the Shiv Sena MLA who brought a large proportion of his Maratha and Chambhar supporters on side, thereby eroding yet further the fragile bonds of chawlness.

For the largely Dalit Buddhist-led opposition movement, the impatience with which the redevelopment's mostly Maratha champions greeted their objections was yet another manifestation of casteism. Neither Anish nor any his Dalit Buddhist friends presented the dispute in religious terms, but when listening to their discussions on the matter it was hard to avoid reading a subtext of superstitious Hindus blindly 'hypnotised' by the false future promised by their political leaders, and rational Buddhists asking logical, sceptical questions as they had been doing for thousands of years.

Notes

1   Maharashtra Housing and Area Development Authority.

Epilogue: a neighbourhood at the end of history?

Loose ends: further tales of the city

I penned much of the above in draft form in 2019, imagining that I would return to Mumbai the following year. A global pandemic thwarted this hope, and I was not able to return until April 2022. In the face of my fears of over five years earlier, all 32 buildings were still standing and it was hard to resist anthropomorphising them as proud and obdurate, like some of the leading lights of the protest movement. But time had not stood still, despite the rupture of nearly two years' intermittent lockdown. While the sample flat remained in place, the entire *kabaddi maidan* had been closed off with blue corrugated fencing. Ten buildings had already been largely vacated, including Chawls C and D whose residents were among those at the forefront of the pro-redevelopment lobby, and there were shutters on many of the windows and wooden bars on some of the doors.

On the other side of the site, my friends at the Jay Bhim Katta predicted that their buildings would remain untouched for another five years or so. The protest movement was still in force and had crystallised into five key demands that were being made to the state housing minister, including the scrapping of the pre-1996 eligibility restriction and reiteration of the need for residents' consent prior to the issue of a written agreement. Should these demands not be met, Mahendra and Manish informed me, the next step would be to take the matter to court.

Ambedkar Jayanti that year was a particularly raucous affair after two years of half-hearted attempts to celebrate in a manner compatible with pandemic restrictions. The focal points of the festivities were the temporary structures erected outside the chawls. Most of these were celebratory in theme, focusing on the Constitution or on Ambedkar's intellectual heritage in the form of Buddha, Shivaji and Phule. The display outside Chawl H was overtly political in tone, however, with black cardboard cut-outs of protesting figures raising their fists and waving placards with Marathi messages such as 'The *maidan* is gone but our right to our homes unites us' and 'From democracy to oppression'. Looming above them was a grey image of a chawl, set against a brooding sky, flanked by busts of Shivaji and Ambedkar.

But amid these signs that the battle lines were drawn as they were in 2017, I found something unexpected. Walking past Chawls C and D one evening, I noticed lights on in some of the windows. Round the corner, the space between Hindu-dominated Chawls R1 and R2 had been taken over by a large tent in which preparations for the Ram Navami festival were in full swing. Who were these Hindus that were staying on in defiance of the eviction notice?

A group of men sitting in the tent told me that around half the residents of their buildings had refused to move, in the continued absence of a written agreement. On another occasion I bumped into a boy from Chawl C. He remembered me but I had entirely forgotten him until he reminded me that I had been impressed by his ability to solve a Rubik's Cube. He explained that Ram Patil had 'diluted' the minds of the Satyam Krida Mandal committee and persuaded them to move to the transit camp. Those who remain, like his family, have come to agree with the opposition movement and their insistence on the need for a written agreement prior to moving. When I mentioned this to Manish, he assured me that many of his Hindu neighbours had come round to his way of thinking on the matter.

This struck me as a positive development, not only because it seemed to promise more leverage for the protest movement, but also because it showed that the 'multi-cultural gusto' of the anti-redevelopment protests in *Praan Jaaye Par Shaan Na Jaaye* was perhaps coming to the BDD Chawls after all. At the same time, did this mean abandoning one of my pet theories, that chawlness and shared chawl history were not sufficient to transcend community divisions, and that this insufficiency was laid bare by the redevelopment plans that had so hypnotised the neighbourhood's Hindus? A further complication came in the form of a rumour, relayed to me by a Dalit Buddhist academic with strong connections to the BDD Chawls, that some of those originally opposed to the redevelopment had in fact ended up taking the biometric test and shifting to the transit accommodation.

With a little distance, I feel my initial interpretation was valid at the time – there *was* a clear divide between the mostly Hindu, Shiv

Sena-supporting cheerleaders for the redevelopment, under the charismatic authority of Ram Patil, and the largely Dalit Buddhist opposition movement with its nerve centre at the Jay Bhim Katta where the equally charismatic Mahendra, Sayaji and Anish held sway. Is it really surprising that after years of inertia and pandemic lockdown, minds might change, particularly when confronted with the sharp reality of having to leave their homes without a watertight formal guarantee of having a new home to move back to? It is surely also understandable that the long delay might lead to the opposite phenomenon: principled opposition yielding to a more self-interested desire for a new, free flat.

But it is probable that even in 2017 I was too easily seduced into a seeing a binary, while, away from the core clusters of support and opposition, the actual picture was more ambiguous. After all, I knew several Marathas back then, including Sushil, who had aligned themselves against community lines to the opposition movement. Quite possibly there were Dalit Buddhists who, privately at least, were already frustrated with the protests and impatient to move on. Whatever the messy, shifting reality of the situation, neoliberal capitalist logics of progress have prevailed, and in the closing months of 2022 the first of the chawl buildings were demolished, including Chawls C and D and Chawls R1 and R2, the protest movement finally browbeaten by the state.

Much else has happened in the intervening years, both in the BDD Chawls and across India. On 31 December 2018, a party of 46 set off by bus from the Jay Bhim Katta to Bhima Koregaon for the celebrations the following day. I was not with them, but I understand from social media posts and WhatsApp messages we exchanged after the event that the visit was enjoyable and trouble-free. Over the year that had passed, however, aftershocks from the January 2018 clashes were felt across India in ways that were profoundly troubling.

A series of reports published independently by different fact-finding committees in early 2018 revealed the extent of disagreement over what had happened. In January, a report by the RPI(A)-affiliated Deputy Mayor of Pune pointed to the 'significant role' of Sambhaji Bhide and another *Hindutva* leader called Milind Ekbote in stoking the violence (Chari and Satheesh, 2018). Two months later, a report by Captain Smita Gaikwad for the Forum for Integrated National Security (FINS) think-tank highlighted allegations that the Elgaar Parishad, a conference held in conjunction with the battle celebrations, was part of a Maoist 'strategy to mislead Dalit youth by brainwashing them and attracting them towards violent anti-democratic ways' (Tushar Damgude quoted in Gaikwad, 2018).

Although First Information Reports were filed against both Milind Ekbote and Sambhaji Bhide, only Ekbote was arrested, while no charges were pressed against Bhide, leading some to speculate over political bias despite police claims of insufficient evidence (Dey, 2018). At the time of writing Bhide remains at large and never far from fresh controversy.

Evidence of a Maoist plot, conversely, was apparently sufficient to facilitate the arrest of multiple human rights activists, lawyers and writers, in June and August 2018, for their supposed connection to the Elgaar Parishad. Among these was Anand Teltumbde, whose work has immeasurably enriched my understanding of contemporary Dalit Buddhist society and is cited throughout this book. After an initial raid on his home in August 2018, he was arrested in February 2019 and released shortly afterwards, before being rearrested in April 2020 and held behind bars until late 2022.

To the annoyance of some Dalit activists, the original Bhima Koregaon celebrations and violence were almost completely overshadowed by the endless debates over the Elgaar Parishad arrests. The whole of India, it seemed, had an opinion on these arrests, and these were expressed in news articles, lectures, vigils, blog posts, tweets, WhatsApp circulars, Facebook rants and memes. But, as so often happens when debates escalate at such scale, instead of a billion-part counterpoint covering all the nuances of the country's vast social, political and cultural terrain, what seemed to emerge was more like a binary standoff between two forces: those aligned towards the political left, often referred to in India as 'liberals', who deplored the arrests as a symptom of the ever darker turn the government was taking, and those on the conservative right who cheered them on as an essential intervention against the virus of anti-nationalism.

Soon another virus began to circulate. The single most disconcerting image I saw in the early stages the Covid-19 pandemic was a video from Fawaz of a totally silent Delisle Road. Later Anish shared a video of socially-distanced residents of Chawl F cheering the return of Pradeep, who had been hospitalised. As the Modi government enacted one of the world's strictest lockdowns, the everyday chawlness of proximity and easy companionship was drastically curtailed, but the emergency-mode chawlness was mobilised in force. Tejaswini's daughter explained in a WhatsApp message that residents were allowed to walk around their own buildings and into others' rooms but were not allowed to go outside except for shopping, for two hours in the morning. The whole BDD Chawls collectively decided that only two people from each floor, selected on a rotating basis each week, would go out and shop on their neighbours' behalf.

Meanwhile, the Gramastha Mandals emptied out as residents returned to their villages. Unlike the migrant labourers who made arduous journeys on foot back to villages in Uttar Pradesh and beyond, the BDD Chawls bachelors mostly travelled home in chartered buses and private cars. Many were required to quarantine for 28 days in village schools or empty farmhouses, and I heard about incidences of violence at the hands of frightened villagers, although Sandesh told me his brother's quarantine featured plenty of hanging about outside playing cards with family members who had ostensibly come to deliver food.

After the lockdown ended, many stayed on for many months in their villages. Some, like Tukaram, were able to work from home, while others, like Sunil from Kingaon, lost their Mumbai jobs and found temporary work in the village. Most eventually returned to Mumbai in 2021 or early 2022 and took advantage of the new messes that had opened to feed them. I spent a few happy afternoons and evenings hanging out in various Gramastha Mandals in spring 2022 and, scooping rice and *bhaji* from a metal tiffin stack with my fingers, I could indulge myself briefly in the fiction that nothing had really changed.

An anthropologist's anxieties: methods and ethics revisited

My own relationship to my health changed irrevocably while doing fieldwork. One night in early May I felt a lump, small and rubbery, in the corner of my groin. There was no pain – it was curiously pleasant to the touch in fact – and, half asleep, I wondered if this was my spleen. The next morning it was still there, and I fell to googling. It was obviously an enlarged lymph node, and the UK's National Health Service website indicated it was probably a sign of infection. But I felt fine, so I scanned down the list of rarer, more serious possible causes. None of them looked good: HIV, tuberculosis, lupus and, at the bottom, almost like an afterthought, 'Could it be cancer?'

And so began a five-month journey of visits to the doctor, blood tests and anxiety. I discovered several more enlarged lymph nodes in the weeks that followed, each discovery a queasy spike of despair. HIV was quickly ruled out, as were diabetes and various fungal infections. As the game of elimination led down the path to malignancy, I became intimately familiar with the symptoms of every possible cancer, and the year-on-year risks of a 30- to 35-year-old man contracting each. In June I was diagnosed with syphilis, an unfortunate but easily treatable side effect of my being in a long-distance non-monogamous relationship. At first this was a cause for relief, but my anxieties returned as the lymph nodes refused to shrink after a penicillin injection. Perhaps the syphilis was a red herring? Perhaps I also had an incurable lymphoma? At my lowest ebb I convinced myself that I had a brain tumour.

By October, the lymph nodes had started to subside and with them my fears. Since then, I have largely edited this chapter out of my Mumbai memories, although I no longer take my health for granted in the unthinking way I did before fieldwork. In many ways I was lucky. There were many moments of happiness during this period and, throughout, I remained immersed in fieldwork, which provided a necessary distraction and a feeling of worth deriving from a sense that whatever was wrong with my physical body, I was still building a body of research. Some readers may regard this as toxic but in my case it seemed to work. Many anthropologists have been far less lucky than me, and the stories of friends and colleagues, and those in 'Field of screams', Amy Pollard's classic 2009 study of young ethnographers having a miserable time (which I read obsessively in a spirit of self-boosting schadenfreude), are so often stories of loneliness, shame, guilt, paranoia, illness, fear and regret.

I did not discuss my health concerns in any but the broadest sense with my research participants. I already felt that they saw me as rather fragile and prone to illness, and I hated this role. Every time somebody remarked on the weight I had lost, or the weakness of my arms, or asked me if *'tabiyat down hai?'* (is my condition 'down'?) I felt a rush of anxiety trailed by a cloud of shame. Indeed, shame came easily to me that year: shame at living in a flat, not a chawl; shame at my inability to stomach long overnight bus journeys to visit friends' villages; shame at being too afraid to ride on a motorbike to Bhima Koregaon; shame at my lack of fluency in Hindi and Marathi.

I also avoided the topic because of the uncomfortable questions it would raise about my sexuality. With a few exceptions I never came out in the BDD Chawls, and my interlocutors rarely asked me questions about my romantic life or marriage plans. I struggled to imagine how they would react to my having a boyfriend in the UK, and even more so to my meeting men in Mumbai. The fact that I was perfectly at ease discussing such personal topics with friends from other strands of my Mumbai life – English-medium educated academics and creatives, among others – is unquestionably classism on my part. I heard little to suggest that many in the BDD Chawls held homophobic views, yet the longer I avoided disclosing my queerness, the more remote the possibility of ever doing so seemed. The few people that I did tell were entirely accepting and did not seem particularly fazed, although cautioned me to be selective in who else I told.

I therefore kept sex and fieldwork at arm's length. But in the Introduction (see 'The "why" and the "how": on ethics and methods') I omitted part of the story: while I never allowed sexuality to become an object of study, it invisibly guided the research choices I made. The Gramastha Mandals, for example, were not only virgin ethnographic territory on which I could leave my mark, but they were also intensely tactile, homosocial places with a prevailing atmosphere that always seemed on a knife-edge between banter and flirtation. I was scrupulous in avoiding any temptation to take advantage of this state of affairs, but even so I instinctively gravitated to these spaces and felt just a little more at home and alive in them than I did when visiting Tejaswini and her daughters or hanging out with Gunjan at her stall. Just as my whiteness and maleness impacted the lens through which I viewed the BDD Chawls, so did my sexuality, and it does not feel too much of a stretch to speculate that a heterosexual (male) or asexual researcher might have approached the site in a different way, notwithstanding all the other identities and experiences informing their field methods.

A very different question of methods and ethics only crossed my mind long after leaving the field. One early reader, encountering Vikas' reflections on his roommates' penchant for hard drinks that brought them home in a 'stuporous position', asked me whether I was laughing at Vikas when I wrote this passage.[1] This flummoxed me as I was fond of Vikas and found his requests (that continued after I returned home) for clarification on the meaning of recondite terms like 'withal' and 'prolixity' immensely endearing. And, yes, I often smiled when these requests came through, and we certainly *both* laughed when he used the word 'stuporous'. But if I am indeed laughing at Vikas, am I also laughing at Sayaji with his requests for Ganesh's surname and date of birth; at Mohan, for his obsessive admiration of Shivaji; at Tukaram for his cynicism and image-consciousness? Perhaps the line between affection and mockery is thinner than I realised, especially when operating across a significant power differential, but throughout the writing process I have been mindful of including only such vignettes as shed light on the book's broader arguments, and as far as possible have tried to position *myself* as the butt of any jokes.

In *Decolonizing Methodologies,* Maori activist and professor Linda Tuhiwai Smith turns the tables by listing some of the questions that indigenous activists often ask of researchers: 'Is her spirit clear? Does he have a good heart? What other baggage are they carrying? Are they useful to us? Can they fix up our generator? Can they actually do anything?' (2021, p. 10). I suspect my interlocutors quickly divined that I would be the last person to turn to for practical assistance such as fixing a generator, but as far as I can gauge, they made a favourable judgement on my heart and spirit. The resulting burden of responsibility has been heavy, not least as I have tried to navigate writing the book I want to write while respecting the desires of those that feature in it. For Anish, my usefulness is bound up with my ability to spread Ambedkar's message to a wider audience outside India, something I have in an extremely small way been able to do, albeit not necessarily in quite the manner he would have envisaged. Tukaram, meanwhile, developed a jokey catchphrase, 'I will show you' to convey an unspecific threat should I write about him in a bad light.

Whether, based on this study he will take it upon himself to 'show' me remains to be seen, but I am conscious that, to date, I have only managed to share small extracts of my research with him and others at the BDD Chawls. I gave printouts of an early publication (Galton, 2018) to my friends at the Jay Bhim Katta, and, much later on, used WhatsApp to share the link to an article about Gramastha Mandals I wrote for *Scroll* (Galton, 2022). Most usefully, perhaps, I was able to give Manish a copy of the relevant files pertaining to the BDD Chawls from the Maharashtra State Archives that he would not otherwise have had access to. But, as Tuhiwai Smith argues, 'reporting back' is a never a one-off endeavour, and sharing *knowledge,* as opposed to sharing *information* entails a long-term commitment of trying to explain research, ideas and theories in a way that resonates with participants rather than simply handing out a written report as a one-off act (2021, pp. 16–17). I still have a very long way to go on this journey, and as a next step I hope to get this book translated into Marathi or Hindi, mindful of the many further ethical questions this process will raise.

Conclusion: history lessons for a contested world

The premise of this book has been that of history as a battleground with very real consequences for the future. In his November 2022 speech in Assam, Amit Shah informed the audience that a nation without pride in its 'glorious past' can never aspire to a 'bright future', and that no matter how much India's history has been 'distorted and tampered with', there is nothing to stop the 'correct history' being written now (PTI, 2022). The history the Minister for Home Affairs was referring to was one in which heroic fighters, most of them Hindu, defended India against a long line of 'religiously fanatic' Muslim invaders. Some of my Maratha friends would probably nod at this in sympathy but for their Dalit Buddhist neighbours such rhetoric epitomises false history. Nevertheless, from a very different perspective that should not be simplistically understood as a direct counterpoint to Amit Shah's position, the Buddhists also argue for the need to correct the distortions of history and uncover the glorious past to ensure a bright future. For them, religious fanaticism is principally the preserve of Hindus, the intergenerational victims of a millennia-old duping at the hands of invading Aryans who imposed fake gods and caste hierarchy on the rational Buddhist population.

I set out, in the Introduction, to understand as an anthropologist how such historical debates play out at an everyday neighbourhood level. Here I approach this question by asking a slightly different one: *why* is history so hyper-visible in the BDD Chawls? From the buildings themselves, symbols of a working-class past dominated by the textile industry and a convivial mode of living now threatened with extinction, to the *kattas* and the corridors where gods and historical superhumans all but leap off the walls and into the chawls – why was all this so foreign to me? My adolescence in middle-class southwest England took place against a backdrop of (a)political calm, between the Cold War and the War on Terror, and I never doubted that liberal democracy was humanity's final destination, the end of history (cf. Fukuyama, 1992). I was comfortable enough to have no real need for history to help navigate the everyday or to stake a claim in society. At school, history was a colourful and wide-ranging subject featuring Egyptians, Romans, Tudors, Victorians, Bolsheviks and Nazis. With hindsight, I sympathise with hip-hop intellectual Akala's description of his own history lessons as 'little more than aristocratic nationalist propaganda' (2019, p. 75), but at the time I found it fascinating, provided it did not impinge too obviously on my daily reality.

Back in the BDD Chawls, the everyday salience of the historical, the legendary and the mythical is the result of centuries of instrumentalising and contestation. The ubiquitous images of a godlike Shivaji speak differently to different viewers precisely because of this legacy. Govind Pansare decries the 'false history' of Shivaji that has been deployed by self-interested politicians from the British rulers to the Shiv Sena, and the tendency to turn a great man into a god (2015, pp. 88–96). When Mohan and Tukaram extol Shivaji's Hindu nationalist tolerance in the face of Islamic intolerance, they draw – indirectly, perhaps – on the heritage of Tilak, who fused anticolonial resistance with Brahmanic anti-Muslim sentiment in his nationalist celebrations of Shivaji's life (Hansen, 2001, pp. 30–1). These projects to stake a claim in the 'spiritual domain' of an envisaged future India (Chatterjee, 1993, pp. 5–6) continued long after independence in the renaming of city landmarks, such as Victoria Terminus to Chhatrapati Shivaji Maharaj Terminus in 1996. For the non-Brahman movement, conversely, Shivaji was *kulwadi bhushan* (the 'pride of peasants'), as much a symbol of resistance to Brahmanic hegemony as a totem of anti-imperialism (Hansen, 2001, pp. 30–1; O'Hanlon, 1983. p. 3). This is the legacy I encountered among my Dalit Buddhist friends at the Jay Bhim Katta, although their Shivaji, like that of their Maratha neighbours, has been heavily shaped by school textbooks, even if they now contest the contents of these books.

Only after returning home did it occur to me that maybe all this was not so foreign, after all. The day after I arrived back in the UK in 2018, a group of fellow students from SOAS staged their own historical contestation at a north London café called Blighty which they branded as 'Winston Churchill themed' and a 'colonial and gentrifying presence' in the neighbourhood (Blighty Café Protest, 2018). To a brunching crowd they read out extracts from Heathcote Williams's (2015) poem 'Great Britain's Greatest Beast – Winston Churchill', which stitches together Churchill's own words to reach the inevitable conclusion that 'Churchill was a racist'. In the words of one of the protest organisers, who later faced a vile and sustained campaign of racism in the right-wing tabloid press for her involvement:

> Schooling teaches us about the Second World War and the role played by Churchill, the UK's great wartime leader. There is currently a resurgence in celebrating war-era British history ... [and] The Blighty Café, with its sculpture of Churchill and nostalgic menu, is a part of this trend. But, as is often the case with major historical figures, the reality is inconveniently complex and inconveniently challenging. Aside from the racist views quoted in the poem, Churchill also expressed Islamophobic, antisemitic and anti-Irish views. He had striking miners shot in Wales.
>
> (Hussain, 2018)

While the target of the protest was arguably misdirected (the owner himself claims the café celebrates the Commonwealth rather than glorifying Churchill, and is involved in a range of community and international microfinance initiatives (Evans, 2018)), it sits within a wider trend of reckoning with the 'false', or at least simplistically self-congratulatory history of Britain's place in the world over the past 200–300 years, and an excavation and (re)-centring of alternative, often decolonising histories.[2] For many of those doing this work, like journalist Afua Hirsch, this is not an intellectual abstraction but an urgent grappling with the 'prejudices, problems and hypocrisy' of 'everyday British life' that have so negatively impacted their own lives (Hirsch, 2018, p. 26).

Seeing how thinkers from minoritised communities in my own country have turned to history to claim space in a re-examined national narrative has helped me to better appreciate the importance of history in my Dalit Buddhist interlocutors' worlds. In particular, the privileging of Ambedkar over Gandhi as a nationalist hero; the insistence on his centrality in the Constitution Drafting Committee; the heavy emphasis of his role in creating reservations for marginalised castes – all these make more sense to me when considered not only as a phenomenon characteristic to India, where the idiom of hero-worship bordering on deification permeates society (cf. Pansare, 2015, p. 88), but also recognisable as an example of a more widespread impulse to reclaim one's history – and thereby future – from one's oppressors. That Ambedkar himself was, among many other roles, a historian, is significant in this regard, not least in the way Ambedkar's history-making underpins the 'true' nationalism of ancient Buddhist rationalism and constitutional equality claimed by the regulars at the Jay Bhim Katta.

Again, while Anish and his friends' alternative history is highly specific to their circumstances within contemporary India, alternative nationalisms rooted in particular readings of history can be found in many other parts of the world too. I have already noted the UK Labour Party's attempts to forge a 'progressive patriotism' in the face of an increasingly jingoistic Conservative Party. In Egypt, robust traditions of nationalism exist among the Coptic Christian minority who, akin to Dalit Buddhists in India, 'seek an ideological space for the Copts within Egypt' (van der Vliet, 2009, p. 282).[3] They also draw on ancient history to do so, in this case through a discourse of pan-religious national unity based on a perceived historical continuity with Egypt's glorious Pharaonic past (Wood, 1998, 182–5).

All of this brings us back to Maura Finkelstein's question I posed in Chapter 1: 'not whether these stories are *true* but instead what these stories *do*?' (2019, p. 144). We have seen how, for Dalit Buddhists, parallel narratives of oppression and emancipation both highlight the persistence of caste inequalities in India at large while acknowledging significant improvements to their own personal circumstances (Chapter 2); and how the claim to be Indian, firstly and lastly, appears to be a claim to space in the history, present and future of the nation that is compatible with a critique of the current Hindu-nationalist dispensation (Chapter 4). We have seen how Gramastha Mandal migrants sublimate their present marginalisation in BDD Chawls society, despite typically sharing a language, religion and caste with the resident families that surround them, by pointing to the role of their fathers and grandfathers in establishing the Mitra Mandals that they now feel excluded from (Chapter 3); and how histories of village caste divisions are used to justify the reconfiguration of these divisions in the BDD Chawls (Chapter 5). And we have seen how stories of locked and unlocked doors (Chapter 1) and appeals to a shared Maharashtrian identity and history (Chapter 6) are not sufficient to unite communities in a common position with respect to the redevelopment proposals (Chapter 7) that are now a reality.

It is easy to be seduced into viewing the world in polarised terms – blue–saffron, secular–religious, left–right, conservative–liberal, reactionary–progressive, capitalist–socialist, Republican–Democrat, Leave–Remain – in an attempt to make sense of the confusion, or to maintain or dismantle the status quo. But in doing so we risk being wrongfooted by the exceptions that fall outside the binaries – the women and ethnic minorities who voted for Trump, the gay men who eagerly embrace the most capitalist forms of heteronormativity, the devout Muslims who passionately support queer rights. The 'three tales of the city' I told in the Introduction are themselves binaries: Bombay to Mumbai, mill to mall, multicultural cosmopolis to segregated dystopia, but, as I have shown, the Marathi-centric concept of 'Mumbai' is more widespread and fragmented than at first appears (Chapter 6). We have also seen that many residents of the village of mills have found some space, however tenuous, in the city of malls (Chapters 1, 3 and 5) and that the BDD Chawls has always, to an extent, been a place characterised by spatial segregation of communities (Chapter 5).

Above all, it is the unique stories of individuals and their capacity and propensity to change that disrupts our easy drift into binary thinking. No individual is firstly and lastly a Hindu or a Buddhist, a migrant or a family resident, a Maharashtrian, or even an Indian. Pseudonymisation notwithstanding, Anish is, firstly and lastly, Anish, while Tukaram, transcending and subsuming all his other identities, is pre-eminently Tukaram. Anish's experiences and world views may overlap considerably with those of Sayaji, Manish and Mahendra, but as we have seen, there are differences too, especially in their understandings of history. The same applies to Tejaswini and Gunjan, perhaps even more so. Likewise, there is a great deal of variety in the attitudes and aspirations held by different Gramastha Mandal residents, and in the extent to which they engage in the social life of the neighbourhood. Moreover, none of these identities are static. Not only will one resident of Jhambe Gramastha Mandal not have exactly the same strength of attachment to Jhambe village as another will, but his own sense of belonging at any given time may well be stronger or weaker than it was five years, five months, five days or even five hours ago. And a resident of the BDD Chawls who was staunchly in support of the redevelopment proposal in 2017 might feel very differently in 2022.

Intercommunity friendships and marriages also complicate the narrative of polarisation, even if power differentials along the dominant-marginalised axis mean that simply 'having Dalit friends' might not in itself prompt a Maratha to question their caste privilege, and marrying a dominant-caste Hindu is unlikely to confer any social prestige on a Dalit. But, if nothing else, these cases indicate that the boundaries between communities are porous and remind us that love and friendship do not always fit neatly with groupthink and ideology. I still smile, confused but oddly comforted, when I remember that Mahendra, so stridently opposed to Hinduism, is married to a Hindu who continues to worship her 'fake' gods.

In the end, I have not written the book I originally set out to write, and the sociolinguistic study of a central Mumbai street awaits its better-qualified author. Neither have I written the book Anish would have liked me to write – a biography of Ambedkar from the perspective of his followers – although this niche has already been expertly filled by several others. Instead, I have captured a slice of chawl life at a specific moment in time, a generation after the decline of the mills but before the last remaining vestiges of twentieth-century Lower Parel are destroyed in Mumbai's attempts to transform itself into a new Shanghai. In doing so, I have given an outsider's perspective on two communities (Dalit Buddhist and Maratha Hindu) and also on two modes of living (resident families and migrant bachelors), between which there is limited interaction and considerable misunderstanding. If I have made a theoretical contribution, it has been to build an understanding of how contested narratives of history play out in the daily life of a divided neighbourhood and how different communities invoke the legacies of certain superhuman, or even godlike, figures in fashioning their politics and their cultural identities. The resulting story is both utterly unique to the BDD Chawls and recognisably universal.

Notes

1. See 'Boredom, beer and bhajans' in Chapter 3
2. To take just two examples, Sathnam Sanghera's (2021) *Empireland* traces the legacies of the British empire to illustrate the extent to which the UK remains rooted in its colonial past, while David Olusoga's (2016) documentary 'Black and British: a forgotten history' unearths strands of British history that have long been sidelined and suppressed.
3. See also ElGendi, 2017.

Bibliography

Adarkar, N. 2011. 'Salaries and wages: Girgaon and Girangaon', in Adarkar, N. (ed.) *The Chawls of Mumbai: Galleries of life*. Delhi: ImprintOne, pp. 15–25.

Adarkar, N. and Menon, M. 2004. *One Hundred Years, One Hundred Voices – The Millworkers of Girangaon: An oral history*. Calcutta: Seagull Books.

Akala. 2019. *Natives: Race and class in the ruins of empire*. London: Two Roads.

Aloysius, G. 1997. *Nationalism without a Nation in India*. New Delhi: Oxford University Press.

Ambedkar, B.R. 1982a. 'B.L.C. Debates, Vol. XXIII', in Moon, V. (ed.), *Dr Babasaheb Ambedkar, Writings and Speeches* (Vol. 2). Bombay: Education Department, Government of Maharashtra, pp. 381–2.

Ambedkar, B.R. 1982b. 'On the creation of a separate Karnatak province', in Moon, V. (ed.), *Dr Babasaheb Ambedkar, Writings and Speeches* (Vol. 2). Bombay: Education Department, Government of Maharashtra, pp. 189–96.

Ambedkar, B.R. 1982c. 'Dr Ambedkar at the Round Table Conferences', in Moon, V. (ed.), *Dr Babasaheb Ambedkar, Writings and Speeches* (Vol. 2). Bombay: Education Department, Government of Maharashtra, pp. 503–792.

Ambedkar, B.R. 1987a. 'Revolution and counter-revolution', in Moon, V. (ed.), *Dr Babasaheb Ambedkar, Writings and Speeches* (Vol. 3). Bombay: Education Department, Government of Maharashtra, pp. 151–429.

Ambedkar, B.R. 1987b. 'Riddles in Hinduism', in Moon, V. (ed.), *Dr Babasaheb Ambedkar, Writings and Speeches* (Vol. 4). Bombay: Education Department, Government of Maharashtra, pp. 5–362.

Ambedkar, B.R. 1990a. 'Who were the Shudras', in Moon, V. (ed.), *Dr Babasaheb Ambedkar, Writings and Speeches* (Vol. 7). Bombay: Education Department, Government of Maharashtra, pp. 9–229.

Ambedkar, B.R. 1990b. 'Pakistan, or the partition of India', in Moon, V. (ed.), *Dr Babasaheb Ambedkar, Writings and Speeches* (Vol. 8). Bombay: Education Department, Government of Maharashtra, pp. 1–483.

Ambedkar, B.R. 1993. 'The untouchables and the Pax Britannica', in Moon, V. (ed.), *Dr Babasaheb Ambedkar, Writings and Speeches* (Vol. 12). Bombay: Education Department, Government of Maharashtra, pp. 75–147.

Ambedkar, B.R. 2013. *The Annihilation of Caste with Reply to Mahatma Gandhi*. Diamond Jubilee special issue. Mumbai: Government of Maharashtra.

Ambedkar, B.R. 2014a. 'Adoption of the Constitution', in Moon, V. (ed.), *Dr Babasaheb Ambedkar, Writings and Speeches* (Vol. 13). Bombay: Education Department, Government of Maharashtra, pp. 1161–219.

Ambedkar, B.R. 2014b. 'Statement by Dr B. R. Ambedkar in explanation of his resignation', in Moon, V. (ed.), *Dr Babasaheb Ambedkar, Writings and Speeches* (Vol. 14-II). Bombay: Education Department, Government of Maharashtra, pp. 1317–27.

Ambedkar, B.R. 2014c. 'The rise and fall of the Hindu woman: Who was responsible for it?', in Moon, V. (ed.), *Dr Babasaheb Ambedkar, Writings and Speeches* (Vol. 17-II). Bombay: Education Department, Government of Maharashtra, pp. 109–29.

Ambedkar, B.R. 2014d. 'Do not depend on God or superman', in Moon, V. (ed.), *Dr Babasaheb Ambedkar, Writings and Speeches* (Vol. 17-III). Bombay: Education Department, Government of Maharashtra, pp. 88–9.

Anderson, B. 1991. *Imagined Communities: Reflections on the origin and spread of nationalism* Revised and extended edition. London: Verso.
Anderson, S., Francois, P., Kotwal, A. and Kulkarni, A. 2016. 'Distress in Marathaland'. *Economic and Political Weekly,* 51 (51): 14–16.
Anthony, D.W. 2007. *The Horse, the Wheel and Language: How Bronze-Age riders from the Eurasian steppes shaped the modern world.* Princeton: Princeton University Press.
Appadurai, A., 2000. 'Spectral housing and urban cleansing: Notes on millennial Mumbai'. *Public Culture,* 12 (3): 627–51.
Bakker, H. 1986. *Ayodhya: The history of Ayodhya from the 7th century BC to the middle of the 18th century.* Groningen: E. Forsten.
Bakshi, S.R. and Sharma, S. K. 2000. *The Great Marathas.* New Delhi: Deep & Deep Publications.
Bare Acts Live. 2018. 'Maharashtra State Reservation (of seats for admission in educational institutions in the State and for appointments in the public services and posts under the State) for Socially and Educationally Backward Classes (SEBC) Act, 2018'. http://www.bareactslive.com/MAH/mh849.htm (accessed 8/12/22).
Beltz, J. 2004. 'Introduction', in Jondhale, S. and Beltz, J. (eds), *Reconstructing the World: B.R. Ambedkar and Buddhism in India.* New Delhi: Oxford University Press, pp. 97–119.
Beltz, J. 2005. *Mahar, Buddhist and Dalit: Religious conversion and socio-political emancipation.* New Delhi: Manohar.
Bénéï, V. 2008. *Schooling Passions: Nation, history and language in contemporary western India.* Stanford, CA: Stanford University Press.
Berliner, D. (ed.). 2016. 'Anthropology and the study of contradictions'. *HAU: Journal of Ethnographic Theory* 6 (1): 1–27.
Béteille, A. 1992. *Society and Politics in India: Essays in a comparative perspective.* New Delhi: Oxford University Press.
Bhattacharya, A. 2018. 'Bhima Koregaon and the Dalits' never-ending search for a nation'. *The Wire,* 5 January. https://thewire.in/caste/bhima-koregaon-dalits-never-ending-search-nation (accessed 24/2/23).
Birkvad, I.R. 2020. 'The ambivalence of Aryanism: A genealogical reading of India-Europe connection'. *Millennium: Journal of International Studies* 49 (1).
Blighty Café Protest. 2018. https://vimeo.com/255423060 (accessed 29/12/22).
BMC Elections, 2017. 'BMC New Ward No 198 Municipal Civic Elections 2017'. BMC Elections. https://www.bmcelections.com/ward-no-198-g-south-ward-brihan-mumbai-municipal-corporation-mcgm/ (accessed 8/12/22).
Bourdieu, P. 2003. *Firing Back: Against the tyranny of the market.* London: Verso.
Caru, V. 2011. 'The making of a working-class area, the Worli BDD Chawls (1920–40)', in Adarkar, N. (ed.), *The Chawls of Mumbai: Galleries of life.* Delhi: ImprintOne, pp. 26–36.
Caru, V. 2019. '"A powerful weapon for employers?": Workers' housing and social control in interwar Bombay', in Kidambi, P., Kamat, M. and Dwyer, R. (eds) *Bombay before Mumbai: Essays in Honour of Jim Masselos.* London: Hurst & Co., pp. 213–35.
Chandavarkar, R. 1994. *The Origins of Industrial Capitalism in India: Business strategies and the working classes in Bombay, 1900–1940.* Cambridge: Cambridge University Press.
Chandavarkar, R. 2004. 'From neighbourhood to nation: The rise and fall of the left in Bombay's Girangaon in the twentieth century', in Adarkar, N. and Menon, M. (eds) *One Hundred Years, One Hundred Voices – the Millworkers of Girangaon: An oral history.* Calcutta: Seagull Books, pp. 7–80.
Chandran, R. 2017. 'Mumbai tenants paying 30 cents rent oppose revamp of century-old homes'. *Reuters,* 5 June. https://www.reuters.com/article/india-landrights-housing-idUKL5N1FH0B6 (accessed 24/2/23).
Chari, M. 2018a. 'People with saffron flags allegedly attack Dalits going to Bhima Koregaon memorial near Pune'. *Scroll.in,* 1 January. https://scroll.in/latest/863444/people-with-saffron-flags-allegedly-attack-dalits-heading-to-bhima-koregaon-memorial-near-pune (accessed 24/2/23).
Chari, M. 2018b. 'Thousands rally in Mumbai to demand the arrest of alleged instigator of Bhima Koregaon violence'. *Scroll.in,* 26 March. https://scroll.in/article/873408/thousands-rally-in-mumbai-to-demand-the-arrest-of-alleged-instigator-of-bhima-koregaon-violence (accessed 24/2/23).
Chari, M. and Satheesh, S. 2018. 'Tensions over 300-year-old history hold the key to the Bhima Koregaon violence – not a Maoist plot'. *Scroll.in,* 15 Sept. https://scroll.in/article/894403/

tensions-over-300-year-old-history-hold-the-key-to-the-bhima-koregaon-violence-not-a-maoist-plot (accessed 24/2/23).

Chatterjee, P. 1993. *The Nation and its Fragments: Colonial and postcolonial histories*. Princeton, NJ: Princeton University Press.

Chatterji, A.P, Hansen, T.B. and Jaffrelot, C. 2019. (eds) *Majoritarian State: How Hindu nationalism is changing India*. New York, NY: Oxford University Press.

Cohn, B. 1955. 'The changing status of a depressed caste', in Marriott, M. (ed.), *Village India: Studies in the little community*. Menasha, WI: American Anthropological Association, pp. 53–77.

Coleman, A. 1985. *Utopia on Trial: Vision and reality in planned housing*. London: Shipman.

Dandekar, H.C. 1986. *Men to Bombay, Women at Home: Urban influence on Sugao village, Deccan, Maharashtra, India, 1942–1982*. Ann Arbor: Centre for South and Southeast Asian Studies, University of Michigan.

Das, B. 2000. 'Moments in a history of reservations'. *Economic and Political Weekly*, 35 (43/44): 3831–4.

Das, P.K. 1995. 'Manifesto of a housing activist', in Patel, S. and Thorner, A. (eds) *Bombay: Metaphor for Modern India*. New Delhi: Oxford University Press. pp. 213–47.

Daut, M. 2021. 'Napoleon isn't a hero to celebrate'. *New York Times*, 18 March. https://www.nytimes.com/2021/03/18/opinion/france-year-of-napoleon.html (accessed 10/2/23).

De, R. 2018. *A People's Constitution: The everyday life of law in the Indian Republic*. Histories of Economic Life. Princeton, NJ: Princeton University Press.

Deshingkar, P. and Farrington, J. (eds). 2009. *Circular Migration and Multilocational Livelihood Strategies in Rural India*. New Delhi: Oxford University Press.

Deshpande, A. and Ramachandran, R. 2017. 'Dominant or backward? Political economy of demand for quotas by Jats, Patels and Marathas'. *Economic and Political Weekly* 52: 81–92.

Deshpande, P. 2007. *Creative Pasts: Historical memory and identity in western India, 1700–1960*. New York, NY: Columbia University Press.

Deshpande, R. and Palshikar, S. 2017. 'Political economy of a dominant caste', in Nagaraj, R. and Motiram, S. (eds) *Political Economy of Contemporary India*. Cambridge: Cambridge University Press, pp. 77–97.

Dey, A. 2018. 'Bhima Koregaon case: Pune police is not pressing charges against Hindutva leader Sambhaji Bhide'. *Scroll.in*, 31 August. https://scroll.in/article/892601/bhima-koregaon-case-pune-police-is-not-pressing-charges-against-hindutva-leader-sambhaji-bhide (accessed 9/12/22).

Dhupkar, A. 2017. 'Residents oppose govt decision on BDD Chawls redevelopment'. *Mumbai Mirror*, 3 April. https://mumbaimirror.indiatimes.com/mumbai/other/residents-oppose-govt-decision-on-bdd-chawl-redevelopment/articleshow/57982341.cms (accessed 24/2/23).

D'Monte, D. 2002. *Ripping the Fabric: The decline of Mumbai and its mills*. New Delhi: Oxford University Press.

Doniger, W. 2009. *The Hindus: An alternative history*. London: Penguin Press.

Doran, C. 2017. 'Nationalism is not a dirty word'. *Journal of Socialomics*, 6(3): 207.

Echanove, M. and Srivastava, R. 2014. 'Mumbai's circulatory urbanism', in Angelil, M. and Hehl, R. (eds), *Empower! Essays on the Political Economy (+ Political Ecology) of Urban Form*. Berlin: Ruby Press, pp. 82–113.

ElGendi, Y. 2017. 'Coptic commemorative protests and discourses of Egyptian nationalism: A Visual Analysis'. *Middle East – Topics & Arguments* 8: 45–56.

Evans, C. 2018. 'Activists stormed my Blighty cafe. But we're about community, not colonialism'. *The Guardian*, 31 January. https://www.theguardian.com/commentisfree/2018/jan/31/cafe-blighty-protesters-community-colonialism (accessed 29/12/22).

Express Web Desk, 2018. 'Mumbai bandh highlights: Jignesh Mevani appeals for peace, says state govt must ensure rule of law'. *The Indian Express*, 3 January. https://indianexpress.com/article/cities/mumbai/mumbai-bandh-live-updates-dalit-marathas-clashes-pune-bhima-koregaon-5008377/ (accessed 24/2/23).

Fernandes, L. 2006. *India's New Middle Class: Democratic politics in an era of economic reform*. Minneapolis: University of Minnesota Press.

Fernandes, N. 2013. *City Adrift: A short biography of Bombay*. New Delhi: Aleph Book Company.

Finkelstein, M. 2011. 'The chronotype of a chawl: A ghost story in three acts', in Adarkar, N. (ed.), *The Chawls of Mumbai: Galleries of life*. Delhi: ImprintOne, pp. 49–57.

Finkelstein, M. 2019. *The Archive of Loss: Lively ruination in mill land Mumbai*. Durham, NC: Duke University Press.

Firstpost, 2018. 'Shiv Sena supports reservation demands for Maratha community, goes against party's stance under Bal Thackeray'. *Firstpost,* 31 July. https://www.firstpost.com/politics/shiv-sena-supports-reservation-demands-for-maratha-community-goes-against-partys-stance-under-bal-thackeray-4855671.html (accessed 24/2/23).

Fiske, A. and Emmrich, C. 2004. 'The use of Buddhist scriptures in B.R. Ambedkar's The Buddha and His Dhamma', in Jondhale, S. and Beltz, J. (eds), *Reconstructing the World: B.R. Ambedkar and Buddhism in India.* New Delhi: Oxford University Press, pp. 97–119.

Fitzgerald, T. 2004. 'Analysing sects, minorities, and social movements in India: The case of Ambedkar, Buddhism and Dalit(s)', in Jondhale, S. and Beltz, J. (eds), *Reconstructing the World: B.R. Ambedkar and Buddhism in India.* New Delhi: Oxford University Press, pp. 267–82.

Fuchs, M. 2004. 'Buddhism and Dalitness: Dilemmas of religious emancipation', in Jondhale, S. and Beltz, J. (eds), *Reconstructing the World: B.R. Ambedkar and Buddhism in India.* New Delhi: Oxford University Press, pp. 97–119.

Fukuyama, F. 1992. *The End of History and the Last Man.* New York, NY: Free Press.

Gadgil, M. 2017. 'BDD chawl redevelopment receives no bids'. *Mumbai Mirror,* 15 February.

Gaikwad. S. 2018. 'Report on Koregaon-Bhima riot Jan 1, 2018'. Forum for Integrated National Security.

Gallinews, 2017. 'BDD Chawl Ke Redevelopment Project ka Virodh karnewale ko Police ne kiya Giraftar'. *Gallinews.com,* 22 April. https://gallinews.com/bdd-chawl-ke-redevelopment-project-ka-virodh-karnewale-ko-police-ne-kiya-giraftar/ (accessed 24/2/23).

Galton, J. 2018. 'Celebrating the Battle of Koregaon: Contested histories and the (de-)colonial Dalit subject'. *SOAS Journal of Postgraduate Research,* 11: 63–84.

Galton, J. 2022. 'In busy Mumbai, gramastha mandal dormitories offer the comfort of the village in the city's heart'. *Scroll.in,* 15 May. https://scroll.in/article/1023180/in-busy-mumbai-gramastha-mandal-dormitories-offer-the-comfort-of-the-village-in-the-citys-heart (accessed 29/12/22).

Gangar, A. 2011. 'Chalchitra/chawlchitra: The representation of Mumbai's chawls in Hindi films', in Adarkar, N. (ed.), *The Chawls of Mumbai: Galleries of life.* Delhi: ImprintOne, pp. 89–100.

Gardner, A. 2010. *City of Strangers: Gulf migration and the Indian community in Bahrain.* Ithaca, NY: ILR Press.

Gavaskar, M. 2010. 'Mumbai's shattered mirror'. *Economic and Political Weekly,* 45 (7): 17–22.

Geertz, C. 1998. 'Deep hanging out'. *The New York Review of Books,* October 22nd.

Geertz, C. 2000. 'Deep play: Notes on the Balinese cockfight', in Geertz, C. (ed), *The Interpretation of Cultures: Selected essays.* New York, NY: Basic Books, pp. 412–54.

Gellner, E. 1983. *Nations and Nationalism.* Oxford: Blackwell.

Ghannam, F. 2002. *Remaking the Modern: Space, relocation and the politics of identity in a global Cairo.* Berkeley: University of California Press.

Glaeser, E. 2011. *The Triumph of the City: How urban spaces make us human.* London: Macmillan.

Golwalkar, M.S. 1939. *We, or Our Nationhood Defined.* Nagpur: Harihareshwar Printing Press.

Gombrich, R. 1988. 'How the Mahayana began'. *Journal of Pali and Buddhist Studies,* 1: 29–46.

Gore, M.S. 1970. *Immigrants and Neighbourhoods: Two aspects of life in a metropolitan city.* Bombay: TISS.

Gorringe, H. 2008. 'The caste of the nation: Untouchability and citizenship in South India'. *Contributions to Indian Sociology,* 42 (1): 123–49.

Government of Maharashtra, 2016. Sanctioned Modification to Regulation 33(9) of Development Control Regulations for Greater Mumbai, 1991.

Gudavarthy, A. 2018. *India After Modi: Populism and the right.* London: Bloomsbury India.

Guha, R. 2002. 'The darling of the dispossessed' (originally published in *The Hindu*). http://ramachandraguha.in/archives/ambedkar-the-hindu.html (accessed 12/12/22).

Gundimeda, S. 2015. *Dalit Politics in Contemporary India.* Basingstoke: Taylor and Francis.

Gupta, D. 2005. 'Whither the Indian village: Culture and agriculture in "rural" India'. *Economic and Political Weekly,* 40 (8): 751–8.

Guru, G. 2016. 'Nationalism as the framework for Dalit self-realization'. *Brown Journal of World Affairs,* 23 (1): 239–52.

Habib, S.I. 2017. 'Introduction', in Habib, S. I. (ed.), *Indian Nationalism: The essential writings.* New Delhi: Aleph Book Company, pp. 1–36.

Hansen, T.B. 1999. *The Saffron Wave: Democracy and Hindu nationalism in modern India.* Princeton, NJ: Princeton University Press.

Hansen, T.B. 2001. *Wages of Violence: Naming and identity in postcolonial Bombay*. Princeton, NJ: Princeton University Press.

Hansen, T.B. and Verkaaik, O. 2009. 'Introduction – urban charisma: On everyday mythologies in the city'. *Critique of Anthropology*, 29: 5–26.

Hanwate, M. 2017. 'Developers turn backs on tenders for BDD chawl redevelopment plan'. *Mumbai Live*, 28 February. https://www.mumbailive.com/en/infrastructure/builders-thwart-bdd-redevelopment-plans-once-again-8462 (accessed 24/2/23).

Harris, A., 2008. 'From London to Mumbai and back again: Gentrification and public policy in comparative perspective'. *Urban Studies* 45 (12): 2407–28.

Haygunde, C. 2022. 'Hindutva leader Sambhaji Bhide dropped from Koregaon Bhima violence case: Police to SHRC'. *The Indian Express*, 5 May. https://indianexpress.com/article/cities/pune/sambhaji-bhide-koregaon-bhima-violence-case-police-7901767/ (accessed 24/2/23).

Heuzé, G. 1995. 'Cultural populism: The appeal of the Shiv Sena', in Patel, S. and Thorner, A. (eds) *Bombay: Metaphor for modern India*. Bombay: Oxford University Press, pp. 213–47.

Hirsch, A. 2017. 'Toppling statues? Here's why Nelson's column should be next'. *Guardian*, 22 August. https://www.theguardian.com/commentisfree/2017/aug/22/toppling-statues-nelsons-column-should-be-next-slavery (accessed 10/2/23).

Hirsch, A. 2018. *Brit(ish): On race, identity and belonging*. London: Vintage.

Holt, J. 2016. 'Introduction' in Holt, J. (ed), *Buddhist Extremists and Muslim Minorities: Religious conflict in contemporary Sri Lanka*. New York, NY: Oxford University Press, pp. 1–17.

Holwitt, p. 2017. 'Strange food, strange smells: Vegetarianism and sensorial citizenship in Mumbai's redeveloped enclaves'. *Contemporary South Asia* 25: 333–46.

Hussain, H. 2018. 'I read a poem at Blighty Cafe: The brunch empire which celebrates Britain's imperial history'. *Gal-dem*, 15 February. https://gal-dem.com/blighty-cafe-celebrates-imperial-history/ (accessed 29/12/22).

Ilaiah, K. 1996. *Why I Am Not a Hindu: A Sudra critique of Hindutva, philosophy, culture, and political economy*. Calcutta: Samya; Distributed by Bhatkal Books International.

Jaffrelot, C. 1996. *The Hindu Nationalist Movement and Indian Politics, 1925 to the 1990s: Strategies of identity-building, implantation and mobilisation (with special reference to Central India)*. London: Hurst & Co.

Jaffrelot, C. 2005. 'For a theory of nationalism'. In Dieckhoff, A. and Jaffrelot, C. (eds), *Revisiting Nationalism*. New York, NY: Palgrave Macmillan.

JanMohamed, A. 2019. 'Rohit Vemula's revolutionary suicide', in Chatterji, A. P, Hansen, T. B. and Jaffrelot, C. (eds), *Majoritarian State: How Hindu nationalism is changing India*. New York, NY: Oxford University Press.

Jaoul, N. 2006. 'Learning the use of symbolic means: Dalits, Ambedkar statues, and the state in Uttar Pradesh'. *Contributions to Indian Sociology* 40: 175–207.

Jaoul, N. 2012. 'The making of a political stronghold: A Dalit neighbourhood's exit from the Hindu Nationalist riot system'. *Ethnography* 13: 102–16.

Jaoul, N. 2016. 'Citizenship in religious clothing? Navayana Buddhism and Dalit emancipation in late 1990s'. *Focaal – Journal of Global and Historical Anthropology* 76: 46–68.

Jeelani, G. 2017. 'From love jihad, conversion to SRK: 10 controversial comments by UP's new CM Yogi Adityanath'. *Hindustan Times*, 6 April. https://www.hindustantimes.com/assembly-elections/from-love-jihad-conversion-to-srk-10-controversial-comments-by-up-s-new-cm-yogi-adityanath/story-5JW2ZFGZzAdIZeIcjcZCNM.html (accessed: 5/12/22).

Jones, R., Cox, D., Dionne, E.J., Galston, W., Cooper, B. and Lienesch, R. 2016. 'How immigration and concerns about cultural changes are shaping the 2016 election: Findings from the 2016 PRRI/Brookings Immigration Survey'. Washington: Public Religion Research Institute.

Judah, B. 2016. *This is London: Life and death in the world city*. London: Picador.

Junghare, I. 1988. 'Dr Ambedkar: The hero of the Mahars, ex-untouchables of India'. *Asian Folklore Studies* 47: 93–121.

Kamdar, M. 1997. 'Bombay/Mumbai: The postmodern city'. *World Policy Journal* 14: 75–88.

Kapilacharya. 1967. *Shiv Sena Speaks*. Bombay: Marmik.

Kasianov, G. 2022. 'The war over Ukrainian identity'. *Foreign Affairs*, 4 May. https://www.foreignaffairs.com/articles/ukraine/2022-05-04/war-over-ukrainian-identity (accessed 29/12/22)

Kaul, N. 2017. 'Rise of the political right in India: Hindutva-development mix, Modi myth and dualities'. *Journal of Labour and Society*, 20 (4): 523–48.

Kaur, R. 2003. *Performative Politics and the Cultures of Hinduism: Public uses of religion in western India*. Delhi: Permanent Black.

Keer, D. 1971. *Dr Babasaheb Ambedkar: Life and mission*. Bombay: Popular Prakashan.

Kharat, S. 2009. 'The bone merchant', in Dangle, A. (ed.), *Poisoned Bread: Translations from modern Marathi Dalit literature* (trans. Adarkar, P.). Hyderabad: Orient Black Swan, pp. 123–9.

Kidambi, P. 2001. 'Housing the poor in a colonial city: The Bombay Improvement Trust, 1898–1918'. *Studies in History*, 18: 57–79.

Kidambi, P. 2007. *The Making of an Indian Metropolis: Colonial governance and public culture in Bombay, 1890–1920*. Aldershot: Ashgate.

Koppikar, S. 2018. 'Underlying Maharashtra's Dalit protests, a tangle of old caste struggles and new Hindutva assertion'. *Scroll.in*, 3 January. https://scroll.in/article/863644/underlying-maharashtras-dalit-protests-a-tangle-of-old-caste-struggles-and-new-hindutva-assertion (accessed 24/2/23).

Kosambi, M. 1995. 'British Bombay and Marathi Mumbai', in Patel, S. and Thorner, A. (eds) *Bombay: Mosaic of modern culture*. Bombay: Oxford University Press, pp. 3–24.

Krishnan, S. 2000. *The Murder of the Mills: A case study of Phoenix Mills*. Mumbai: Girangaon Bachao Andolan.

Kulkarni, A.R. 1996. *Marathas and the Maratha country*. New Delhi: Books & Books.

Kumar, M. 2009. 'Reservations for Marathas in Maharashtra'. *Economic and Political Weekly* 44: 10–12.

Kumar, S. and Ansari, K. 2022. 'The alliance matrix: Dalit-Muslim unity or Dalit-Pasmanda unity?' *Economic and Political Weekly*, 57 (22). https://www.epw.in/engage/article/alliance-matrix-dalit-muslim-unity-or-dalit (accessed 24/2/23).

Kumar, U. 2015. 'Prof Vimal Thorat delivers lecture on Dalit feminist writing at MIT'. TwoCircles.net. https://twocircles.net/2015may24/1432488896.html (accessed 24/2/23).

Kumbhojkar, S., 2012. 'Contesting power, contesting memories: The history of the Koregaon Memorial'. *Economic and Political Weekly*, 47: 103–7.

Kunduri, E. 2018. 'Beyond *khet* (field) and factory, *gaanv* (village) and *sheher* (city): Caste, gender and the (re)shaping of migrant identities in urban India'. *South Asia Multidisciplinary Academic Journal*, 19.

Laine, J.W. 2003. *Shivaji: Hindu king in Islamic India*. Oxford: Oxford University Press.

Laine, J.W. 2011. 'Resisting my attackers, resisting my defenders: Representing the Shivaji narratives', in Schmalz, M.N. and Gottschalk, P. (eds), *Engaging South Asian Religions Boundaries, Appropriations, and Resistances*. Albany, NY: State University of New York Press, pp. 153–72.

Leeson, L. 2019. 'Our land: Creative approaches to the redevelopment of London's Docklands'. *International Journal of Heritage Studies*, 25 (4): 365–379.

LeftWord, 2015. 'Publisher's note' in Pansare, G. 2015. *Who Was Shivaji?* (trans. Narkar, U.). New Delhi: LeftWord.

Lele, J. 1995. 'Saffronization of the Shiv Sena: The political economy of city, state and nation', in Patel, S. and Thorner, A. (eds), *Bombay: Metaphor for modern India*. Bombay: Oxford University Press. pp. 213–47.

Limbale, S. 2009. 'The bastard', in Dangle, A. (ed.) *Poisoned Bread: Translations from modern Marathi Dalit literature* (trans. Agrawal, D.). Hyderabad: Orient Blackswan, pp. 130–42.

Lloyd, D. 1997. 'Nationalisms against the state', in Lowe, L. and Lloyd, D. (eds), *The Politics of Culture in the Shadow of Capital*. Durham, NC: Duke University Press, pp. 173–97.

Maharashtra Housing and Building Laws, 2014. 'The Development Control Regulations for Greater Mumbai, 1991 [as modified up to the 21st June, 2014]'. http://maharashtrahousingandbuildinglaws.com/the-development-control-regulations-for-greater-mumbai-1991/ (accessed 16/12/22).

Malinowski, B. 1922. *Argonauts of the Western Pacific: An account of native enterprise and adventure in the archipelagos of Melanesian New Guinea*. New York: E. P. Dutton.

Masoodi, A. 2017. 'The changing fabric of Dalit life'. *Livemint*, 21 April. https://www.livemint.com/Leisure/avsrwntNuBHG3THdAb5aMP/The-changing-fabric-of-Dalit-life.html (accessed 24/2/23).

Masselos, J. 2019. 'Remembering Bombay: Present memories, past histories', in Kidambi, P., Kamat, M. and Dwyer, R. (eds) *Bombay Before Mumbai: Essays in honour of Jim Masselos*. London: Hurst & Co., pp. 305–14.

Massey, D. 1991. 'A global sense of place'. *Marxism Today*, June 1991. https://banmarchive.org.uk/marxism-today/june-1991/a-global-sense-of-place/ (accessed 2/1/23).

McCann, C. 2017. 'Separate but equal? Gender segregation in UK schools'. *Oxford Human Rights Hub* https://ohrh.law.ox.ac.uk/separate-but-equal-gender-segregation-in-uk-schools/ (accessed 12/12/22).

McGrew, W. 2016. 'Gender segregation at work: "Separate but equal" or "inefficient and unfair"' https://equitablegrowth.org/gender-segregation-at-work-separate-but-equal-or-inequitable-and-inefficient/ (accessed 12/12/22).

Mehta, S. 2004. *Maximum City: Bombay lost and found*. London: Review.

Mehta, K. 2011. 'The terrain of home, and within urban neighbourhoods (a case of Bombay chawls)', in Adarkar, N. (ed.), *The Chawls of Mumbai: Galleries of life*. Delhi: ImprintOne, pp. 81–8.

Mhaskar, S. 2013. 'Encountering "inclusion" and exclusion in post-industrial Mumbai: A study of Muslim ex-millworkers' occupational choices', in Skoda, U., Nielsen, K.B. and Fibiger, M.Q. (eds), *Navigating Exclusion, Inclusion Engineering: Entangled social processes in India*, London: Anthem Press, pp. 149–63.

Mhaskar, S. 2018. 'Ghettoisation of economic choices in a global city: A case study of Mumbai'. *Economic and Political Weekly*, 53 (29): 29–37.

Mhaskar, S. and Sapkal, R.S. 2022. 'Backward or forward? Examining the contemporary caste status of Marathas'. *Economic and Political Weekly*, 57 (16).

Mines, D.P. 2005. *Fierce Gods: Inequality, ritual, and the politics of dignity in a south Indian village*. Bloomington: Indiana University Press.

Mirror Now. 2017. 'BDD Chawls residents say no to biometric survey – The News'. https://www.youtube.com/watch?v=heguBkUT3VU&feature=youtu.be (accessed 16/12/22).

Mishra, P. 2013. 'A temple for god of cricket Sachin Tendulkar in Bihar'. *Hindustan Times*, 20 November. https://www.hindustantimes.com/india/a-temple-for-god-of-cricket-sachin-tendulkar-in-bihar/story-ETQfMpSOLsrPb1eSZdv8ZM.html (accessed 24/2/23).

Mosse, D. 2012. *The Saint in the Banyan Tree: Christian and caste society in India*. Berkeley: University of California Press.

Mumbai Housing and Area Development Board. 2016. E-Tender Notice No. EE/PPD/MB/BDD/2169/2016. http://www.eoicaracas.gov.in/docs/BDD_Tender_Notice1.pdf (accessed 21/12/22).

Mungekar, B.L. 2007. 'State, Market and the Dalits', in Michael, S. (ed.), *Dalits in Modern India: Vision and values*. New Delhi; Thousand Oaks, CA: SAGE.

Nag, S. 2009. 'Nehru and the Nagas: Minority nationalism and the post-colonial state'. *Economic and Political Weekly*, 44 (49): 48–55.

Namishray, M. 2018. 'Who was revolutionary Dalit poet Namdeo Dhasal really?' *Forward Press*, 20 June. https://www.forwardpress.in/2018/06/who-was-revolutionary-dalit-poet-namdeo-dhasal-really/ (accessed 8/12/22).

Nelson Society. 2020. 'Nelson and the slave trade: A position statement by the Nelson Society'. https://nelson-society.com/nelson-and-the-slave-trade-a-position-statement-by-the-nelson-society/ (accessed 10/2/23).

Nehru, J. 2004. *The Discovery of India*. New Delhi: Viking/Penguin Books India.

O'Hanlon, R. 1983. 'Maratha history as polemic: Low caste ideology and political debate in late nineteenth-century western India'. *Modern Asian Studies* 17: 1–33.

O'Hanlon, R. 1985. *Caste, Conflict, and Ideology: Mahatma Jotirao Phule and low caste protest in nineteenth-century western India*. Cambridge: Cambridge University Press.

Olusoga, D. 2016. 'Black and British: A forgotten history' (documentary). BBC Two. https://www.bbc.co.uk/programmes/b082x0h6 (accessed 24/2/23).

Omvedt, G. 1976. *Cultural Revolt in a Colonial Society: The non-Brahman movement in western India, 1873 to 1930*. Bombay: Scientific Socialist Education Trust.

Omvedt, G. 1994. *Dalit and the Democratic Revolution: Dr Ambedkar and the Dalit movement in colonial India*. New Delhi: Sage Publications.

Omvedt, G. 2003. *Buddhism in India: Challenging Brahmanism and caste*. London: SAGE.

Omvedt, G. 2006. *Dalit Visions: The anti-caste movement and the construction of an Indian identity* Revised edition. New Delhi: Orient Longman.

Orwell, G. 1945. 'Notes on nationalism'. *Polemic* 1 (May 1945). Also available: https://www.orwellfoundation.com/the-orwell-foundation/orwell/essays-and-other-works/notes-on-nationalism/ (accessed 6/12/22).

Osella, C. and Osella, F. 2000. 'Migration, money and masculinity in Kerala'. *Journal of the Royal Anthropological Institute* 6 (1): 117–33.

Palmié, S. and Stewart, C. 2016. 'Introduction: For an anthropology of history'. *HAU: Journal of Ethnographic Theory* 6 (1): 207–36.

Panjwani, N. 1984. 'Living with capitalism: Class, caste and paternalism along industrial workers in Bombay'. *Contributions to Indian Sociology*, 18: 267–92.

Pansare, G. 2015. *Who Was Shivaji?* (trans. Narkar, U.). New Delhi: LeftWord.

Parliament of India, 1953. 'The Andhra State Bill debate, 2nd Sept 1953 (continued)'. Official debates of the Rajya Sabha. https://rsdebate.nic.in/bitstream/123456789/588187/1/PD_04_02091953_7_p844_p924_3.pdf (accessed 6/12/22).

Parry, J. 2003. 'Nehru's dream and the village "waiting room": Long-distance labour migrants to a central Indian steel town'. *Contributions to Indian Sociology*, 37 (1–2): 217–49.

Pawar, D. 2009. 'We are kings' (extract from *Baluta*) in Dangle, A. (ed.), *Poisoned Bread: Translations from modern Marathi Dalit literature* (trans. Adarkar, P.). Hyderabad: Orient BlackSwan, pp. 98–105.

Pawar, J.V. 2017. *Dalit Panthers: An authoritative history* (trans. Sonawane, R.). New Delhi: The Marginalised.

Pendse, S., Adarkar, N. and Finkelstein, M. 2011. 'Overview' in Adarkar, N. (ed.), *The Chawls of Mumbai: Galleries of life*. Delhi: ImprintOne, pp. 1–11.

Phadke, M. 2016. 'SoBo to get cheaper homes with revamp of BDD chawls'. *Hindustan Times*, 27 August. https://www.hindustantimes.com/mumbai-news/sobo-to-get-cheaper-homes-with-revamp-of-bdd-chawls/story-yP27k4V63SPp6TzlCanGfN.html (accessed 24/2/23).

Phadke, S., Khan, S. and Ranade, S. 2011. *Why Loiter? Women and risk on Mumbai streets*. New Delhi: Penguin.

Phoenix Palladium. N.d. 'About the Mall'. https://phoenixpalladium.com/about-us (accessed 19/12/22).

Pinto, J. and Fernandes, N. 2003. *Bombay, Meri Jaan: Writings on Bombay*. New Delhi: Penguin.

Pollard, A. 2009. 'Field of screams: Difficulty and ethnographic fieldwork'. *Anthropology Matters*, 11 (2): 1–24.

Prakash, G. 2011. *Mumbai Fables: A history of an enchanted city*. Princeton, NJ: Princeton University Press.

PTI. 2017. 'Maharashtra CM Devendra Fadnavis to launch BDD chawls redevelopment project on Saturday'. *The Indian Express*, 20 April. https://indianexpress.com/article/india/maharashtra-cm-devendra-fadnavis-to-launch-bdd-chawls-redevelopment-project-on-saturday-4621508/ (accessed 24/2/23).

PTI. 2018a. 'Pune: Violence mars Bhima Koregaon battle anniversary event'. *The Indian Express*, 1 January. https://indianexpress.com/article/india/pune-violence-mars-bhima-koregaon-battle-anniversary-event-mevani-5007857/ (accessed 24/2/23).

PTI. 2018b. 'Riots over Dalits' Koregaon-Bhima battle anniversary celebration in Pune kills 1, destroys 50 cars'. *India Today*, 1 January. https://www.indiatoday.in/india/story/violence-mars-bhima-koregaon-battle-anniversary-event-1120253-2018-01-01 (accessed 24/2/23).

PTI. 2019. 'Over 1,000 scientists, scholars sign petition demanding withdrawal of citizenship bill'. *The Economic Times*, 10 December. https://economictimes.indiatimes.com/news/politics-and-nation/over-1000-scientists-scholars-sign-petition-demanding-withdrawal-of-citizenship-bill/articleshow/72454503.cms?from=mdr (accessed 24/2/23).

PTI. 2021. 'Lord Buddha inspiration for India's Constitution, says PM Modi'. *The Hindu*, 20 October. https://www.thehindu.com/news/national/lord-buddha-inspiration-for-indias-constitution-says-pm-modi/article37085897.ece (accessed 6/12/22).

PTI. 2022. 'No one can stop us from rewriting history to free it from distortions: Amit Shah', *The Indian Express*, 25 November. https://indianexpress.com/article/india/no-one-can-stop-us-rewriting-history-free-distortions-amit-shah-8288780/ (accessed 19/12/22).

Public Works Department. 1922. File No 35/II 'Tenders – Development Department Chawls'.

Public Works Department. 1924. File No 65/3 'Petition from Mr V M Hassan for the fragment of his bills in connection with the construction of chawls at Delisle Road'.

Public Works Department. 1925. File No 65A/10 'Petition from Messrs J.C. Gammon Ltd, contractors, for payment of bills in connection with the construction of chawls at Delisle Road'.

Public Works Department. 1938. File No 2032/36-I (1937–8).

Punekar, S.D., Varickayil, R., Desai, A.R., Dighe, S., Savur, M., Ganesh, K., Nair, M.N.V. and Bidwai, P. (eds), 1988. *Labour Movement in India: Documents*. New Delhi: Indian Council of Historical Research; Popular Prakashan.

Puranik, A. 2015. 'Mumbai: How BDD Chawl residents react to redevelopment news'. *Mid Day*, 24 November. https://www.mid-day.com/mumbai/mumbai-news/article/mumbai--how-bdd-chawl-residents-react-to-redevelopment-news-16708191 (accessed 24/2/23).

Queen, C. 2004. 'Ambedkar's Dhamma: Source and method in the construction of engaged Buddhism', in Jondhale, S. and Beltz, J. (eds), *Reconstructing the World: B.R. Ambedkar and Buddhism in India*. New Delhi: Oxford University Press, pp. 97–119.

Radhyesham, J. 2018. 'Real tussle between right-wingers & Marathas'. *Times of India*, 4 January.

Rajmani, R. 2018. 'Bhima Koregaon and the Savarna gaze'. *News Laundry*, 5 January. https://www.newslaundry.com/2018/01/05/bhima-koregaon-savarna-gaze-media-dalits-caste (accessed 24/2/23).

Rajshekar, V.T. 1987. *Dalit: The Black Untouchables of India*. Atlanta, GA: Clarity.

Ramteke, S. 2018. 'Dr Ambedkar's thoughts on female empowerment', in Rani, H. P. and Kesari, M. (eds) *Women in higher education in India: Perspectives and challenges*. Newcastle upon Tyne: Cambridge Scholars Publishing, pp. 97–101.

Ranganathan, M. 2008. *Govind Narayan's Mumbai: An urban biography from 1863*. London: Anthem Press.

Ranjan, P. 2020. 'Going back to Nehru: Why secular nationalism is the only way to avoid balkanization of India'. *The Week*, 6 April. https://www.theweek.in/news/india/2020/04/06/going-back-to-nehru-why-secular-nationalism-is-the-only-way-to-avoid-balkanization-of-india.html (accessed 8/12/22).

Rao, A. 2009. *The Caste Question: Dalits and the politics of modern India*. Berkeley: University of California Press.

Rao, R. 2020a. 'Nationalisms by, against and beyond the Indian state'. *Radical Philosophy* 2.07: 17–26.

Rao, R. 2020b. 'The CAA protests shake the bounds of Indian secular morality'. *The Caravan*, 29 January. https://caravanmagazine.in/politics/caa-protests-shake-old-bounds-indian-secular-morality (accessed 24/2/23).

Reuters. 2019. 'Berlin police scuffle with activists at gentrification protest'. *Reuters*, 2 May. https://www.reuters.com/article/us-may-day-germany-berlin-idUSKCN1S74O6 (accessed 24/2/23).

Ring, L.A. 2006. *Zenana: Everyday peace in a Karachi apartment building*. Bloomington: Indiana University Press.

Roberts, N. 2016. *To Be Cared For: The power of conversion and foreignness of belonging in an Indian slum*. Oakland, CA: University of California Press.

Robinson, E. 2016. 'Radical nostalgia, progressive patriotism and Labour's "English Problem."' *Political Studies Review* 14 (3): 378–87.

Rodrigues, E. and Gavaskar, M., 2003. *Emancipation and Dalit Politics. Bombay and Mumbai: The city in transition*, pp.137–60.

Rothberg, M. 2019. 'Notes on historical comparison in the age of Trump (and Erdoğan)'. *Massachusetts Review*, 60 (4): 818–26.

Rowe, W.L. 1973. 'Caste, kinship and association in urban India', in Southall A .W. (ed), *Urban Anthropology: Cross-cultural studies of urbanization*. New York, NY: Oxford University Press, pp. 211–50.

Roy, S. 2007. *Beyond Belief: India and the politics of postcolonial nationalism*. Durham, NC: Duke University Press.

Saigal, S. 2021. 'Maratha reservation: a timeline of events'. *The Hindu*, 5 May. https://www.thehindu.com/news/cities/mumbai/maratha-reservation-a-timeline-of-events/article34487593.ece (accessed 24/2/23).

Sambhaji Brigade. n.d. http://www.sambhajibrigade.in/ (website no longer available).

Sanatan Sanstha, 2022. 'About us' https://www.sanatan.org/en/about-us (accessed 7/12/22).

Sanghera, S. 2021. *Empireland: How imperialism has shaped modern Britain*. New York, NY: Viking Books.

Savarkar, V.D. 1949. *Who Is a Hindu?* Poon: S.P. Gokhale.

Schalk, P. 2006. 'The political suspension of ethics: Proposals for a historical study of reversal of values in a situation of martial conflict in Lanka', in Alback, T. (ed), *Exercising Power: The role of religions in concord and conflict*. Åbo: Donner Institute for Research in Religious and Cultural History, pp. 312–21.

Schonthal, B. 2016. 'Configurations of Buddhist nationalism in modern Sri Lanka', in Holt, J. (ed), *Buddhist Extremists and Muslim Minorities: Religious conflict in contemporary Sri Lanka.* New York, NY: Oxford University Press, pp. 1–17.

Schonthal, B. and Walton, M. 2016. 'The (new) Buddhist nationalisms? Symmetries and specificities in Sri Lanka and Myanmar'. *Contemporary Buddhism,* 17 (1): 81–115.

Sen, A. 2007. *Shiv Sena Women: Violence and communalism in a Bombay slum.* Bloomington: Indiana University Press.

Shaban, A. 2010. *Mumbai: Political economy of crime and space.* Hyderabad: Orient Blackman.

Shah, A. 2009. 'Brick kiln workers from Jharkhand: The labour of love', in Deshingkar, P. and Farrington, J. (eds), *Circular Migration and Multilocational Livelihood Strategies in Rural India.* New Delhi: Oxford University Press, pp. 177–201.

Shah, A. 2022. [Twitter]. 24 November. https://twitter.com/AmitShah/status/1595800885250392065?ref_rc=twsrc%5Etfw%7Ctwcamp%5Etweetembed%7Ctwterm%5E1595800885250392065%7Ctwgr%5E43858600fe7ebfdfa68464170f2105002c04129b%7Ctwcon%5Es1_&ref_url=https%3A%2F%2Findianexpress.com%2Farticle%2Findia%2Fno-one-can-stop-us-rewriting-history-free-distortions-amit-shah-8288780%2F (accessed 19/12/22).

Shaikh, J. 2005. 'Worker politics, trade unions and the Shiv Sena's rise in central Bombay'. *Economic and Political Weekly,* 40 (18): 1893–900.

Shaikh, J. 2011. 'Translating Marx: Mavali, Dalit and the making Mumbai's working class, 1928–1935'. *Economic and Political Weekly* 46 (31): 65–73.

Shaikh, M.A. 2016. *I Want to Destroy Myself* (trans. Pinto, J.). New Delhi: Speaking Tiger.

Shani, G. 2008. *Sikh Nationalism and Identity in a Global Age.* New York, NY: Routledge.

Shetty, P. 2011. 'Ganga Building Chronicles', in Adarkar, N. (ed.), *The Chawls of Mumbai: Galleries of life.* Delhi: ImprintOne, pp. 26–36.

Shivasundar. 2023. 'Opinion: BJP-RSS's decolonising project merely a cover for re-Brahmanisation'. *The News Minute,* 5 January. https://www.thenewsminute.com/article/opinion-bjp-rss-s-decolonising-project-merely-cover-re-brahmanisation-171602 (accessed 10/2/23).

Shourie, A. 1997. *Worshipping False Gods: Ambedkar, and the facts which have been erased.* New Delhi: ASA Publications.

Simpson, E. 2013. *The Political Biography of an Earthquake: Aftermath and amnesia in Gujarat, India.* London: Hurst & Co.

Smith, L.T. 2021. *Decolonizing Methodologies: Research and indigenous peoples,* 3rd edition. London: Zed Books.

Srivastava, K. 2019. 'Bombay HC upholds Maratha quota: BJP, Shiv Sena snatch issue from Congress, NCP ahead of state polls'. *Firstpost,* 28 June. https://www.firstpost.com/politics/bombay-high-court-upholds-maratha-quota-bjp-shiv-sena-snatch-quota-issue-from-congress-ncp-ahead-of-state-polls-6898541.html (accessed 24/2/23).

Srivastava, R. and Echanove. M. 2014. 'Modern Mumbai: Revisiting BDD Chawls'. *Urbz* http://www.urbz.net/articles/morden-mumbai-revisiting-bdd-chawls (accessed 19/12/22).

Steinman, E. 2019. 'Why was Standing Rock and the #NoDAPL campaign so historic? Factors affecting American Indian participation in social movement collaborations and coalitions'. *Ethical and Racial Studies,* 42 (7): 1070–90.

Sutar, K.D. 2018. 'Maharashtra caste clashes: Sambhaji Bhide says he is innocent, violence a political conspiracy'. *India Today,* 5 January. https://www.indiatoday.in/india/story/sambhaji-bhide-maharashtra-caste-clashes-sangli-shivaji-sambhaji-1123570-2018-01-05 (accessed 24/2/23).

Sutar, K.D. 2019. 'Maratha reservation issue fails to dent BJP's vote share among Marathas and OBCs'. *India Today,* 6 June. https://www.indiatoday.in/india/story/maharashtra-bjp-maratha-1543840-2019-06-06 (accessed 24/2/23).

Tamburo, E. 2020. 'Regulating technologies, authority, and aesthetics in the resettlement of Taipei military villages'. *Focaal – Journal of Global and Historical Anthropology,* 86.

Tarlo, E. 1996. *Clothing Matters: Dress and identity in India.* London: Hurst & Co.

Tarlo, E. 2000. 'Welcome to history: A resettlement colony in the making', in Tarlo, E., Dupont, V. and Vidal, D. (eds), *Delhi: Urban Space and Human Destinies.* New Delhi: Manohar, pp. 51–74.

Taylor, C. 1994. 'The politics of recognition' in Gutmann, A (ed) *Multiculturalism and the Politics of Recognition.* Princeton, NJ: Princeton University Press.

Tejani, S. 2013. 'The necessary conditions for democracy: B. R. Ambedkar on nationalism, minorities and Pakistan'. *Economic and Political Weekly,* 48 (50): 111–19.

Teltumbde, A. 2007. 'Khairlanji and its Aftermath: Exploding Some Myths'. *Economic and Political Weekly* 42 (12): 1019–25.

Teltumbde, A. 2009. 'Reservations within reservations: A solution'. *Economic and Political Weekly* 44 (41/42): 16–18.

Teltumbde, A. 2012. 'On the death of Bal Thackeray and the grief of Athavale'. *Countercurrents,* 5 December https://countercurrents.org/teltumbde051212.htm (accessed 8/12/22).

Teltumbde, A. 2016. *Dalits: Past, present and future.* New Delhi: Routledge India.

Thapar, R. 2005. 'Some appropriations of the theory of Aryan relating to the beginnings of Indian history', in Trautmann, T. R. (ed.), *The Aryan Debate.* New Delhi: Oxford University Press, pp. 106–28.

Tharoor, S. 2016. *An Era of Darkness: The British empire in India.* New Delhi: Aleph Book Company.

The Hindu Bureau, 2022. 'Seven years after Govind Pansare's death, Bombay HC transfers case to ATS'. *The Hindu,* 3 August.
https://www.thehindu.com/news/national/hc-transfers-probe-into-activist-govind-pansare-murder-case-to-maharashtra-ats-from-cid/article65720802.ece (accessed 7/12/22).

The Wire, 2018. 'Constitution in Hand, Bhim Army's Chandrashekhar Azad Marches to Ayodhya'. *The Wire,* 26 November. https://thewire.in/communalism/constitution-in-hand-bhim-armys-chandrashekhar-azad-marches-to-ayodhya (accessed 24/2/23).

Times of India. 1988. 'Reconstruct chawls, urges delegation'. *Times of India,* 8 October.

Times of India. 1990. 'Plan to renovate BDD Chawls'. *Times of India,* 13 September.

Times of India. 2007. 'Decision on redevpt of BDD chawls deferred'. *Times of India,* 7 September.

TNN. 2017. 'Dalits gear up for show of strength on Republic Day'. *Times of India,* 24 January. https://timesofindia.indiatimes.com/city/rajkot/dalits-gear-up-for-show-of-strength-on-republic-day/articleshow/56742232.cms (accessed 24/2/23).

TNN. 2018. 'Cops look on as mobs hold city to ransom'. *Times of India,* 4 January. https://timesofindia.indiatimes.com/city/mumbai/cops-look-on-as-mobs-hold-city-to-ransom/articleshow/62358763.cms (accessed 24/2/23).

Trautmann, T.R. 2005. 'Introduction', in Trautmann, T. R. (ed.), *The Aryan Debate.* New Delhi: Oxford University Press, pp. xiii–xliii.

Truschke, A. 2022. '"Decolonizing" Indians through Hindutva ideological control'. *Free Voice,* 29. https://shuddhashar.com/decolonizing-indians-through-hindutva-ideological-control/ (accessed 10/2/23).

Tsing, A. 2000. 'The Global Situation'. *Cultural Anthropology,* 15: 327–60.

Upadhyay, S.B. 2004. *Existence, identity and mobilization: The cotton millworkers of Bombay, 1890–1919.* New Delhi: Manohar.

Valunjkar, T.N. 1996. *Social Organization, Migration and Change in a Village Community.* Poona: Deccan College.

van der Veer, P. 1994. *Religious Nationalism: Hindus and Muslims in India.* Berkeley: University of California Press.

van der Vliet, J. 2009. 'The Copts: "Modern sons of the pharaohs"?' *Church History and Religious Culture* 89 (1–3): 279–90.

Venkataramakrishnan, R. 2018. 'Are Dalits really oppressed? Five predictable responses to the Bhima Koregaon bandh'. *Scroll.in,* 3 January. https://scroll.in/article/863684/are-dalits-really-oppressed-five-predictable-responses-to-the-bhima-koregaon-bandh (accessed 24/2/23).

Vergès, F. 2021. *A Decolonial Feminism* (trans. Bohrer, A.). London: Pluto Press.

Vernekar, R. 2017. '5,904 families of BDD chawls to get free houses!' *The Afternoon Despatch & Courier,* 22 April.

Vivekananda, S. 1973. 'The Future of India', in: *The Complete Works of Swami Vivekananda* (Vol. 3). Calcutta: Advaita Ashrama, pp. 285–304.

Wacha, D. 1920. *Shells from the Sands of Bombay: My recollections and reminiscences 1860–1875.* Bombay: Indian Newspaper Company.

Warrier, S.G. 2017. 'Mumbai floods: Why India's cities are struggling with extreme rainfall'. *Hindustan Times,* 29 August. https://www.hindustantimes.com/india-news/mumbai-floods-why-india-s-cities-are-struggling-with-extreme-rainfall/story-wsWPNy2MXh4b9JYTqtA0QJ.html (accessed 24/2/23).

Willliams, H. 2015. 'Great Britain's Greatest Beast – Winston Churchill'. *Stopwar.org,* 24 January https://www.stopwar.org.uk/article/heathcote-williams-winston-churchill-great-britain-s-greatest-beast/ (accessed 29/12/22).

Williams, R.V. 2006. *Postcolonial Politics and Personal Laws: Colonial legal legacies and the Indian state*. New Delhi: Oxford University Press.

Wood, M. 1998. 'The use of the pharaonic past in modern Egyptian nationalism'. *Journal of the American Research Center in Egypt* 35: 179–96.

Yengde, S. 2018. 'Ambedkar's foreign policy and the ellipsis of the 'Dalit' from international activism'. In Teltumbde, A. and Yende, S. (eds), *The Radical in Ambedkar: Critical reflections*. New Delhi: Allen Lane.

Yeshwantrao, N. 1999a. 'Cabinet okays redevelopment of 207 BDD chawls on poll-eve'. *Times of India,* 31 July.

Yeshwantrao, N. 1999b. 'BDD chawl residents are peeved at being equated with slum-dwellers'. *Times of India,* 11 August.

Yuval-Davis, N. 2012. 'An autochthonic scent of memory?' *Feminist Review,* 100: 154–60.

Zachariah, B. 2011. *Playing the Nation Game: The ambiguities of nationalism in India*. New Delhi: Yoda Press.

Zakaria, R. 2021. *Against White Feminism*. London: Penguin Books.

Zaman, R. 2022. 'Why Assamese historians and writers are protesting against the BJP's celebration of Lachit Borphukan'. *Scroll.in,* 24 November. https://scroll.in/article/1038074/why-assamese-historians-and-writers-are-protesting-against-the-bjps-celebration-of-lachit-borphukan (accessed 19/12/22).

Zelliot, E.M. 1996a. 'The nineteenth century background of the Mahar and non-Brahman movements in Maharashtra', in Zelliot, E. M. (ed), *From Untouchable to Dalit: Essays on the Ambedkar movement*. New Delhi: Manohar, pp. 33–52.

Zelliot, E.M. 1996b. 'Learning the use of political means: The Mahars of Maharashtra', in Zelliot, E.M. (ed), *From Untouchable to Dalit: Essays on the Ambedkar movement*. New Delhi: Manohar, pp. 86–125.

Index

References to notes are indicated by n.

Adarkar, Neera: *The Chawls of Mumbai: Galleries of Life* 19, 29, 31, 43, 79
Adik, Ramrao 32
Adityanath, Yogi 104
adivasi see Scheduled Tribe
Afghanistan 115, 128n4
Afzal Khan 157
alcohol 88–9
Aloysius, G. 103, 111, 125
Ambedkar, Dr Bhimrao Ramji 'Babasaheb' 4, 7, 8, 16, 18, 126
 and Ayodhya 128n13
 and Buddhism 112, 113, 114–17
 and Chambhars 121
 and Congress Party 170
 and Constitution of India 54, 57, 107–9, 199
 and emancipation 64–5, 66
 and gender relations 68
 and godlike status 19–20, 52, 56–9, 72–3
 and history 116, 199
 and independence movement 111, 152–3
 and Jay Bhim Katta 55, 56
 and nationalism 21, 101, 103
 and non-Brahman movement 170
 and politics 59–60, 61–2
 and Republic Day 53–4
 and Shivaji 107, 157–8, 174n9
Ambedkar, Prakash 129n20, 170
Ambedkar, Ramabai 55, 122
Ambedkar Jayanti celebrations 57, 58–9, 73, 107, 189–90
Amosu, Vagiri 111
Anderson, Benedict 18, 103, 110, 111
Annihilation of Caste, The (Ambedkar) 66, 113, 153
anthropology 18
anti-nationalism 105, 106, 111, 129n20, 150, 154
Aryan Invasion Theory 18, 21, 103, 115–17, 128n11
Ashoka, Emperor 112, 117
Ashoka Chakra 112–13, 121, 125, 128n6
Asli-Naqli (film) 43–4
Athawale, Ramdas 60, 123, 170, 185
Aurangzeb, Emperor 17, 160
autochthony 93
Ayodhya 15, 16, 118–19, 124
Azad, Chandrashekhar 118, 128n13

Babri Masjid 15, 118, 128n13
bachelor living *see* Gramastha Mandals
backwardness 11, 175n12
Bahujans 67–8, 75n13, 162, 163
Banias 11
Bansode, Kisan Fagoji 170
Barphukan, Lachit 17
BDD Chawls 1, 2–9, 24–6, 173, 186–8
 and Ambedkar 58–9
 and class 20, 45–7
 and Covid-19 pandemic 192–3
 and history 197–8
 and *kattas* 41–3
 and Koregaon 153–4
 and layout 29–31
 and open-door culture 35–9
 and politics 59–63
 and prison history 39–41
 and redevelopment plans 31–5, 176–86, 189–91
 and Shiv Sena 12, 166
 and textile workers 13
 and women 68–71
 see also Buddha Vihar; chawlness; Gramastha Mandals; Jay Bhim Katta
beef-eating 104, 138, 140
Bénéï, Veronique 129n20, 160
Berliner, David 52
bhadang (puffed rice snack) 81
Bhajan Mandals 89
Bhatt, Gaga 163
Bhide, Sambhaji 161–2, 173, 191, 192
Bhima Koregaon celebrations *see* Koregaon, Battle of (1818)
bhoomipujan (ground-breaking ceremony) 177, 178, 182–6
biometric tests 180–1, 183, 184, 187, 190
BJP (Bharatiya Janata Party) 12, 60–1, 123, 165, 183–4
 and nationalism 102, 104–5, 108
BMC (Brihanmumbai Municipal Corporation) 14, 75n8, 167
Bodu Bala Sena 113
Bohra Muslims 11
Bombay *see* Mumbai
Bombay Development Department or Directorate (BDD) 5, 50n5, 139
Bombay (City) Improvement Trust 27n5
boredom 87–9, 96
BORI (Bhandarkar Oriental Research Institute) 161

214 FAKE GODS AND FALSE HISTORY

Brahmans 21, 22, 52, 115–16, 172–3; *see also* non-Brahman movement; Peshwa
British Empire 18, 24, 156, 172, 201n2
 and Dalits 123, 150
 and Koregaon 151–2, 173
 and prisons 39–40, 41
 and voting rights 109
Buddha 56, 58, 73, 129n21
Buddha and His Dhamma, The (Ambedkar) 62
Buddha Vihar (temple) 100–1, 107, 119, 121–4
Buddhism 8, 21, 18, 74n2, 118
 and false history 112–17
 and Protestant Buddhism 114, 124
 and scientific rationalism 112–14
 see also Dalit Buddhists

Caru, Vanessa 31, 41, 139
caste 4, 10, 20, 27n9, 44
 and Gramastha Mandals 130–6, 138–41
 and history 199–200
 and nationalism 111
 and reforms 109
 and villages 137–8, 146–8
 see also Bahujans; Brahmans; Chambhar community; Dalit Buddhists; Depressed Classes; Marathas; reservations; Scheduled Castes
cattle 104; *see also* beef-eating
Chambhar (Chamar) community 10, 12, 120–1, 129n16, 170
Chandra, Bankim 112
Chatterjee, Partha 103, 111–12
Chattopadhyay, Tarinicharan 112
chawlness 20, 31, 36–9, 43–4, 48–9, 49, 187, 188
 and everyday 119–21
chawls 5, 10; *see also* BDD Chawls
Chhatrapati Melas 164
Chhatrapati Shivaji Maharaj *see* Shivaji Bhonsle
Christianity 30, 105, 113, 114, 128n7, 199
Churchill, Winston 16, 18, 198
circular migration 80–1, 141–3
Citizenship (Amendment) Act (CAA) (2019) 128n4, 129n20
class 44–6, 92–3; *see also* castes; middle classes; working-classes
closed-door culture 20, 31, 38, 39–41
clothing 65–6, 75n12
colonialism 5, 12, 17, 110–12; *see also* British Empire
communism 165, 166
Congress Party 32, 41, 61, 63, 171, 179, 183, 184
 and independence movement 152–3, 170
 and Marathas 164–5, 166
Constitution of India 7, 10, 126, 129n20, 199
 and Ambedkar 54, 57, 107–9
 and reservations 65
contested spaces 101, 119
contradictions 52–3
cotton 13; *see also* textile mills
Covid-19 pandemic 23, 189, 192–3
cricket 38–9, 56

Dalit Buddhists 4, 7, 30
 and Ambedkar 57–9, 72–3
 and Brahmans 172–3
 and Buddha Vihar 100–1
 and Chambhars 120–1
 and chawlness 119–21
 and clothing 65–6
 and Constitution of India 107–9
 and emancipation 20, 64–5
 and Ganesh 51–2
 and gender relations 67–72
 and Gramastha Mandals 130–6, 138–41, 145–7, 148
 and Hindus 73–4
 and history 18, 19, 197, 199
 and independence 111
 and Jay Bhim Katta 53–6
 and Koregaon 151–2, 154–5
 and Marathi identity 169–70
 and Muslims 129n20
 and nationalism 101–2, 103, 104, 105–6, 124
 and oppression 63–4, 66–7
 and recognition 125–6
 and redevelopment 22–3, 177–86, 188, 190–1
 and reservations 10–11
 and RPI(A) 60–2
 and Shivaji 149–51, 157–9
 and villages 21–2
Dalit Panthers 61–2, 69, 123, 126
Dalitstan 106, 124, 125, 128n3
Dandekar, Hemlata 137, 147
 Men to Bombay, Woman at Home 79
Das, P.K. 171
Dattatreya, Bandaru 105–6
Davar, Cowasji 13
Delhi 186
Delisle Road *see* BDD Chawls
Depressed Classes 109
Deshpande, P.L.: *Batatyachi Chal* 5
Dhale, Raja 123
Dhammachakra Pravartan Din (Religious Conversion Day) 57, 62, 173
Dharmanna, Kusuma 111
Dhasal, Namdeo 69, 170
difference 30–1, 49, 98–9, 125–7
D'Monte, Darryl 15
dormitories *see* Gramastha Mandals

East India Company 11, 151
economics 84–5
education 10, 11, 68, 84, 141, 159–60
Egypt 34, 199
Ekbote, Milind 191, 192
Elgaar Parishad 191–2
emancipation 63–7, 108, 199
employment 10, 11, 12, 64, 167–8
 and Gramastha Mandals 82–5, 97–8, 99n7, 140–1
 see also textile mills
Erdogan, Recep Tayyip 105

Fadnavis, Devendra 11, 168, 177
fake gods 19–20, 150, 157; *see also* Ambedkar, Dr Bhimrao 'Babasaheb'; Ganesh

INDEX   215

false history 21, 196–7, 198–9
　and British Empire 151–3
　and Buddhism 112–17
　and Shivaji 150, 156–60
feminism 75n15
Fernandes, Leela 46
Fernandes, Naresh 9, 42, 170–1
Finkelstein, Maura 38, 48, 97, 199
　The Archive of Loss 31
Fitzgerald, Timothy 59
flags 53, 60, 104, 112–13, 125, 155
　and saffron-coloured 154, 155, 167, 174
food 61, 81, 86–7, 89; *see also* beef-eating; vegetarianism

Gaikwad, Captain Smita 191
Gandhi, Indira 166
Gandhi, Mahatma 54, 58, 109, 123, 199
　and assassination 164
　and independence movement 111
Ganesh 20, 51–2, 58, 73
Ganesh Chaturthi festival 20, 51–2, 58, 75n16, 175n11
Gardner, Andrew 85
Geertz, Clifford and Hildred 2
Gellner, Ernest 18, 103
　Nations and Nationalism 110–11
gender relations 52–3, 67–72
Ghats 10, 13, 31
Girangaon 2, 5, 13, 45
gods *see* fake gods
Godse, Nathuram 164
Golwalkar, M.S. 117
Gore, M.S. 141–2
Gorringe, Hugo 125
Gramastha Mandals 8–9, 16, 19, 20–2, 25, 76–81
　and caste 130–6, 138–41, 199–200
　and Covid-19 pandemic 23, 193
　and difference 98–9
　and eligibility criteria 133–5, 145–6
　and intercommunity mixing 145–7, 148
　and male environment 195
　and Mitra Mandals 89–90, 92–5
　and recreation 86–9
　and redevelopment 187–8
　and relocation 143–4
　and village attachment 95–7
　and working life 82–5, 97–8
Great Britain 16, 17–18, 102–3, 198–9, 201n2; *see also* British Empire; London
Gujaratis 11, 12, 31, 104, 169, 170–2
Gupta, Dipankar 146
Gupta Empire 116, 117
Guru, Gopal 113, 125
gurus 160–2

Habib, Irfan 105
Hedgewar, K.B. 127n2
Heuzé, Gérard 63
high-rise development 12–13, 34–5, 144–5, 176
High Street Phoenix 15, 45
Hinduism 4, 7, 12, 15, 17
　and Ambedkar 124
　and Aryans 114–17
　and Ayodhya 118–19
　and Buddhism 18, 73–4, 74n2
　and festivals 95
　and Ganesh 51–2
　and gender relations 68, 71
　and Gramastha Mandals 130–6, 138–41, 145–7, 148
　and Koregaon 154–5
　and nationalism 103–5, 106
　and redevelopment 182–6, 188, 190–1
　and rules 113
　see also Marathas; Shivaji Bhonsle
history 16–20, 23, 49, 102–3, 197–200
　and Buddhism 114–17, 121–4
　and India 111–12
　see also chawlness; false history
Holwitt, Pablo 171
homosexuality 194–5
housing 5–6, 13, 144–5, 169, 171; *see also* Gramastha Mandals; redevelopment

Ilaiah, Kancha 67–8, 128n14
imperialism 16, 17–18, 111, 172; *see also* colonialism
Independence Day 95, 101, 104, 123, 138
India 7, 17, 56, 196–8
　and Buddhism 114–15
　and flag 125
　and history 111–12, 112–17
　and independence movement 111, 123, 152–3
　see also Constitution of India; Mumbai; nationalism
Indian National Congress *see* Congress Party
indigenous people 17, 195–6
internationalism 126
internet 87–8, 98
Islam 105, 113, 114, 128n7, 172; *see also* Muslims

jails 39–41
Jainism 117, 169, 171
Jaoul, Nicolas 65
Japan 113–14
Jats 168
Jay Bhim Katta 25, 42, 53–6, 157–8
　and women 68–70
Jijabai 160, 161
Jones, Sir William 128n8

kabaddi 4, 38, 43, 89, 93–4, 100
Kabir 122
Kamala Mills 14, 45
Kambale, Babasaheb 10
Kashmir 106, 124
Katkarwadi 76, 78, 82, 96
kattas (seating areas) 41–3, 49; *see also* Jay Bhim Katta
Khairlanji massacre 67, 146
Khalistan movement 106
Khotachiwadi 29
Kolhapur District 10, 71, 78–9, 81, 86, 89, 98,129n20
Konkan 10, 13, 27n8, 31, 86, 99n10, 136, 170
Koregaon, Battle of (1818) 22, 23, 151–5, 158, 162, 163, 191–2

Krishnan, Shekhar: *The Murder of the Mills: A case study of Phoenix Mills* 14
Kshatriya status *see* Marathas: caste status
Kunbi community 11

Laine, James 16
   Shivaji: Hindu King in Islamic India 7, 11, 160–1
language 2, 23, 26n1, 115; *see also* Marathi language
Lankesh, Gauri 156
Lloyd, David 123–4
Lloyd, Sir George 5
locked doors *see* closed-door culture
London 34, 49, 92, 176

Mahabharata 112, 118
Mahaparinirvan Divas 59, 61
Mahar *see* Dalit Buddhists
Maharashtra 11–12, 150, 159–60, 165
   and identity 169–71, 172–4
Mahipati 174n7
majoritarianism 17–18, 21, 103, 104, 105
Malalasekera, Dr G.P. 129n21
malls *see* shopping malls
Manav Vansh Shastra (Ambedkar) 7, 107
Maoism 191–2
Maratha Seva Sangh 161
Marathas 10, 11, 12, 162–9
   and BDD Chawls 30
   and Buddha Vihar 100–1
   and caste status 11, 150, 162–9, 164, 173, 174n9
   and chawlness 119–21
   and history 19
   and identity 172–4
   and redevelopment 22–3, 185–6
   and Shivaji 118, 150, 156–7, 159–60, 173–4
   and villages 21–2
Marathi language 4, 10, 169–70
Marathon Futurex building 13, 15, 34, 45
marches 167
Massey, Doreen 49
Mehta, Kaiwan 37
Mehta, Suketu: *Maximum City* 9
messes 86–7, 98
   and *khanavalwalis* 86
MHADA (Maharashtra Housing and Area Development Authority) 14, 33, 34
   and redevelopment 179–82, 183–4, 185–6
Mhaskar, Sumeet 140
middle classes 20, 31, 46–7
migration 5, 12, 13, 27n4, 92
   and caste 132, 137–8
   and nationalism 105
   and urban settlement 142–3
   see also circular migration; Gramastha Mandals
mills *see* textile mills
minorities 105, 106
Mistry, Rohinton 9
Mitra Mandals 21, 42–3, 49, 62–3
   and Gramastha Mandals 89–90, 92–5
MNS (Maharashtra Navnirman Sena) 156–7
Modi, Narendra 12, 104, 105, 124, 162

Mohite, S.H. 160
money order economy *see* remittances
monsoon 39
Moon, Meenakshi 68, 69
More, R.B. 58
mosques 15
Mughals 17, 157, 163
Mukherjee, Hrishikesh 43–4
Müller, Max 115
Mumbadevi 12, 26n2
Mumbai 9–10, 11–13
   and caste 137–8
   and class 44–5
   and Gujaratis 169, 170–2
   and language 23, 26n1
   and name changes 27n11
   and property ownership 142–3, 144–5
   and riots 15–16
   and textile industry 13–15
   see also BDD Chawls; Samyukta Maharashtra movement; Shiv Sena
music 89
Muslims 15–16, 17, 104
   and Ayodhya 118–19
   and BDD Chawls 30
   and CAA 128n4
   and discrimination 140
   and nationalism 129n20
   and rights 109
   and Shivaji 156, 157, 159, 160, 161
Myanmar 113

Nagarkar, Kiran: *Ravan and Eddie* 5, 37
Narayan, Govind 15–16
nationalism 7, 16, 17, 101–7, 123–4, 199
   and Ambedkar 107–10
   and Buddhists 21, 114
   and Hinduism 18
   and history 112–17
   and Koregaon 154, 155
   and meaning 110–12
   and Shiv Sena 12
   and Shivaji 155
   and universalism 125–7
Nazi Germany 115, 117
NCP (Nationalist Congress Party) 166
Nehru, Jawaharlal 103, 109–10, 116–17, 123
   and Ashoka Chakra 128n6
   The Discovery of India 7, 106–7, 112
   and independence movement 111
   and nationalism 126
Nelson, Horatio 16, 172
N.M. Joshi Marg *see* BDD Chawls
non-Brahman movement 164–5, 170

open-door culture 20, 31, 35–9
oppression 63–4, 66–7, 108, 172–3, 199
Other Backward Classes (OBC) 11, 75n11
Owaisi, Asaduddin 129n20

Pakistan 107, 128n4, 186
Pallonji, Shapoorji 33, 34, 176
Pansare, Govind 150
   Shivaji kon hota? 156, 157
Parsis 11
parties 37

Patidars (Patels) 168
patriotism 110, 199
Pawar, J.V. 123
  Dalit Panthers: An authoritative history 61–2
Pawar, Sharad 166
Peninsula Corporate Park 45
Peshwa 66, 151–2, 163, 164, 173
Phoenix Mills 14–15
Phule, Jyotirao 'Mahatma' 55, 56, 68, 116, 121
  and Brahmans 174n6
  and Peshwa 164
  and Shivaji 158
Phule, Savitribai 55, 68, 121, 155
Pinto, Jerry 9
police 30, 100–1
politics 59–63, 80, 81, 109; *see also* BJP; Congress Party; nationalism; RPI(A), Shiv Sena
populism 21, 104, 105
Praan Jaaye Par Shaan Na Jaaye (film) 176, 187, 190
Prakash, Gyan 79
protest 108, 129n20, 198
  and redevelopment 22–3, 149, 176, 177–82, 189, 190
  see also riots
Pune 143, 144, 161
Purandare, B.M. 156
Pushyamitra 116

racism 198
Rajshekar, V.T. 128n3
Ram, Lord 15, 56, 74n3, 118, 162
Ramayana 112
Ramdas 160–1, 174n7
Ranade, M.G.: *Rise of Maratha Power* 159
Rao, Anupama 57
recognition 125–7
redevelopment 16, 22–3, 31–5, 149, 176–7, 189–91
  and Buddhist opposition 177–82
  and Girangaon 45
  and Gramastha Mandals 187–8
  and Hindu support 182–6
religion *see* Buddhism; Christianity; Hinduism; Islam; Sikhism
religious riots 10, 15–16, 30
remittances 84–5, 99n9
Republic Day 7, 53–4, 57, 58, 104, 108
reservations (quotas) 10–11, 64–5, 75n11, 199
Ring, Laura 186
riots 10, 15–16, 30, 165
Roberts, Nathaniel 137
Rohidas (Ravidas) 122
RPI(A) (Republican Party of India (Athawale)) 59–63, 71, 74, 113, 123
RSS (Rashtriya Swayamsevak Sangh) 102, 127n2

saffron (colour) 154, 155, 161, 162, 167, 174
Samant, Datta 14
Sambhaji Brigade 161–2
Samyukta Maharashtra movement 11, 12

Sanatan Sanstha 156
sanghas (monastic communities) 112
Satyashodhak Samaj ('Truth-Seeking Society') 116, 164, 168, 170
Savarkar, Vinayak Damodar 105, 124
Scheduled Caste (SC) 11, 59, 65, 109, 130, 174
Scheduled Tribe 11, 65, 75n13
SEBC *see* Socially and Educationally Backward Class
secessionist movements 106
secularism 114
segregation (demographic) 10, 15–16, 31, 74, 186
  and Gramastha Mandals 130–6, 138–41
Sen, Atreyee 2, 119
Shah, Alpa 85
Shah, Amit 17, 18, 103, 196–7
Shahuji Maharaj of Kolhapur 121–2, 164
Shaikh, Malika Amar: *I Want to Destroy Myself* 69, 72
Shaista Khan 157
Shiv Sena 11, 12, 15, 22
  and Dalits 170
  and Ganesh Chaturthi 175n11
  and Gujaratis 171–2
  and Marathas 165–6, 168
  and redevelopment 188
  and Shivaji 150, 156
Shivaji Maharaj, Chhatrapati (Bhonsle) 11, 17, 20, 22, 118
  and Buddhism 122, 149–51
  and coronation 163, 174n9
  and gurus 160–1, 174n7
  and Hindu nationalists 155
  and history 156–60
  and images 55–6
  and Koregaon 163
  and legacy 172, 173, 197–8
  and nationalism 107
  and non-Brahman movement 164
  see also Laine, James; Marathas: caste status
Shivaji Park 61–2
shopping malls 2, 14, 15, 46, 48, 65
  and employment 83–4
Shourie, Arun: *Worshipping False Gods: Ambedkar, and facts which have been erased* 56–7
Shudras (labourers) 10, 163, 174n9
Sikhism 106, 128n7
Simpson, Edward 186
Singh, V.P. 168
slums 29, 45, 186
smartphones 87–8, 98
social clubs *see* Mitra Mandals
Socially and Educationally Backward Class (SEBC) 11, 150, 168
South India 12, 111, 125, 165, 171
Sri Lanka 113, 114, 124, 129n18
strikes 13–14, 154–5

Tarlo, Emma 186
Taylor, Charles 125, 126
technology 87–8, 98
Teltumbde, Anand 67, 75n11, 146, 192

textile mills 2, 5, 10, 13–15
   and Gramastha Mandals 82, 99n7
   and Muslims 140
Thackeray, Bal 12, 165, 168, 171
Thackeray, Raj 171
Thackeray, Uddhav 171
Tharoor, Shashi: *An Era of Darkness* 152
Tilak, Bal Gangadhar 115, 117, 155
trade unions 13–14, 166
transit accommodation 34, 38, 179, 183, 187, 190
Trump, Donald 105, 160
Tsing, Anna 110
Tuhiwai Smith, Linda: *Decolonizing Methodologies* 24, 195–6
Tukaram 122, 160–1

Ukraine 17, 102
uncleanliness 140
United States of America (USA) 16–17, 105, 175n13, 176

universalism 125–7
unlocked doors *see* open-door culture
untouchables *see* Dalit Buddhists
Urban Renewal Schemes 179–80

varna 10, 27n9
vegetarianism 145, 169, 171, 173, 175n16
Vemula, Rohith 105–6
VHP (Vishva Hindu Parishad) 118, 128n12
villages 14, 74, 137–8, 141–3, 146–8; *see also* Gramastha Mandals
violence 154–5, 162, 164–5, 191–2; *see also* riots
Vishnu 15, 56

Who Were the Shudras (Ambedkar) 116
women's rights 68, 75n14–15
work *see* employment
working classes 13, 47
Worli 5, 7, 31, 41, 120

Milton Keynes UK
Ingram Content Group UK Ltd.
UKHW020250251123
433210UK00002B/36